The Third Way

Nijhoff Law Specials

VOLUME 87

The titles published in this series are listed at *brill.com/nlsp*

The Third Way

A Plea for a Balanced Cannabis Policy

By

Cyrille Fijnaut
Brice De Ruyver

BRILL
NIJHOFF

LEIDEN | BOSTON

Translation by Mark van Dyck

Library of Congress Cataloging-in-Publication Data

Fijnaut, Cyrille, 1946- author.
[Derde weg. English.]
The third way : a plea for a balanced cannabis policy / by Cyrille Fijnaut, Brice De Ruyver.
pages cm. -- (Nijhoff law specials ; volume 87)
"Translation by Mark van Dyck."
Includes bibliographical references and index.
ISBN 978-90-04-29318-2 (pbk. : alk. paper) -- ISBN 978-90-04-29319-9 (e-book : alk. paper) 1. Marijuana--Law and legislation--Europe. 2. Marijuana--Law and legislation--Netherlands. 3. Marijuana--Law and legislation. 4. Cannabis. 5. Drug legalization. I. Ruyver, B. De (Brice) author. II. Title.
KJC8970.N35F5513 2015
362.29'5561--dc23

2015022904

This publication has been typeset in the multilingual "Brill" typeface. With over 5,100 characters covering Latin, IPA, Greek, and Cyrillic, this typeface is especially suitable for use in the humanities.
For more information, please see www.brill.com/brill-typeface.

ISSN 0924-4549
ISBN 978-9004-29318-2 (paperback)
ISBN 978-9004-29319-9 (e-book)

Contents

Preface VII

1 **General Introduction: A Way Out of the Deadlock** 1
- 1.1 The Subject of this Discourse 1
- 1.2 A Framework of Basic Concepts 3
- 1.3 The Structure of this Book 6

2 **The United Nations and Cannabis Policy** 9
- 2.1 Introduction 9
- 2.2 The Conventions of 1912, 1925, 1931 and 1936 9
- 2.3 The Conventions of 1961 and 1968 11
- 2.4 The Current Debate within the United Nations 15
- 2.5 Conclusion 19

3 **Cannabis Policy in the Americas** 21
- 3.1 Introduction 21
- 3.2 The Prohibition Era in the United States, 1919–1933 22
- 3.3 The American Legalization Debate in the 1980s 26
- 3.4 The Legalization of Cannabis in the Americas 30
  - 3.4.1 *The Development in the United States* 31
  - 3.4.2 *The Development in Canada* 51
  - 3.4.3 *The Development in Uruguay* 57
- 3.5 Conclusion 60

4 **Cannabis Policy in the European Union** 66
- 4.1 Introduction 66
- 4.2 The Origin of the Policy Pursued: Two Committees of Inquiry 66
- 4.3 The Schengen Agreement and Drug Policy 70
- 4.4 The Present Drug Policy of the European Union 72
  - 4.4.1 *Is there Room for the Legalization of Cannabis?* 73
  - 4.4.2 *The Gravity of the Cannabis Problem* 77
- 4.5 The Current Policy Developments in the Member States 80
- 4.6 Conclusion 88

5 **The Dutch Cannabis Policy** 89
- 5.1 Introduction 89
- 5.2 The Naive Starting Point in the 1970s and 1980s 90
- 5.3 The Ratification of the Convention Against the Smuggling of Drugs 94

5.4 The Reconsideration of the Policy in 1996 and 2004 97
5.4.1 *The Tightening of the Coffeeshop Policy* 98
5.4.2 *The Fight Against Illicit Cannabis Cultivation* 99
5.4.3 *The Legalization of Cannabis for Medical Use* 101
5.5 The Development, Organization and Functioning of the Illicit Cannabis Cultivation 102
5.6 The Cannabis Problem and the Problem of the Coffeeshops 107
5.6.1 *The Zeeland Border Area: Terneuzen* 108
5.6.2 *The Brabant Border Area: Task Force B5* 112
5.6.3 *The Limburg Border Area: Maastricht* 115
5.6.4 *The Problems in the Inner City of Amsterdam* 127
5.7 The Tolerated Sale and Use of Cannabis Around 2010 130
5.8 The Proposals of the Van de Donk Committee 132
5.8.1 *The Revision of the Coffeeshop Policy* 135
5.8.2 *The Struggle Against Illicit Cannabis Cultivation* 151
5.9 Conclusion 156

6 General Conclusion: Towards a Third Way 161
6.1 The Reformulation of the Question 161
6.2 A Preliminary Matter: The Reconsideration of the Drug Treaties 162
6.3 The Regulation of Alcohol and Tobacco: A Good Example? 168
6.4 The Legalization of Cannabis in the European Union: The American Way? 179
6.4.1 *The Green Gold Rush* 180
6.4.2 *The One-Sidedness of the Economic Approach* 182
6.4.3 *The Main Objectives of Legalization* 184
6.4.4 *The Real Consequences of Legalization* 187
6.4.5 *The Neglect of Public Health* 190
6.4.6 *The Harmfulness of Cannabis Use* 194
6.5 The Regulation of Cannabis in the European Union: A Proposal for Discussion 199
6.5.1 *The Principles of the Proposal* 199
6.5.2 *The Prevention of Cannabis Use by Young People* 201
6.5.3 *Three Acceptable Forms of Cultivation and Consumption* 202
6.5.4 *A Highly Controversial Matter: The Establishment of a Closed Production and Distribution System* 204
6.5.5 *The Needs for (Cross-Border) Law Enforcement* 207
6.5.6 *The Abolition of the Coffeeshops* 208

Bibliography 211
Index 228

Preface

It is a question with a long history: what is sensible when it comes to developing and implementing a policy with regard to products which are certainly in the case of regular use harmful, but which at the same time exert a strong attraction, even so strong that people (may) become dependent on or addicted to them? This question relates to many illicit drugs, but these days it is, both nationally and internationally, mainly related to the policy regarding the production, distribution and consumption of cannabis. Generally speaking, the legalization of cannabis in the South American country Uruguay and in some states of the United States of America, in particular Colorado and Washington State, has given a powerful impetus to the discussion about the cannabis policy.

In the Netherlands, that discussion has become increasingly relevant over the past years because of the struggle of coffeeshop owners and political parties – especially the PvdA (Labour Party) and D66 (Democrats 66, a social-liberal party) – against the coffeeshop policy of I. Opstelten, the Minister of Security and Justice in the Rutte I and Rutte II cabinets. In Belgium, the public discussion is not linked to a coffeeshop problem. That is why in Belgium the discussion has a less offensive character than in the Netherlands. However, for a variety of reasons – statements by leading persons, the discovery of big cannabis plantations, and so on – also in Belgium the discussion sometimes runs high. It was not a coincidence that in January 2014 the then Minister of Social Affairs and Public Health, L. Onkelinx, asked the General Drugs Policy Cell to give an account of the state of the cannabis policy and to examine whether that policy should be adapted in one direction or the other.

So today, the cannabis policy is not something like a ship upon a calm and windless sea, on the contrary. More than ever it divides people and raises tempers. With the result that the public discussion about what should happen is largely dominated by two camps: the supporters and the opponents of legalization. In our opinion that, all in all simple, conflict is not in line with the complexity of the problem and therefore we will propose, in this discourse, a Third Way: the golden mean between both extremes.

The reason we have written this discourse, is that for many years already we are involved in discussions about cannabis policy as well as in research into the problems which – in part as a consequence of that policy, but also due to entirely other factors – are related to the cultivation, distribution and consumption of cannabis. It seems appropriate to add that both of us have built up the necessary experience not only thanks to projects in our own countries, but also by working closely together in 2008 in the cross-border research project on drug-related crime in the Euregio Meuse-Rhine. Especially the latter project has forced us to face the fact that, although radical positions in the cannabis discussion have the advantage of their simplicity, they do not do justice to reality, and certainly not to international reality. Therefore the main target of this discourse is to realize a breakthrough in the current discussion and to present, in the form of a Third Way, an alternative approach.

In the Dutch edition of this book the developments in both the Netherlands and Belgium are discussed, but in this English-language edition the developments in Belgium are left out. The principal reason to focus entirely on the Netherlands, is that since the 1960s, the Dutch cannabis policy, in contrast with the Belgian one, has been an important point of reference in the international discussion about the policy that should be pursued regarding the use of cannabis. A second reason is related to the first: in international and foreign literature about cannabis policy the developments in the Netherlands are often depicted in an incomplete or one-sided manner, which has a negative impact on the quality of the international debate about what has happened and what should happen now. The corresponding chapter in this book is a purposeful attempt to rectify as much as possible the existing image of the situation in the Netherlands.

It is obvious that during the writing of this discourse we have made use of the wide range of sources that, in the course of many years, have become available to us. To fully update our source material, we have called in the assistance of Ch. Colman, and we cordially thank her for all the support she has given us the past months. We would also like to thank all the researchers who responded constructively on our request for a copy of their recent reports. In this context, we especially want to mention Prof. Dr. A. Spapens and Dr. E van der Torre.

Tilburg-Gent, January 2015
Cyrille Fijnaut and Brice De Ruyver

CHAPTER 1

General Introduction: A Way Out of the Deadlock

1.1 The Subject of this Discourse

As already indicated in the preface, the discussion concerning the legalization of cannabis is not only taking place in Belgium and the Netherlands, but also in North and South America. However, a lot more can be told about it. The same discussion is also going on in a number of other member states of the European Union and within the United Nations. So we may state that we are dealing with a *glocal* discussion. In other words, a discussion which takes place both globally and locally, and at all the intermediate (sub)continental levels. It could hardly be otherwise. Within the framework of the United Nations countries have engaged themselves – by way of treaties – to a certain worldwide drug policy, which also affects their cannabis policy. Because of the nowadays available, enormous and worldwide transportation, communication and payment possibilities, it should not be neglected that also the drug trade is operating on a global scale.

Thus, to ensure a balanced local or national discussion about the drug policy, the participants to that discussion have to pay attention not only to the local situation, but also to the worldwide context. But in the heat of the debate this is easily forgotten and the international context is not, or not always sufficiently, taken into account. The pamphlets that some time ago stirred the constantly simmering discussion about the legalization of cannabis in Belgium and the Netherlands have conclusively demonstrated this.

In the *Manifest Joint Regulation,* on 31 January 2014 published by a group of Dutch mayors, they make it seem as if they are the first ones in history to reveal the shady sides of the policy of tolerance. In their cry of distress, they furthermore state that the Netherlands does not have to care a bit about the policy the member states of the European Union, in mutual consultation, for many years already are pursuing, and that none of the things that are happening in some American states are at variance with the drug treaties of the United Nations. So the writers of the pamphlet clearly do not worry about the serious problems a singular approach by a European member state will create in the relations with the surrounding countries and the member states of the European Union in general. Neither do they seem to care about the fact that the legal foundation of what is happening in some American states is both more complicated and much more problematic than they suppose.

 | DOI 10.1163/9789004293199_002

The pamphlet *Cannabis: bis?* (*Cannabis: a second look?*) presented by a few Belgian academics on 18 November 2013 has the same flaws. In that pamphlet it is continuously, though without any argumentation, suggested that the drug policy, and therefore also the cannabis policy, still has the characteristics of a "war on drugs". In line with this unproven statement, it is also repeatedly postulated that the cannabis policy of the European Union is in essence an offshoot of such a repressive policy. However, everybody who seriously examines the European cannabis policy cannot but conclude that this representation of the facts is totally incorrect.

Consequently, it is not out of proportion to declare that both pamphlets do not deliver a constructive contribution to the discussion about the most appropriate cannabis policy in Belgium and the Netherlands and, at a larger scale, the European Union and the United Nations. On the contrary, they narrow the discussion to the question whether or not cannabis should be legalized, and they divide people who participate or want to participate in that discussion into supporters and opponents of legalization. This way they encourage a war of positions which inevitably drags the discussion into a deadlock.

Yet, neither these pamphlets, nor the deadlock related with them, were the reason to write this treatise on cannabis policy. As already indicated in the preface, the authors of this discourse have previously worked together on the analysis of drug problems in their home regions, and since then have always retained their interest in the subject. Closely watching, nationally as well as internationally, what is happening in the field of cannabis, they have noticed that year after year the prevailing policy comes under greater pressure. At the national level, both the Netherlands and Belgium are confronted with the problem of the apparently unstoppable illicit production of cannabis, and as far as the Netherlands is concerned there is the problem of the meanwhile impressive number of legal procedures related to the policy aimed at reducing the problems caused by coffeeshops.

At the international level, that is: in the surrounding countries and therefore in the European Union, there is of course also the discussion about the best way to deal with the illicit production and distribution of cannabis. But there is more than that. In particular the legalization of cannabis in some North American states and one South American country weighs heavily on the European cannabis policy discussion, and also on the cannabis policy discussion which, precisely in relation to the mentioned development, is going on within the United Nations.

And so a crucial question arises: what does a balanced drug policy and more specific a balanced cannabis policy suitable for the next years and decades look like? By this we mean a policy which distinguishes itself by starting points, objectives and means that not only take account of the nature, extent and development of the cannabis phenomenon as such, but also, and directly associated with this, of the developments in the cannabis policies pursued by Belgium and the Netherlands, the (surrounding member states of the) European Union, the Americas and the United Nations. In other words a policy that, because it is so realistic, will be able to gain nationally and internationally enough support and therefore has a chance to be successfully implemented. In this discourse we focus the crucial question of what a balanced drug policy looks like entirely on the cannabis policy, because due to the legalization debate, that part of the drug policy is now evolving the most. But it is obvious that the same question can also be focused on the heroin policy, the cocaine policy and the policy regarding synthetic drugs.

1.2 A Framework of Basic Concepts

In the drug policy discussion often all sorts of terms are used indifferently. Of course, this leads to a confusion that does not advance the clarity and the significance of the discussion. Therefore it is important to specify right from the start the meaning that is attributed to the term "legalization" in this treatise.

First of all it is useful to keep in mind that something that is not legal, cannot be regulated. This may seem trivial, but it is not. Sometimes, for instance, people think the production of cannabis can be regulated without legalizing the drug. That is definitely a misconception. Regulation of cannabis only becomes possible if the drug is legalized. Legalization precedes regulation. And by legalization is meant, in this discourse, that the drug – from the production phase to the consumption phase – is removed from criminal law. No exceptions can be made, irrespective of the purpose for which or the context or the way in which the drug is produced, traded and distributed. Consequently, we think that in principle it does not matter whether the legalization is aimed at the medical or the recreational use of the drug. Though we will not deny that some countries do indeed make this distinction and follow the path of legalization only to a certain extent, for instance by legalizing the production et cetera of cannabis for medical use but not for recreational use. We refer to the Netherlands, where there is a strict legal framework for the production and distribution of medical cannabis, but not for the production and distribution of recreational cannabis.

These days regulation actually means that, generally speaking, the authorities determine the conditions under which cannabis is allowed to be produced, traded, sold and consumed. Obviously, the term "regulation" in itself does not say anything. Many aspects of the production, distribution, sale and use of cannabis can be organized in very different ways. The production, for example, can be assigned to state-owned companies or to commercial enterprises under strict state supervision. The distribution can be assigned to the existing network of pharmacies or to a new network of shops which in several respects have to comply with important rules such as the amount of cannabis they are permitted to sell to a customer at one time. Also relevant in this context: the total level of taxes on the production et cetera of cannabis and the purposes for which the related revenues may be used. Should all the revenues be spent on drug education and prevention programmes and drug addict care? Or perhaps also on the construction of roads and the maintenance of school buildings?

In the second place it is important to emphasize what the term "legalization" in our discourse does *not* stand for. Legalization is not synonymous with decriminalization, in the sense that is commonly attached to the latter term when it is used in relation to drugs. In general, decriminalization refers to the abolition of the punishability of a certain behaviour. Applied to drugs, usually it has to do with the possession of a small amount of drugs for personal use or with the personal use of a small amount of drugs, in this case cannabis. A well-known example is that of Portugal. In 2001, the offence of the possession (for personal use) of all illicit drugs was removed from criminal law and given a place in administrative law. Someone who is caught in the possession of a small amount of drugs has to appear before a multidisciplinary college, a kind of "dissuasion commission".[1] That commission has a wide range of possibilities at its disposal to intervene, such as the suspension of legal proceedings in the case of non-addicted offenders, ordering a fine, limiting the freedom of movement, withdrawal of the driving licence or another licence, up to and including mandated drug treatment.[2] People who have committed other offences are referred to the criminal justice system.

In some – mostly Anglo-Saxon – countries the term "decriminalization" is also used when the penalty for a punishable offence is reduced. For example when the possession of small amounts of drugs is no longer punished with deprivation of liberty but only with a fine. In this form of decriminalization the general prohibition of cannabis remains intact, but a specific part of the prohibition is moderated, tempered. Or, as E. Crick et al. write:

---

1 May and Skrine, 2013, p. 50.

2 In the period 2002–2009, each year about 6,000 administrative proceedings were started, and 60 to 70% of these proceedings were suspended because the drug users involved were considered to be non-dependent users.

> Decriminalization refers to the removal of a certain act (e.g. possession of cannabis) from the realm of criminal law. Under such a policy, prohibition remains the rule, but the act is considered a civil offence rather than a criminal one. Civil sanctions could include fines, warnings or treatment but the threat of a criminal record is removed.[3]

Sometimes the latter kind of decriminalization is called *de iure* decriminalizaton, because it literally puts an end to a form of punishability. The existence of *de iure* decriminalization suggests there is also something like *de facto* decriminalization. That term is applicable when the punishability of a certain behaviour is not abolished, but the prosecution of the offenders by the public prosecutor's office is dropped or is not a priority within the prosecution policy, provided certain conditions are met.

Regarding these conditions, we can think for instance of the criteria the Dutch Public Prosecutor's Office utilizes to waive prosecution of coffeeshop owners or managers, such as the criterion that the available stock of cannabis in a coffeeshop should not exceed 500 grams or the criterion that it is not allowed to sell cannabis to young people under 18 years of age. Or to give another example, the prosecution of someone who on good grounds can be considered to be a frequent user will *de facto* be waived if he or she within 14 days enrols in an addiction treatment clinic. In cases like these, criminal law is used as a means of pressure to initiate addiction treatment.

These examples show that in practice there is only a paper-thin difference between a decriminalization of the possession of drugs for personal use as realized in Portugal and a *de facto* decriminalization or "depenalization" as it exists for instance in the Netherlands. The European Monitoring Centre for Drugs and Drug Addiction has aptly summarized the situation in the European Union at this point:

> Based on laws passed in Parliament, ministerial directives or prosecutorial guidelines, a varied picture emerges of the overall legal attitude towards personal use of cannabis. Nonetheless, despite the different legal approaches towards cannabis, a common trend can be seen in the development of alternative measures to criminal prosecution for cases of use and possession of small quantities of cannabis for personal use without aggravating circumstances. Fines, cautions, probation, exemption from punishment and counseling are favoured by most European justice systems.[4]

3 Crick, Haase and Bewley-Taylor, 2013, p. 13.

4 Ballotta, Bergeron and Hughes, 2008, vol. 2, p. 111.

1.3 The Structure of this Book

The starting points and the subject matter of this discourse illustrate that the complexity of the cannabis policy problem demands a nuanced approach.

In Chapter 2 we will discuss the treaties concluded in the first decades of the previous century in order to suppress the production and distribution of different (sorts of) vegetable drugs: the The Hague Convention of 1912, the Geneva Convention of 1925, the second Geneva Convention of 1931 and finally the third Geneva Convention of 1936. These treaties play, not so much directly as indirectly, an important role in the present discussion about the cannabis policy that should be pursued. They are indeed the forerunners of the treaties of 1961 and 1988, which, in legal respect, dominate the current cannabis discussion: the Single Convention on Narcotic Drugs of 1961 and the Convention against Illicit Traffic in Narcotic Drugs and Psychotropic Substances of 1988. Obviously, in this book both treaties will mainly be analysed to find an answer to the following question: what do the treaties tell about the production, trade and distribution of cannabis? To conclude Chapter 2, the attitude of the United Nations, regarding the ongoing developments in the cannabis policy, especially in North and South America, is briefly described.

In line with this, in Chapter 3 the developments in the Americas are discussed. The chapter opens with a discussion of the Prohibition, introduced in the United States in 1919 by the activation, through the National Prohibition Act (Volstead Act), of the Eighteenth Amendment of the Constitution of 1917 concerning the ban on the import, the production et cetera of "intoxicating liquors for beverage purposes". The reason we pay attention to the Prohibition is simple: it plays such an important role in the current cannabis discussion. Supporters of legalization continuously make use of that episode of American history to defend their position. But how solid is that defence? Furthermore we look at the discussion about the legalization of cannabis in the United States in the course of the 1980s. That discussion was important because in a way it formed the overture to the (partial) legalization of cannabis for medical purposes in some American states, starting with California, at the end of the 1990s. In Chapter 3 we subsequently examine how, over the past years, the legalization of cannabis has taken shape in two North American states – Colorado and Washington State – and one South American country, Uruguay. In this connection we also pay some attention to the developments in Canada and more specifically in British Columbia. The reason to do so is that the legalization of cannabis for medical purposes in the mentioned Canadian province shows that such a policy, in certain circumstances, can run completely out of control. It also demonstrates the possible repercussions of misgovernment on the developments in the neighbouring countries.

In Chapter 4 we focus on the cannabis policy of and within the European Union. The chapter starts with an exposition on the origin of the drug policy of the European Union and the further development of that policy through "Schengen". Then we look, in general, at the cannabis policy the European Union and its member states are pursuing nowadays, while raising the question: to what extent does that policy, at this moment, offer room for legalization? In addition, we briefly pay attention to the current cannabis policy of some big countries: France, Germany and the United Kingdom. After all we should not forget that if the Netherlands, Belgium or another member state of the European Union would drastically change its cannabis policy, such a change would automatically affect the policies of other member states too. To be able to assess this impact, it is important to have some knowledge of the situation in the other member states.

Chapter 5 is dedicated to the cannabis and coffeeshop policy pursued in the Netherlands since the 1960s. First we examine the policy point towards the cultivation, distribution and consumption of cannabis in the 1960s, 1970s and 1980s. Then we focus on the repeated reconsideration of the Dutch cannabis policy, since 1996, and on the development of cannabis growth over the past years. It is rather obvious that special attention is paid to the shadow of organized crime behind that growth, a shadow that in the course of time has become larger and darker. This development has seriously worsened the cannabis problem. Related to this, we extensively explore the problem of the coffeeshops as it has manifested itself since the 1990s in a number of southern border cities, from Terneuzen to Maastricht, but also in Amsterdam. For a good understanding of the recent developments in the Netherlands – more precisely: the developments since the publication of the report of the Van de Donk Commission in 2009 – a profound insight into the coffeeshop problem is required. Therefore, in the last part of this chapter the findings and recommendations of the Van de Donk Commission will be summarized, as well as the tightening of the policy of tolerance towards the coffeeshops by the Rutte I government. Subsequently both the effects of the changed policy and the actions of a number of coffeeshop owners and a number of mayors against that policy, are listed. Finally, we discuss the parliamentary and extra-parliamentary actions taken by some political parties to force the Minister of Security and Justice, Opstelten, to radically change the cannabis and coffeeshop policy.

In Chapter 6 we argue that by taking a Third Way it is possible to break the deadlock in which the discussion about the cannabis policy, undeniably, has stranded. First the nature of the deadlock is explained. Then we examine how the drug treaties of the United Nations can be adapted to allow for the legalization of cannabis. Of course, the legalization automatically implies the need to regulate the entire cannabis market, from production to consumption. But which approach leads to the best regulation? Can the regulation of alcohol and tobacco serve as a model for the regulation of cannabis? And if not, what should be done? Should the (member states of the) European Union use the regulation of cannabis in some American states as a source of inspiration? Is that regulation, with regard to the interests at stake – economic interests, public health interests and the interests of law enforcement –, sufficiently balanced to deserve a warm welcome at this side of the Atlantic? Based on the answers to these questions we, at the end of Chapter 6, present a proposal for a balanced discussion about the cannabis policy in the European Union. Last but not least we pay special attention to the Dutch coffeeshop, which for many years already is depicted by supporters of cannabis legalization as a major step in the right direction. The question is: is there still a future for the coffeeshop?

CHAPTER 2

The United Nations and Cannabis Policy

2.1 Introduction

As indicated in the general introduction, in this chapter first we discuss the drug conventions of 1925, 1931 and 1936 which, as a result of the The Hague Convention of 1912 and under the auspices of the League of Nations, were concluded to suppress the production and distribution of (different sorts of) vegetable drugs.

Next we pay attention to those provisions in more recent conventions of the United Nations – more precisely the conventions of 1961 and 1988 – which are the most relevant for the cannabis policy. What do they tell about the production of, and the trade in cannabis and what about the possession for personal use and the use of this drug?

Finally, we examine the development of the discussion about the legalization of cannabis as it is taking place today at the level of the United Nations, especially with regard to the developments occurring in North and South America. Is that discussion creating any room for the legalization of cannabis, in any form whatsoever? Or at least room for a debate about the usefulness or uselessness of such a policy change?

2.2 The Conventions of 1912, 1925, 1931 and 1936

The conventions concluded in 1925, 1931 and 1936 were not the first conventions aimed to reduce, all over the world, the production and distribution of (derivatives of) opium and cocaine. The very first convention of that kind was the The Hague Convention of 1912. This treaty had been brought about mainly at the insistence of the United States and was meant to urge the parties concerned to limit, in the first place in their own countries, the production, the sale and the use of the mentioned narcotic drugs to medical and scientific purposes.[1] The international impact of this treaty should not be underestimated and is demonstrated by the fact that in 1914 it led to the Harrison Narcotic Act, which was intended to restrict the import, production and use of opium in the United States. Moreover, this act became the cornerstone of the drug policy that after the First World War was propagated by the United States with ever more fervour all over the world.[2]

1 Société des Nations, 1937, pp. 258–260. See also De Ruyver, 1986, pp. 495–496.

2 Bewler-Taylor, 2001, pp. 24–27, and Knepper, 2011, pp. 114–118.

 | DOI 10.1163/9789004293199_003

The first Geneva Convention of 1925 built further on this and included new engagements.[3] The treaty not only aimed to limit the use of the domestic production of opium and cocaine to scientific and medical purposes and to regulate the distribution of these narcotic drugs within that context. It was also meant to tighten, by different sorts of measures, the supervision of the international trade in these drugs, in order to combat the related smuggling and abuse. Furthermore, we should not forget that important parts of the treaty referred to (Indian) hemp (cannabis), and in particular to cannabis resin (hashish).

As to the last-mentioned substances, in article 11, paragraph 1 of the first Geneva Convention it was, among other things stated that, in addition to the measures related to the tightening of the supervision of the international opium and cocaine trade, the parties of the convention committed themselves to forbid the export of hashish and its derivatives to countries where the use of these drugs was prohibited, and to request, in every case in which exportation was permitted, an import certificate from the government of the importing country. In paragraph 2 the parties promised to impede, through effective control, the illicit international trade in cannabis and especially cannabis resin.

Also because the latter provisions in the Geneva convention of 1925 constitute the starting point of the present-day and mainly on the treaty of 1988 based international policy regarding cannabis, it is strange the second Geneva Convention of 1931 did not apply explicitly but only implicitly to this narcotic drug.[4] The 1931 treaty was principally intended as a confirmation of the objectives and measures that were included in the treaties of 1912 and 1925. Anyhow, the treaty of 1931 comprised a number of measures meant to enable a more efficient reduction of especially the production of narcotic drugs. One of these measures was the introduction of quotas per country for the import, export and use of the different (forms of) narcotic drugs.[5]

Often, albeit wrongly, neglected in this context, is the third Geneva Convention of 1936, which aimed to suppress the smuggling of narcotic drugs.[6] This treaty, concluded at the initiative of the *Internationale Kriminalpolizeiliche Kommission*, forced the parties to promulgate, in line with article 2, the necessary legal provisions "for the severe punishment, notably by imprisonment or other forms of deprivation of liberty" of people who performed, or participated in, whatever kind of actions related to the production et cetera of narcotic drugs that were in conflict with the provisions included in the treaties of 1912, 1925

3 Société des Nations, 1937, pp. 261–275. See also *Tractatenblad*, 1961, no. 151.

4 Société des Nations, 1937, p. 3.

5 In this connection, see also Addens, 1939, pp. 58–92, and *Tractatenblad*, 1961, no. 152.

6 *Tractatenblad*, 1959, no. 48.

and 1931 (also conspiracy and attempts had to be punishable). According to the articles 5–9 of the treaty the parties were obliged to prosecute foreigners who committed these offences at their territories, and under certain conditions they had to extradite suspects to other countries. Article 11 stipulated that each of the parties had to establish a central bureau responsible for the prevention of the offences concerned, the ensurance of the prosecution of suspects and the communication with similar bureaus in other countries.[7]

It is certainly important to mention the third Geneva Convention in the context of this discourse, because as a result of that treaty, cannabis was almost automatically put on a par with the other narcotic drugs. Thus it became one of the prohibited narcotic drugs whose production, distribution et cetera from that time on had to be restrained by, in principle, the criminal justice system. What had made such a radical turnaround in the drug policy possible? Why had cannabis, without much discussion, been given a place in the treaty? These are obviously important questions, and to be able to answer them we have to focus on the United States.

As stated by P. Andreas and E. Nadelmann some years ago, the punitive turn in the international drug policy – also with regard to cannabis – has indeed to be attributed to the United States in the first place. According to both scientists, since 1930 federal drug fighters in the United States have been pleading:

> for the global criminalization of cannabis and its treatment on a par with heroin and cocaine, despite abundant scientific evidence questioning the need for such a punitive approach.

The driving force behind the campaign was H. Anslinger. In the 1920s this official of the United States Treasury Department had played an important role in the international fight against the smuggling of alcohol and in 1930 he was appointed commissioner of the newly established Federal Bureau of Narcotics of the Treasury Department.[8]

2.3 The Conventions of 1961 and 1968

In 1961 The Hague and Geneva Conventions – with the exception of the Geneva Convention of 1936 – were replaced by the Single Convention on Narcotic

7 Bewley-Taylor, 1999, pp. 40–41.

8 Brunn, Par and Rexed, 1975, pp. 125–126; Andreas and Nadelmann, 2006, p. 43, pp. 123–124; and Knepper, 2011, pp. 128–129, 136–137.

Drugs, which at some points was adapted in 1971 by means of a protocol.[9] The convention also aimes to limit the use of narcotic drugs to medical and scientific purposes. The preamble of the convention states that, in order to achieve this goal, all over the world effective measures have to be taken against the abuse of narcotic drugs. The vast assortment of measures included in the convention not only comprises the setting-up of international supervision through, among other things, an International Control Comittee. It also contains a large number of measures the signatory parties – on their own and in cooperation with other countries – have to take to restrain the production and smuggling of narcotic drugs. Furthermore it obliges the parties in a number of ways to combat these kinds of behaviour via the criminal justice system.

Cannabis ("the flowering or fruiting tops of the cannabis plant"), the cannabis plant and cannabis resin ("the separated resin, crude or purified, obtained from the cannabis plant") are explicitly submitted to the provisions of the convention (article 1). They are included in both Schedule I and Schedule IV of the convention and are therefore subjected to most of the measures of control that apply to opium and cocaine. For a good understanding it is important to indicate more precisely which aspects have to be controlled in the first place:

- The term "Production" refers to "the separation of opium, coca leaves, cannabis and cannabis resin from the plants from which they are obtained";
- "Manufacture" is defined as "all processes, other than production, by which drugs may be obtained";
- And "Illicit traffic" (smuggling) means "cultivation of or trafficking in drugs contrary to the provisions of this convention".

It has to be remarked that the convention has left some room for the legal production of narcotic drugs, including cannabis. Articles 29 and 30, for instance, offer the signatory parties the possibility to make the production as well as the trade and also the delivery of narcotic drugs, dependent on a licence, unless the production, trade or delivery is entrusted to one or more state-owned enterprises. In case a licence is granted to persons or companies, they are, of course, obliged to monitor the compliance with the terms of the licences.

9 *Tractatenblad*, 1962, no. 30 and *Tractatenblad*, 1980, no. 184. See also De Ruyver, 1986, pp. 499–500. The Vienna Convention of 1971 regarding the psychotropic substances is left out of consideration in this discourse because the production et cetera of cannabis did not play a role in that convention.

Article 31 stipulates that, in principle, parties cannot knowingly allow the export of narcotic drugs to any country or region, unless it is in accordance with their laws and regulations. When the import and export of narcotic drugs are not done by a state-owned enterprise, these activities have to be subjected to an extensive system of licences. Additionally it is stated in article 33 that parties are not allowed to permit the possession of narcotic drugs "except under legal authority".

There are some provisions which (also) apply specifically to cannabis. In connection with the discussion about the desirability of the legalization of cannabis we have to refer to article 22, in which it is stated that whenever a party is of the opinion that, because of the prevailing conditions in the country or a territory of the state party, the prohibition of the cultivation of cannabis is the most suitable measure to protect public health and welfare, the party concerned has to prohibit that cultivation, also in order to prevent the diversion of narcotic drugs into the illicit traffic. Article 28 then offers the possibility to cultivate cannabis for industrial purposes (fibre and seed) and horticultural purposes, provided that the necessary measures are adopted to prevent the misuse of, and the illicit traffic in, the leaves of the cannabis plant. Of course, the Single Convention does not allow the cultivation et cetera of cannabis for commercial purposes.

In 1988 the Single Convention was completed by the Convention against Illicit Traffic in Narcotic Drugs and Psychotropic Substances.[10] According to the preamble, the latter treaty was the result of a strong concern about:

> the magnitude of and rising trend in the illicit production of, demand for and traffic in narcotic drugs and psychotropic substances, which pose a serious threat to the health and welfare of human beings and adversely affect the economic, cultural and political foundations of society.

In line with this a number of more specific reasons to draft the new convention are enumerated. For instance the fact that illicit drug traffic is an international criminal activity and that the revenues of this illicit traffic enable international criminal organizations "to penetrate, contaminate and corrupt the structures of government, legitimate commercial and financial business, and society at all its levels". There is also the desire "to eliminate the root causes of the problem of abuse of narcotic drugs and psychotropic substances, including the

10 *Tractatenblad*, 1990, no. 94. For the English edition of the treaties discussed here, see De Ruyver, Vermeulen, Vander Beken, Vander Laenen and Geenens, 2002, pp. 72–144.

illicit demand for such drugs and substances and the enormous profits derived from illicit traffic".

The core of the 1988 convention – certainly in view of the discussion about the appropriate cannabis policy – is the very long article 3 about "Offences and sanctions". Paragraph 1 of that article forces all parties to adopt the necessary measures to establish a number of acts, when committed intentionally, as criminal offences under their domestic law. Spread over 3 subparagraphs (a., b. and c.) and 11 sub-subparagraphs (a.i., a.ii.,…, c.iv.) the acts concerned are enumerated. In the context of this discourse in particular the following acts are important:

- Paragraph 1, a.i.: "The production, manufacture, extraction, preparation, offering, offering for sale, distribution, sale, delivery on any terms whatsoever, brokerage, dispatch, dispatch in transit, transport, importation or exportation of any narcotic drug or any psychoactive substance contrary to the provisions of the 1961 Convention, the 1961 Convention as amended or the 1971 Convention";
- Paragraph 1, a.ii.: "The cultivation of opium poppy, coca bush or cannabis plant for the purpose of the production of narcotic drugs contrary to the provisions of the 1961 Convention and the 1961 Convention as amended";
- Paragraph 1, a.iii.: "The possession or purchase of any narcotic drug or psychoactive substance for the purpose of any of the activities enumerated in i. above".

In paragraph 2 of article 3 it is explicitly stated that each signatory party has to adopt, "subject to its constitutional principles and the basic concepts of its legal system", the necessary measures to establish the following acts as criminal offences: "the possession, purchase or cultivation of narcotic drugs or psychotropic substances for personal consumption" contrary to the provisions of the aforementioned 1961 and 1971 conventions. The importance of this part of article 3 can hardly be overestimated, because it provides the possibility to divert, under certain circumstances, the individual drug user from the criminal justice system. Many countries use this provision at prosecution level.

Paragraphs 4 and 5 are related to, on the one hand, sanctions and measures which must be possible to impose and "which take into account the grave nature of these offences" (for example imprisonment, fines, confiscation). On the other hand, they are related to the factual circumstances the authorities have to take into account to determine the gravity of the committed offences, such as the involvement of an "organized criminal group" or the use of violence or arms by the offenders.

In paragraph 6 it is stated that "any discretionary legal powers" related to the prosecution of persons for offences established in accordance with article 3 should be exercised "to maximize the effectiveness of law enforcement measures in respect of those offences, and with due regard to the need to deter the commission of such offences". Paragraph 7 requests the parties to ensure that their competent authorities bear in mind the seriousness of the committed offences as well as the circumstances in which they were committed when considering the parole or early release of convicted persons. Paragraph 8 stipulates that in determining the statute of the limitations period, special attention has to be paid to the case in which an alleged offender has evaded the administration of justice.

Furthermore especially article 14 is relevant in the context of our discourse. It deals with the eradication of the illicit cultivation of plants containing narcotic drugs and with the elimination of the illicit demand for narcotic drugs and psychotropic substances. Paragraph 2 of article 14 states that each state party has to take "appropriate measures":

> to prevent illicit cultivation of and to eradicate plants containing narcotic or psychotropic substances, such as opium poppy, coca bush and cannabis plants, cultivated illicitly in its territory.

In the next sentence it is indicated that in the context of these measures the fundamental human rights have to be respected and due account has to be taken of traditional licit uses, at least if there is historic evidence for such uses, and of protection of the environment. Considering the central theme of the 1988 convention – the cross-border struggle against the illicit traffic in narcotic drugs and psychotropic substances – it is not surprising that many provisions are related to the establishment of jurisdiction and the supply of bigger and smaller forms of legal assistance. Innovative types of cooperation are made possible, such as the transfer of proceedings for criminal prosecution and the appropriate use of controlled delivery.[11]

2.4 The Current Debate within the United Nations

It is obvious that since the coming into force of the drug conventions of 1961 and 1988, there has been a lot of discussion, including at the level of the United Nations, about the rationale, the observance and the enforcement of these

11 See Van Kempen and Fedorova, 2014, pp. 97–101.

treaties, also with regard to the cultivation of cannabis. How could it be otherwise, given the ever more intense debates that are going on in a number of member states?

As to the significance of the conventions, it has to be noted that since 1988, especially the United Nations Office on Drugs and Crime in Vienna has revealed in different ways the development of the drug problems in the world. The *World drug report*, published in 2008, is a good example of this.[12] Regarding cannabis the report states that the worldwide production of cannabis herb (marijuana) declined from 45,000 mt (metric tons) in 2004 to 41,400 mt in 2008, and that from 2005 to 2006 the production of cannabis resin (hashish) dropped 10% – from 6,600 mt to 6,000 mt. Though the report remarks that the scale of the production can vary strongly from one (sub)continent to the other. In 2006 cannabis was mainly cultivated in North and South America (55%) and Africa (22%), followed by Asia and Europe. However, from 2004 to 2006 the cultivation of cannabis in Europe increased.[13]

The office is well aware of the unintended negative consequences of the pursued policy: a lucrative and violent black market, the negative impact of law enforcement on the resources available for public health, the diversion of drug problems from one geographic area into another, the problem that pressure on the market for a particular drug can inadvertently promote the use of an alternate drug, and the marginalization of drug consumers by the use of criminal justice against them. Nevertheless, the authors of the report conclude:

> These unintended consequences represent serious challenges as the international drug control system faces its next century, but they should not overshadow its significant achievements. Under the current system of controls, it is highly unlikely that the world will ever face a drug problem like the one that confronted China 100 years ago. (...) No one can know for sure what the world would have looked like without the international drug control system, but it was initiated in response to a profound humanitarian crisis, and that crisis has largely been resolved.[14]

Given these findings and conclusions it is not at all remarkable that the International Narcotics Control Board of the United Nations both before and after 2008 has taken the clear stand that each of the signatory parties has to put the conventions concerned accurately and decisively into practice, and that

12 United Nations Office on Drugs and Crime, 2008.

13 United Nations Office on Drugs and Crime, 2008, p. 14.

14 *Ibid.*, p. 21.

the drug problems are no reason to diminish attention.[15] On the contrary, the board stated in 2002:

> these new trends make it all the more urgent for them to find new ways to substantially reduce the illicit demand for drugs.[16]

So, according to this organization, the flexibility of the conventions was and is very limited. That is why in 2002 and the following years, the board rather strongly criticized the Dutch coffeeshop.[17] Pleas from opponents of the prevailing cannabis policy were not welcomed with applause and understanding within the institutions of the United Nations. Not only for formal reasons, but also for reasons that had everything to do with the practical significance of the conventions concerned.

The conclusion of D. Bewley-Taylor and C. Hallam in 2008 in the Beckley Foundation report about cannabis policy, for instance, was diametrically opposed to the above-cited conclusion the United Nations Office on Drugs and Crime drew that same year from a survey of the worldwide developments in the realm of drugs:

> it concludes that current control regimes are either ineffective or inconsistent, and challenges policy makers to confront these realities, and agree a more rational way forward for international cannabis control.[18]

In the following years the board moderated its resistance against the medical use of cannabis, but continued its strong opposition against the recreational use of it. The developments that were happening in Colorado, Washington State and Uruguay in 2011–2012 were in any case regarded as violations of the 1961 convention. In its annual report of 2012 the board qualified the developments in the two first-mentioned states as:

> a significant challenge to the objective of the international drug control treaties to which the United States is a party.

15 International Narcotics Control Board, 2008, pp. 107–115.

16 See International Narcotics Control Board, *Flexibility of Treaty provisions as regards harm reduction approaches*, Vienna, September 30, 2002, Seventy-fifth Session, Restricted E/INCD/2002/W.13//SS.5.

17 Jelsma, Blickman and Bewley-Taylor, 2014, pp. 8–11.

18 Bewley-Taylor and Hallam, 2008, p. 1.

At this occasion the bureau also voiced its disapproval of the situation in California, where the lack of control on the use of cannabis for medical purposes has resulted in the frequent recreational use of this narcotic drug. In the same annual report the bureau urged the American government "to ensure full compliance with the international drug control treaties in its entire territory".[19]

So, it is no surprise that the "Political declaration" and the accompanying "Plan of action on international cooperation towards an integrated and balanced strategy to counter the world drug problem", which were adopted at the 52nd session of the Commission on Narcotic Drugs in 2009, do not leave any room for the legalization of cannabis, nor, as a consequence, for such a broad interpretation of the treaties that a kind of quasi-legalization would be possible. Both policy documents are aimed at the complete eradication or a substantial decrease of the illicit cultivation of "opium poppy, coca bush and cannabis plant", a considerable reduction of the illicit demand for "narcotic drugs and psychotropic substances", as well as a serious diminution of the production, trade and distribution of "psychotropic substances, including synthetic drugs". In these strategic policy documents not a single word is said about cannabis legalization, in any form or variant whatsoever.

The same is true for the declaration about the mentioned policy published by the Commission on Narcotic Drugs at its 57th session, which took place in Vienna from 12 to 14 March 2014.[20] In that declaration the worldwide negative consequences of the drug problem are summed up and the member states are urged to diligently fulfil the commitments they have made in order to achieve in a "comprehensive, integrated and balanced" way the targets of the conventions concerned. Moreover, the concern is expressed that:

> illicit cultivation of opium poppy, coca bush and cannabis plant and illicit drug production, manufacture, distribution and trafficking remain a major challenge in countering the world drug problem.

In his statement at the 57th session of the Commission on Narcotic Drugs in Vienna, the president of the International Narcotics Control Board, R. Yans, among other things pointed out that his board had never declared war on anyone

---

19 International Narcotics Control Board, 2013, pp. 11–12, p. 31, 36, 116. See also Jelsma, Blickman and Bewley-Taylor, 2014, pp. 12–13, and A. Travis, "Relaxation of US cannabis laws 'violates UN drug conventions'", *The Guardian*, 5.3.2013.

20 United Nations, Commission on Narcotic Drugs, *Draft joint ministerial statement* (...), Vienna, 12.3.2014, E/CN.7/2014/L.15.

or anything, and that the policy that was written down in the conventions had been formulated by the member states in order to combat the abuse of substances they consider(ed) to be very dangerous, such as cannabis.[21] At other occasions, though, Yans spoke plainly negative about the concealed and unconcealed legalization of cannabis in an increasing number of American states. In March 2013 in London, for example, at the presentation of the annual report of 2012, he said the way these states allow the use of cannabis for medical purposes "undermines the humanitarian aims of the drug control system and are a threat to public health and wellbeing".[22] In his opinion the American initiatives open the door for the recreational use of cannabis and are, if only for that reason, in conflict with the conventions concerned.

It is evidently a shortcoming that these and other statements are not substantiated by reports or research data. Their nature is nominal, downright rhetorical. One allows oneself to be convinced by them or not, one believes them or not. No wonder the reports of the commission are an easy target for groups campaigning for the legalization of drugs, and especially cannabis.

In its criticism of the annual report of 2012, the International Drug Policy Consortium says the International Narcotics Control Board ignores the fact that there is already a black market for drugs, which is to a large extent controlled by criminal groups. The consortium also reproaches the board that it ignores the question raised by many governments whether the current drug policy is sustainable and whether the treaties should be revised. Moreover, the consortium accuses the board of suggesting that in case of a reconsideration of the drug policy public health will be lost from sight and cannabis will become amply available for all young people, including minors. *Quod non!*[23]

2.5 Conclusion

The conclusion of this chapter can be rather short. The text of the drug conventions and the commentaries of the institutions that have to ensure the implementation of the treaties leave no doubt about it: the drug conventions do not offer any room for the large-scale production, trade or distribution of

21 United Nations, International Narcotics Control Board, *Discours de* (...), Vienna, 13 March 2014.

22 See, among other things, the article of A. Travis about the presentation of the annual report in *The Guardian*, 4 March 2014 (with the "message from the President" in annex), "UN: cannabis law changes pose 'very grave danger to public health'".

23 International Drug Policy Consortium, 2013, pp. 3–5, 6–7, 9–10.

cannabis for recreational or medical purposes. Considering the responses this explanation of the treaties sometimes provokes, it may be appropriate to add at once that we are not dealing with a dictate of a supranational power, but with a policy that all the countries involved in the treaties have agreed upon. However, in the context of this study a lot more can be said about the drug conventions of the United Nations.

In the first place, it may be regretted that in the roaring 1920s and 1930s the League of Nations, without a serious discussion about the usefulness or uselessness of such a decision, has step by step subjected cannabis to the drug treaties. The same is probably true for the 1961 decision to include this drug in the Single Convention on Narcotic Drugs. But since that decision has indeed been made by the parties concerned, they simply cannot ignore it now: *pacta servanda sunt.* Otherwise they undermine their credibility and almost automatically will come into conflict with parties that refuse to follow their example. Parties which, with regard to cannabis, want to revise the drug treaties have to follow the royal road to achieve this goal, that is: they have to prepare a protocol that makes changes possible and should attempt to acquire sufficient support for it.

In the second place, the institutions which have to supervise the implementation of the drug treaties should spend more time and energy on the current discussion in several continents about the legalization of cannabis. Today, the input of the institutions consists mainly of rather nominal, formal, defensive arguments. Given the seriousness of the discussion and the importance of the developments that have led to it, they should thoroughly explore the backgrounds of the debate and empirically examine the validity of complete or partial alternatives to the present cannabis policy. Should there not explicitly be created room for the provision – upon prescription by a physician – of medical cannabis to seriously ill people? What about the establishment of non-profit cannabis clubs? To what extent home cultivation of cannabis for personal use can be allowed? And which boundaries – in terms of the number of plants or the quantities of cannabis – should be respected in that case?

CHAPTER 3

Cannabis Policy in the Americas

3.1 Introduction

We already indicated that the inclusion of cannabis in the later conventions of the League of Nations was due to the renowned American civil servant Anslinger. He was firmly convinced that the use of criminal justice was necessary "to eradicate the problem of drug addiction". In his opinion, criminal prosecution was needed to restrain both the supply of and the demand for narcotic drugs. He regarded drug users mainly as criminals and only in the second place as addicts. In the United States the cannabis policy advocated by Anslinger resulted in the Marihuana Tax Act of 1937. Through this act cannabis became completely proscribed in the United States. Individuals – from importers to sellers – who, one way or another, were involved in the traffic of this drug could be condemned to large fines (up to 2,000 dollars), five years of imprisonment, or both sanctions simultaneously.[1]

Not only in the United States but also in many other countries, the ongoing criminalization of cannabis is considered to be in sharp contrast with what happened in the United States about eighty years ago: the end of the prohibition of alcohol in 1933. According to many people the example of the American alcohol prohibition demonstrates that any prohibition, including a prohibition of cannabis, is bound to have a negative impact. But is that really the case? Maybe the appearance of negative consequences also depends on the context in which a prohibition is realized? And, if only for that reason, maybe one prohibition is not necessarily similar to the other? And if that is right: what are the arguments for and against a prohibition of cannabis? In the United States these questions again came to the fore in the 1980s. They gave rise to a lot of – more or less organized – discussions about the appropriate answers.

It is relevant to recall the main features of these discussions, because their content had a lot in common with the current debate about the legalization of cannabis. Another important reason to do so, is that these discussions were in a sense a prelude to the legalization of cannabis for medical use in California and more than twenty other American states. It is not exaggerated to claim that this form of legalization has opened the door for the legalization of cannabis for recreational use. In the last part of this chapter we focus on the latter

1 Woodiwiss, 1988, pp. 31–32, and Bewley-Taylor, 1999, p. 42.

 | DOI 10.1163/9789004293199_004

development. But first we discuss the way the federal authorities look at the legalization of cannabis, and then we trace the legalization process in Colorado and in Washington State. Complementary to this, the impact of the legalization of cannabis for medical use in British Columbia is explained. What consequences did it have within the territorial borders of this Canadian province and what did it mean for the export of locally cultivated cannabis to the United States? Given the resemblance between the role of British Columbia (with regard to the United States) and the role of the Netherlands (with regard to the European Union) it is important to pay some attention to the developments in British Columbia. And since these developments cannot be separated from the general cannabis policy of Canada, they have to be embedded in an analysis of that policy.

Finally, we have a closer look at the legalization of cannabis in the South American country of Uruguay. Not at least because many supporters of cannabis legalization believe the Uruguayan approach is a shining example for the rest of the world.

3.2 The Prohibition Era in the United States, 1919–1933

The leading role of the United States within the criminalization movement in the international drug policy in the 1930s, is certainly remarkable given the fact that in 1933 this same country abolished the prohibition of alcohol. In 1919 the anti-alcohol policy had enthusiastically been implemented by American progressives and, as noted above, until the 1930s this policy was vehemently defended by prominent drug fighters such as Anslinger.[2] However, Anslinger was surely not the only defender. Many people were convinced that the prohibition of alcohol would have been a success if the enforcement of the legislation concerned had been organized more effectively.[3]

On request of some members of the famous Wickersham Commission, which was established in 1929 to examine the problem of the enforcement of the prohibition laws, it was stated in the conclusions of the 1931 report of the commission that the prohibition regime was indeed feasible, provided that its enforcement was better organized. All members of the commission agreed that in case the controversial amendment would be revised, the following words would have to be used:

---

2 Kerr, 1985, pp. 185–210.

3 Bewley-Taylor, 1999, p. 37.

> The Congress shall have power to regulate or to prohibit the manufacture, traffic in or transportation of intoxicating liquors within, the importation thereof into and the exportation thereof from the United States and all territory subject to the jurisdiction thereof for beverage purposes.[4]

This conclusion opened the possibility to end the Prohibition Era. And that is exactly what happened in 1933, partly as a consequence of the mentioned report. On 5 December 1933 the Eighteenth Amendment was repealed. Earlier that year, the prohibition regime, laid down in the National Prohibition Act, had already been converted into a licensing regime.[5] In the context of this discourse a detailed description of that memorable episode in American history is not necessary. Nevertheless, a few things are important to mention.

In the first place, it is important to emphasize that the commission attributed the failing enforcement to a large number of political, institutional and psychological circumstances: large-scale corruption in the public administration, a serious lack of cooperation from the states, a lack of cooperation between the various federal services, and a public opinion that increasingly turned against the policy pursued. According to the commission economic reasons also played an important role. The professionalism and, as a consequence, the realized profits within the illicit market, grew faster than the resources provided to effectively combat that market. The huge profit associated with the illicit trade:

> makes possible systematic and organized violation of the National Prohibition Act on a large scale and offers rewards on a par with the most important legitimate industries. It makes expenditure in corruption possible. It puts heavy temptation in the way of everyone engaged in enforcement and administration of the law. It affords a financial basis for organized crime.

Connected to this, the commission made clear that when a law, despite the fact that it is vigorously enforced and leads to a lot of convictions, has only a small deterrent effect, one may wonder if:

> and, after a decade of experience the volume of violations seems to increase steadily and the public attitude is increasingly indifferent or

4 Wickersham Commission, 1931, p. 1, 83.

5 Woodiwiss, 1988, p. 30, and Kerr, 1985, pp. 265–274.

> hostile, the question arises as to whether such a law is, in any proper sense, enforceable.[6]

In the second place, it is important to stress that the commission felt that the prohibition of alcohol had stimulated organized crime in all the logistic phases of the production and distribution process. This applied just as well to the import of illicit alcohol – mainly from Canada, but also from Mexico, the Caribbean and Europe – as to the transport and distribution of foreign or domestic illicit alcohol within the United States. By way of illustration, the commission pointed out that for various reasons "bootlegging had gone on for at least a generation before the National Prohibition Act", but that this form of smuggling was just a trifle in comparison with "the bootlegging of today", characterized by individual violations of the law that are symptoms of:

> an organized system of production and distribution. Those who are found distilling, or transporting, or selling are merely employees. Behind them are the heads of an organization, supplying the capital, making the plans, and reaping the large profits. It is clear enough that the real problem is to reach these heads of the unlawful business. Experience has taught them to carry on their business with impunity and it is in evidence that they are harder to reach than formerly. To catch them calls for a much higher type of enforcement organization and a higher and more experienced type of agents than have been available in the past.[7]

This quotation will quickly conjure up associations with the current situation of the fight against illicit cannabis cultivation in countries such as the Netherlands and Belgium. Therefore it is, in the third place, wise to indicate that one should avoid to make too easy – not to say: cheap or flawed – comparisons between both phenomena. Certainly one should beware of too hastily drawing conclusions regarding the cannabis policy that should be pursued in the Netherlands, Belgium or the European Union.

To begin with, one should realize that the American Prohibition was not part of a policy to which the United States had committed itself by way of a treaty, neither at the level of the American continent nor internationally.

Related to this, it has to be emphasized that in the surrounding countries alcohol was not subjected to any form of prohibition, and so it could rather easily and in large quantities be smuggled across the almost endless borders of

6 Wickersham Commission, 1931, pp. 44–61.

7 *Ibid.*, pp. 21–43, particularly p. 36.

the United States. In other words: although the (American) Prohibition was at odds with the alcohol policy in Canada, Mexico et cetera, it did not, as such, affect (the implementation of) that policy in these countries.

Furthermore, we should not forget that the Prohibition was not related to just one particular type of alcohol-containing drink, but to the whole range of alcoholic beverages. When applied to the situation in Western Europe, the question arises how the inventors of a coffeeshop with a legally regulated "backdoor" intend to deal with the production and distribution of several other organic (and synthetic) drugs (cocaine, heroin, "pills") some visitors of coffee-shops are also using. They also cannot evade the question what to do with the supply of different sorts of cannabis which are not domestically cultivated but are imported, in one form or the other, from Morocco, South America et cetera, and to some extent are still offered for sale in the existing coffeeshops. Are they willing to legally regulate these supplies to "their" coffeeshops? If so, how should that be done? And if not, how to carry the fight against the import and distribution of these illicit forms of cannabis?[8]

In addition, it has to be emphasized that although the Prohibition has given a boost to organized crime in the United States, this type of serious crime in the US does not have its origins in the anti-alcohol policy of that time. Already since the end of the nineteenth century the phenomenon of organized crime had manifested itself over there. Not only in the alcohol market, as mentioned earlier, but also in the drug trade, the gaming sector and the sector of prostitution. Around 1920 many criminal gangs in America had already the infrastructure in place and manpower available to organize the illicit import, production and distribution of alcohol. In that sense, the Prohibition was just another, albeit great, opportunity for Italian as well as Chinese, Jewish and Irish gangs to operate successfully in an enormous black market and to earn a lot of money by doing so.[9]

Therefore, it is no surprise that the abolition of the Prohibition did not mark the end of organized crime in the United States. Not only the criminal groups concerned remained actively involved in trafficking in women and illicit gaming, they also continued, in a variety of illicit ways, their racketeering practices in important legal sectors. Moreover, in New York a number of criminals did not entirely quit the alcohol business. During the Prohibition Era they had bought themselves into production and distribution companies, and after the

8 Fijnaut, 2009, pp. 19–20.

9 Nelli, 1976, pp. 101–140; Asbury, 1990, pp. 299–324; Fried, 1993, pp. 1–43, 90–91, and Durney, 2000, pp. 11–51.

abolition of the Prohibition they kept on earning money from the alcohol business, but now legally.[10]

One should not expect too soon or too much that the introduction of "legal" coffeeshops will drastically reduce organized crime related to coffeeshops. What will the people who now occupy central positions in the illicit cannabis cultivation business do with cannabis harvests not destined for Dutch coffeeshops? Will they stop producing this cannabis? Or will they use it to compete with the "legal" coffeeshops? And/or will they (also) increase the export of cannabis to foreign countries in order to keep up their revenues? And/or will they make larger investments in cannabis cultivation in surrounding or remote countries? And how do the supporters of the "legal" coffeeshop think foreign authorities, which do not endorse such a kind of cannabis legalization, will react to these developments?

3.3 The American Legalization Debate in the 1980s

The background of the Prohibition alone is reason enough to understand why since then also in the United States there have repeatedly been heated discussions about the pursued or needed drug policy. At the end of the 1980s, for example, the debate once again flared up in all fierceness. The conclusion of the 1988 Vienna Convention against illicit traffic was not the sole cause of that discussion. At least equally important were the increasing drug problems in the big cities, the associated expenses – for administration, justice, police, assistance, et cetera – needed to keep these problems more or less under control, the controversial foreign drug policy of the United States in South America and the unstoppable importation of narcotic drugs into North America.

For a better understanding of the debate of that time – which usually took the shape of a debate for or against the legalization of drugs and especially cannabis just like it does today – it is recommended to read the contributions collected in *The drug legalization debate* (1991), a book edited by J. Inciardi, and *Drug legalization: for and against* (1992), a book edited by R. Evans and I. Berent.[11] Of course, there is more literature that is helpful to get an idea of the arguments exchanged in the debate.[12] However, the contributions in the two books mentioned already paint an accurate picture of the drug policy

10 Sutherland, 1934, pp. 189–193; Foot White, 1955, pp. 142–146, and *Proceedings*, 1934, pp. 46–52, 430–432.

11 Inciardi, 1991, and Evans and Berent, 1992.

12 See, for instance, Wisotsky, 1989, and Eldredge, 1998.

discussion in the United States about 25 years ago and demonstrate how much that discussion had in common with the debate at that time in Western Europe as well as with the current discussion in both parts of the world.

One of the topics of the American debate of the late 1980s was, of course, the lessons that should be learned from the Prohibition. The supporters of legalization pointed to the growth of organized crime as a result of the ban on alcohol and its corrupting effect on American society. In the same breath it was often added that these problems did not mean much in comparison with the enormous corruption which meanwhile had taken root in the police force, justice, the administration, business and banking due to the illicit drug prohibition. The opponents of legalization argued, among other things, that although organized crime had increased during the Prohibition, that increase was certainly not due to the Prohibition. Long before that time, organized crime already existed in the United States – as previously mentioned in this chapter. Moreover, the opponents of cannabis legalization emphasized that the Prohibition had resulted in a decrease of the alcohol consumption of Americans and, as a consequence, also a decrease in public drunkenness and other misbehaviour.[13]

Apart from this rather history-oriented dispute regarding the effects of the Prohibition, moral philosophical arguments also played an important role in the debate about the drug policy pursued. Supporters of legalization claimed that the policy pursued resulted in the criminalization of millions of Americans who were found "guilty" of a form of behaviour which, for the rest, had caused no victims. The policy concerned did not only put democratic tolerance in American society severely under pressure, but also engendered huge social costs, for instance by promoting the rise of a society of informers. However, according to opponents of legalization the government had to protect the freedom of its citizens and for that reason was responsible for restraining any behaviour that could disarrange people's lives and/or could pose a considerable threat to the community around them. Supporters of legalization, on the other hand, were of the opinion that such a government exhibited totalitarian traits. The government should not tell citizens what is good and bad for them.[14]

Supporters and opponents of legalization agreed that until then the national and international enforcement of the drug legislation had not produced the desired result. But they disagreed on the conclusions needed to be drawn from the finding. The supporters of legalization argued that, in this context, criminal

---

13 Carter, 1992, p. 92; Moore, 1992, p. 96, and Carter, 1992, p. 94.

14 Nadelmann, 1992, p. 23; Wilson, 1992, p. 35, 40; Bennett, 1992, p. 56; Tully and Bennett, 1992, p. 65, and Friedman, 1992, p. 58.

prosecution and international criminal cooperation were by definition flawed and could never be successful. In other words, the war against drugs had ended in a complete failure. One of their arguments was that since cannabis plants and coca bush can be cultivated all over the world, it is easy to compensate the destruction of these plants in one part of the world by intensifying the cultivation in another part. The opponents of legalization, on their part, stated that the war on drugs was neither won nor lost. Thanks to all the efforts made, the size of the problem and the number of victims were still relatively small. The related costs were considerably lower than suggested by the supporters of legalization. Comparatively, these costs represented only a small part of the annual resources for the promotion of public welfare and the annual resources for personal comfort.[15]

Associated with the latter issue, there was the topic whether the criminalization of the drug market was meaningful or meaningless. Supporters of legalization pointed to the desastrous, counterproductive effects of the criminalization. It meant that millions of Americans were put in jail for possession of drugs – with all the resulting negative consequences for themselves and their entourages. Their dealers, however, usually escaped criminal prosecution and, moreover, made a lot of money on their illicit trade. The opponents of legalization rejected this argument and stated that the massive imprisonment of drug users was not due to the drug legislation as such, but the result of the freedom of people to obey or violate that legislation. For the same reason one should not expect that legalization of drugs would all at once transform drug dealers into law-abiding citizens.[16]

Closely related to this, there was the question of the impact of drug legalization on drug consumption. For the opponents of legalization the answer was clear: the use of drugs, the number of drug addicts and drug-related crime would increase enormously because of the increased availability of drugs. Supporters of legalization refused to accept this doom scenario and continued to believe that legalization would not necessarily lead to an increase of drug use and addiction problems. Among other things they were convinced that once drugs would be legalized, illicit drug traffickers would no longer make large numbers of users addicted to secure their revenues. On this point, and with regard to cannabis, a number of participants in the debate opted for a middle position. They believed that in countries where cannabis use had been

15 Nadelmann, 1992, p. 20, pp. 22–23; Moore, 1992, p. 135; Smith, 1992, p. 84; Tully and Bennett, 1992, p. 71; Bennett, 1992, p. 55, 227; Friedman, 1992, p. 57, and Wisotsky, 1992, p. 189.

16 Nadelmann, 1992, pp. 21–22, p. 27; Brenner, 1992, pp. 173–174, and Tully and Bennett, pp. 67–68.

decriminalized, the total use of the product had remained stable or had even slightly decreased. As to the United States, the use of cannabis would probably increase a little bit after legalization, but not as dramatically as the opponents of legalization predicted. The latter, for their part, referred to the use of alcohol and tobacco. The normalization of these products had created huge problems, especially in urban ghettos. If drugs would also be legalized, the misery in the places mentioned would be incalculable.[17]

This brings us automatically to another big issue in the debate of that time: the comparison between the different luxuries. Was there any reason to treat drugs otherwise than alcohol and tobacco? Supporters of legalization considered it hypocritical to allow the use of alcohol, despite the widespread alcohol abuse, but to prohibit the use of drugs. And the same applied to tobacco. Although it was well-known that smoking is much more perilous than the use of drugs, tobacco use was not punishable whereas drug use was. According to the supporters of legalization, in terms of abuse and damage a false distinction was made between these products. That distinction was nothing but a moral and therefore untenable distinction.[18]

Finally, it has to be remarked that also then there was already a lot of discussion between supporters and opponents of legalization about the way the legalization of drugs could be put in practice. Which drugs should be legalized? What should be understood by legalization? Should only the use be decriminalized, or also the production and distribution? To whom the production and distribution of the legalized drugs might or should be assigned? State-owned companies, supermarkets, pharmacies? Who, and on which conditions, would be allowed to buy and use which drugs? According to the participants in the debate the answers to these questions were not only important in view of the needed public support for the legalization, but also with regard to shifts in the black market. Drug traffickers would automatically start looking for new consuming markets. Yet, the supporters of legalization saw possibilities to translate their opinions in a practical policy. They thought it would be wise to cautiously grant individual traders licences to sell drugs and to raise taxes on these drugs, low enough to avoid the development of a black market.[19]

17 Wilson, 1992, pp. 30–33, p. 36, pp. 39–40; Bennett, 1992, p. 54; Tully and Bennett, 1992, p. 71; Friedman, 1992, p. 52; Nadelmann, 1992, p. 22, 25; Moore, 1992, p. 144; Jonas, 1991, p. 161, and Inciardi and McBride, 1992, p. 39.

18 Brenner, 1992, p. 169; Wilson, 1992, p. 41; Smith, 1992, p. 83; Nadelmann, 1992, p. 35, and Szasz, 1992, p. 265.

19 Rangel, 1992, pp. 14–15; Moore, 1992, p. 134, and Branch, 1992, p. 302.

3.4 The Legalization of Cannabis in the Americas

In the present international discussion, the developments in the American states, Colorado and Washington State, are easily mentioned in one breath with the evolution in Uruguay.[20] On the one hand, this is due to the fact that what is happening in both American states, in some respects resembles to what is at stake in Uruguay: the legalization and, as a consequence, the regulation of cannabis. On the other hand, it should not be forgotten that whereas in the recent past South America mainly figured as the first line of defence in the American war on drugs, this continent is nowadays, through the Organization of American States, involved in a constructive dialogue with the United States on this point.[21]

The starting shot for that dialogue was fired in 2012, at the sixth summit for heads of state and government leaders in Cartagena. There, a number of South American participants came to the conclusion that the war on drugs had ended in a failure and that it was necessary to look for alternatives for the current drug policy. The American government was not willing to go that far. However, some of its members thought it was legitimate to talk about the legalization of drugs.[22] The result of the discussion was that the Organization of American States was set the task to prepare a study about the way drug problems were dealt with in the Americas. In May 2013 the report of the study group concerned was published.[23] In that report four scenarios to cope with drug problems were worked out: *together*, *pathways*, *resilience* and *disruption*. For each of these scenarios the following aspects were examined: how is the drug problem defined, how shall we try to solve it, what is the potential of this approach, and which challenges have to be overcome during implementation?

---

20 Room, 2013. On November 4th 2014 the citizens of Washington D.C. voted in favour of the legalization of cannabis as far as its limited possession and cultivation by adults of 21 or older are concerned. See B. Nuckols, "Washington D.C. residents to vote on marijuana legalization in November", *The Cannabist*, 6.8.2014. On that same day also a majority of Alaskans and a majority of residents of Oregon voted for the complete legalization of cannabis, from its production to its distribution. See the related reports on the website of the Marijuana Policy Project.

21 Nadelmann, 1993, pp. 251–312.

22 See the report of this conference by J. Doward, "'War on drugs' has failed, say Latin American leaders", *The Guardian*, 7.4.2012. Also read the Reuters report, published by *The New York Times* on 27.2.2012: "Napolitano defends US drug war in face of legalization debate". About the war on drugs in South America an awful lot has been written. A good example is De Grazia, 1991.

23 Organization of American States, 2013.

It would lead us too far to give a detailed description of the four scenarios here. At this place, it is important to underline that the second scenario in particular is linked to the developments in the three states mentioned. It contains an image of a future in which a growing number of governments agrees that the prevalent drug policy does not bear the hoped-for fruit, while another number of governments is not inclined to legalize drugs. That makes it very difficult "to reach a consensus on which direction to pursue when looking for new regulatory pathways".

As a result of which several countries start experiments that, in the short run, make their policies deviate from the prevailing drug policy. In the long run it will probably lead, step by step, to a consensus about a new policy. Therefore it is important to take a closer look at the experiments that are conducted in the Americas at this moment. These experiments can be the first signals of a drastic change of the drug policy, which, of course, not only will affect the Americas but also the rest of the world.[24]

3.4.1 *The Development in the United States*

The legalization of cannabis (for recreational purposes) in Colorado and Washington State is inseparably connected with the legalization of cannabis for medical purposes in an increasing number of states. The latter development started in 1996 in California and has certainly not come to a halt since that time. So far, 22 American states have regulated the provision of cannabis for medical use.[25] Although in a number of cases this form of legalization is clearly at variance with the drug treaties of the United Nations, it is increasingly tolerated by the federal authorities, at least at the level of the cannabis users and the specialized retail sector.[26]

In this connection it is remarkable that in medical circles in the United States there are still serious doubts about the therapeutic value of marijuana.[27] In a 2008 report of the American College of Physicians about this matter it is stated that, with a few exceptions, the effectiveness of marijuana

24 *Ibid.*, p. 41, pp. 45–49.

25 National Conference of State Legislatures, 2014. For the developments in the past months, see, for instance, J. Berger, "Medical marijuana is legal in Connecticut, but not yet sold", *The New York Times*, 1.5.2014, and J. McKinley, "New York leaders reach deal on medical marijuana", *The New York Times*, 19.6.2014.

26 Room, 2013, pp. 345–346.

27 C. Saint Louis, "Politicians' prescriptions for marijuana defy doctors and data", *The New York Times*, 26.6.2014.

is certainly not proven: "Additional research is needed to clarify marijuana's therapeutic properties and determine standard and optimal doses and routes of delivery."[28]

This means there is a wide gap between the reasons for which politicians in a number of states – sometimes after much discussion and in some cases also after conflicts with the police, justice and health care, such as happened in California and Arizona[29] – have agreed with the legalization of cannabis for medical use and the scientific evidence supporting the medical benefits of cannabis. That is all the more remarkable because there are also studies which show that, under certain conditions, short-term as well as long-term use of (certain doses of) cannabis can have adverse health effects. Problems such as amnesia, impaired motor skills, addiction, decline of performance, symptoms of chronic bronchitis, paranoia and (chronic) psychosis can arise.[30]

Nevertheless, in October 2009 the Obama Administration has given green light to the development of a policy of tolerance regarding the medical use of cannabis. The government announced that the Justice Department had to employ its resources in an efficient and intelligent way, and that the prosecution of patients using cannabis, as well as the prosecution of recognized shopkeepers who are selling cannabis to this group of users is not in line with that policy starting point. An important prerequisite, however, is that patients and shopkeepers have to adhere strictly to the relevant legislation in the states concerned.[31] The large-scale production and distribution of cannabis is not backed by this policy. That became very clear when in May 2011 federal prosecutors in several states informed the administrations of these states that the Controlled Substances Act "may be vigorously enforced against those individuals and entities who operate large marijuana production facilities".[32]

---

28 American College of Physicians, 2008.

29 S. Moore, "Los Angeles prepares for clash over marijuana", *The New York Times*, 18.10.2009, and M. Lacey, "Legal marijuana in Arizona? Yes for buyers, no for sellers", *The New York Times*, 22.7.2011.

30 In this connection, see Volkow, Baler, Compton et al., 2014.

31 See the Associated Press report in *The New York Times* of 19.10.2009: "New medical marijuana policy outlined", and D. Stout and S. Moore, "US won't prosecute in states that allowed medical marijuana", *The New York Times*, 20.10.2009.

32 Quotation from a letter the federal prosecutor of Arizona sent to the Arizona Department of Health Services on 2.5.2011 (attached to a report about this matter in the blog ("The Authority") of the Hubbard Law Firm, 3.5.2011).

This does not alter the fact that the gradual normalization of the medical use of cannabis in the United States – a result of the policy of tolerance – has paved the way for the legalization of the recreational use of cannabis. However, other forms of normalization have also played an important role. One should also take into account that in recent years some American states have decriminalized the personal possession of small quantities of cannabis. Given the past of American drug policy, it is understandable that in many cases this only happened after fierce discussions between supporters and opponents, but eventually the decision was taken.[33] In turn, this second form of normalization of cannabis use has made the complete legalization of cannabis in the United States a more acceptable topic for discussion. Some opinion polls indicate that nowadays a large majority of Americans support this evolution or at least consider it to be inevitable.[34]

To what extent the Dutch cannabis and coffeeshop policy has served as an example in this development, is hard to say. However, it is a fact that the supporters of legalization, grouped around the Open Society Foundations in New York, always refer to the Dutch policy of tolerance to illustrate the blessings of a different policy. This may explain why in the report on the drug policy of the Netherlands written by the Dutch researchers J.-P. Grund and J. Breeksema and published by the Open Society Foundations in 2013 not much attention is paid to the serious problems that are also related to the coffeeshop policy. Though these problems are not denied, they are not discussed in a balanced way. Obvious examples are the role of organized crime in the illicit cannabis traffic and the huge problems with the maintaining of public order in a number of border municipalities.[35]

3.4.1.1 The Stance of the Federal Authorities

Everybody who reads the White House's strategic policy document *A drug policy for the 21st century* will realize that the Obama Administration is fully aware of the shift in the public discussion about the use of drugs in general and the use of cannabis in particular. The policy document explicitly states:

33 For an outline of that discussion in, for example, Massachusetts, see J. Saltzman, "Drug law puzzles police; many questions on enforcement of new marijuana rules", *The Boston Globe*, 25.12.2008.

34 Denver Post Editorial Board, "Editorial: is marijuana legalization simply inevitable?", *The Cannabist*, 30.7.2014.

35 Grund and Breeksema, 2013.

> While law enforcement will always play a vital role in protecting our communities from drug-related crime and violence, we simply cannot incarcerate our way out of the drug problem. Put simply, an enforcement centric 'war on drugs' approach to drug policy is counterproductive, inefficient, and costly. At the other extreme, drug legalization also runs counter to a public health and safety approach to drug policy. The more Americans use drugs, the higher the health, safety, productivity, and criminal justice costs we all have to bear.

According to this policy plan, the middle of the road approach is preferred by the government. Its Third Way is based on the following principles: emphasis on prevention rather than incarceration, training of health care providers to encourage them to take action before addiction occurs, expansion of the possibilities for treatment for addicted persons, more resources for the reintegration of addicted persons, and a 'smart on crime' approach with regard to the enforcement of the drug legislation. The latter means:

> at the end of the day, we cannot arrest our way out of the drug problem. The Obama Administration has made clear we will not focus limited federal drug enforcement resources on individual drug users. Instead, our drug policy emphasizes the expansion of innovative 'smart on crime' strategies proven to help break the cycle of drug use, crime, arrest, and incarceration.[36]

This creed is repeated time and again in the annual *National drug control strategy*. The 2013 *Strategy* clearly states that the drug policy debate is too radical.[37] One side defends the thesis that "drug legalization is the 'silver bullet' solution to drug control", whereas the other side adheres to "a law enforcement-only 'war on drugs' mentality". Neither of these two approaches, the statement continues, "is humane, effective or grounded in evidence", and thus:

> The Obama Administration supports a 'third way' approach to drug control – one that is based on the results of considerable investment in research from some of the world's preeminent scholars on the disease of addiction.

As to the practical significance of all this when applied to cannabis, the policy plan is less compromise-minded. Under the headings *Eradicate marijuana cultivation* and *Stop indoor marijuana production* it is pointed out in strong terms

36 White House, 2010, pp. 3–4.

37 Office of National Drug Control Policy, 2013, pp. 1–2.

that the police and other services have demolished thousands and thousands of plantations. However, no mention is made of any progress in working out the cited policy vision with regard to the individual user.[38] For a long time it remained unclear how the federal authorities looked at the developments in the states, especially in those states that were on the verge of legalizing cannabis for recreational use.

The Drug Enforcement Administration was the only government agency that vehemently opposed cannabis legalization. The past years this agency has regularly produced ominous publications that point to the large amounts of cannabis that are smuggled into the United States or that, one way or another, are domestically cultivated. Numerous quotations warn people of the dangers of marijuana abuse (not: marijuana use).[39] No wonder that in January 2014 the director of this central service expressed his deep concern about the legalization of cannabis in the states previously mentioned. At that occasion, it was recorded that, in his opinion, taking the path towards legalization "is reckless and irresponsible".[40]

Meanwhile, on 29 August 2013, the Deputy Attorney General – the vice-minister of Justice, so to speak – J. Cole has, in some degree, elucidated the stance of the Obama Administration at this point.[41] That day, in a memorandum addressed at all federal prosecutors, he writes:

> that the American Congress has determined that marijuana is a dangerous drug and that the illegal distribution and sale of marijuana is a serious crime that provides a significant source of revenue to large-scale criminal enterprises, gangs, and cartels. The Department of Justice is committed to enforcement of the Controlled Substances Act (CSA) consistent with those determinations. The Department is also committed to using its limited investigative and prosecutorial resources to address the most significant threats in the most effective, consistent, and rational way.

The threats the Deputy Attorney General subsequently enumerates, are, among other things, the revenues of criminal organizations generated by selling

38 *Ibid.*, p. 45.

39 Drug Enforcement Administration, 2013, and Drug Enforcement Administration, 2014a and 2014b.

40 See the report "DEA admits marijuana legalization 'scares us'" in RT, 16.1.2014.

41 The corresponding press release as well as the memorandum mentioned in the next sentence of the main text is available at the website of the Justice Department: <http://www.justice.gov>. In this connection, see also A. Southall, "US says it won't sue to undo state marijuana laws", *The New York Times*, 29.1.2013.

cannabis, and the transfer of cannabis from a state where it is legalized to a state where that is not the case. To this he adds that the coming into force of the laws concerned in Colorado and Washington State certainly affects the customary cooperation between federal and state services with regard to the fight against drugs, but that the memorandum is based:

> on its expectation that states and local governments that have enacted laws authorizing marijuana-related conduct will implement strong and effective regulatory and enforcement systems that will address the threat those state laws could pose to public safety, public health, and other law enforcement interests.

In line with this, he makes no secret of the fact that:

> This memorandum does not alter in any way the Department's authority to enforce federal law, including federal laws relating to marijuana, regardless of state law. Neither the guidance therein nor any state or local law provides a legal defense to a violation of federal law (...). Even in jurisdictions with strong and effective regulatory systems, evidence that particular conduct threatens federal priorities will subject that person or entity to federal enforcement action, based on the circumstances.

Anyone who thinks that in the United States the prohibition of cannabis is abolished, is wrong. It really is not over yet. Up to now it has only been mitigated in some states. The recent change is not only based on a new federal vision on how to approach drug problems, and the cannabis problem in particular. It is also the result of *Realpolitik* with regard to the cannabis problem. On 4 March 2014 this was once again underlined by the federal prosecutor in Colorado and the deputy administrator of the Drug Enforcement Administration in a statement before a subcommittee in the US House of Representatives about *The Department of Justice's strategy to enforce and prosecute certain marijuana related crimes*:

> Marijuana is the most widely available and commonly abused illicit drug in the United States. (...) Availability increases are due to large-scale marijuana importation from Mexico and Canada, as well as increasing domestic indoor grows and marijuana cultivation in states that have legalized marijuana or passed medical marijuana initiatives.

To deal with this problem, they declared, state and federal authorities have to work closely together "to ensure that our efforts are mutually supportive".[42] According to many press releases from both the Drug Enforcement Administration and the Federal Bureau of Investigation this also means that, just as before and throughout the United States, time after time there will be action taken against the large-scale production and (local, national, or cross-border) distribution of cannabis.[43]

On 23 January 2014 an Obama spokesperson said the president has no intention to legalize cannabis at the federal level. The president considers the developments in Colorado and Washington State as experiments these states are allowed to conduct.[44] The *National drug control strategy 2014* reflects the same vision. In that annual report not a word is said about the experiments in both states. On the contrary, with regard to marijuana the report is entirely focused on the fight against this drug i.e. the battle against open-air plantations, especially at federal territory and, no less important, the fight against indoor plantations. With a certain sense of pride it is revealed in the report that in 2013 the Drug Enforcement Administration and its partners demolished 2,754 indoor plantations.[45] Obama's reserve on this matter is not typical for him. A number of Democratic governors approach the situation the same way, even the governor of California: "I think we ought to kind of watch and see how things go in Colorado."[46]

Whether the recent call by the editorial board of *The New York Times* to revoke the second Prohibition will significantly change that attitude, remains to be seen. By the way it is remarkable that one of the main reasons for revocation put forward by the editorial board is typically American: among the 658,000 people arrested for cannabis possession (FBI figures for 2012) there are

42 Also this statement is available at the website of the Justice Department.

43 These press releases are available at the websites of the government agencies concerned. Only recently, in New York, a Canadian "pot playboy" from Montreal has been sentenced to 27 years in prison for running an international cannabis and cocaine business. See the report in *The Boston Globe*, "Marijuana supplier named pot playboy gets 27 years", 20.8.2014.

44 See R. Reillyryan, "White House says marijuana policy is states' rights issue", *The Huffington Post*, 14.7.2014. See also the report "Obama will kiffen nicht legalisieren" in *Der Spiegel*, 23.1.2014.

45 Office of National Drug Control Policy, 2014, pp. 42–43.

46 A. Nagourney, "Despite support in party, Democratic governors resist legalizing marijuana", *The New York Times*, 5.4.2014.

disproportionately many young black men, and these arrests are "ruining their lives and creating new generations of career criminals".[47]

Over the past months all sorts of reports have made clear that this contradictory development – what is legalized at state level remains prohibited at the federal level – leads to many tensions. For instance, there are problems of a financial nature: not all banks want to be associated with financing the cannabis industry. For a long time the FBI refused access to its data records for the screening of individuals who or companies that, at state level, were applying for a licence. Sometimes it is very difficult or even impossible for researchers to gain access, at the federal level, to the stock of cannabis for scientific purposes which is administered by the National Institute on Drug Abuse. Not so long ago, it became clear that federal authorities are entitled to cut off the supply of water from federal to state territory in case the water is used for the cultivation of cannabis. In several states, and in particular in California, local authorities are also worried about the exhaustion of their territories, and especially about the use – or rather abuse – of water, by all kinds of cannabis growers. Recently activists from Denver went to the local court to complain about the fact that, by paying taxes on cannabis products, they were inadvertently at variance with the Fifth Amendment of the federal Constitution, incriminating themselves of offences that are punishable at the federal level. Henceforth, they would refuse to pay these taxes.[48]

Nevertheless, the increasing legalization of cannabis for medical use and now also for recreational use has ignited a new kind of Gold Rush in the United States. Not only persons who and companies that were already operating in the cannabis industry try to increase their market shares, but also new companies do their utmost to gain a share of the market. In this they are aided by national lobby groups as well as philanthropic financial magnates such as G. Soros. In 2010 Soros donated 1 million dollars for a campaign in California.[49]

---

47 The Editorial Board, "Repeal prohibition, again", *The New York Times*, 27.7.2014.

48 S. Kovaleski, "US issues marijuana guidelines for banks", *The New York Times*, 14.4.2014; G. Johnson, "FBI to allow access to records for marijuana license background checks", *Associated Press*, 11.4.2014; M. Ferner and M. Reilly, "Feds may cut off water for legal marijuana crops", *The Huffington Post*, 19.5.2014; M. Ryzik, "Dry California fights illegal use of water for cannabis", *The New York Times*, 6.8.2014; D. Migoya, "US House OKs bill that could ease marijuana banking issues", *The Cannabist*, 16.7.2014, S. Kovaleski, "Medical marijuana research hits wall of US law", *The New York Times*, 9.8.2014, and J. Ingold, "Is paying pot tax self-incriminating? Activists lose initial court challenge", *The Cannabist*, 22.8.2014.

49 See, for instance, H. Abdullah, "Up in smoke: the Obama's administration's pot politics problem", *CNN.com*, 5.2.2014; C. Miles, "Marijuana legalization is a multi-billion dollar

Thus, it is no wonder that researchers who for a long time already are focussing on the cannabis problem, have started worrying about the "dangerous corporate takeover of the legal marijuana market". One of the best-known among them is J. Caulkins. In the spring of 2014 he expressed his concern that big companies would dominate the cannabis market and would try to lure as many people as possible into the use of cannabis. However, he realized that in the United States it was not possible to assign the sale of cannabis to state-run shops. Not only because at the federal level cannabis is still prohibited, but also because such shops would be loathed by both conservatives and libertarians. Therefore, he developed two alternative models. In the first model, the production and distribution are assigned to non-profit organizations. In the second model, they are entrusted to small cooperatives of users.[50]

3.4.1.2 The Situation in Colorado

In the year 2000 the state of Colorado legalized the production and distribution of cannabis for medical use.[51] Only a few years later this state had become home to "many thriving medical marijuana businesses". This can be deduced, for instance, from the fact that in October 2013 112,149 inhabitants were inscribed in the special register that contains the names et cetera of all inhabitants who – usually because of the (formal) reason they are suffering from severe pain – have an authorization to buy cannabis for medical use.[52] In the wake of this flourishing form of legalization and due to a mixed company of lobbyists – from old-fashioned idealists to big investors – in 2004 a discussion started about the question whether the existing cannabis policy should be extended to the production and distribution of cannabis for recreational use.[53]

On Tuesday 6 November 2012 this discussion resulted in a popular vote on an amendment of the Colorado Constitution to legalize the cultivation et cetera of cannabis for recreational use: the meanwhile generally known *Amendment*

revolution that's sweeping across the USA", <http://www.policymic.com/articles>, and B. Terris, "Big Pot rising: the marijuana industry's first full-time lobbyist makes rounds on Capitol Hill", *The Washington Post*, 12.4.2014.

50 Caulkins, 2014.

51 As to the circumstances in which this happened, see J. Aguilar, "Pivotal Boulder medical marijuana trial blazed way to pot regulation, use", *The Cannabist*, 6.8.2014.

52 N. Snyder, "Is marijuana legal in Colorado?", *Denver.about.com*, 2014.

53 M. Ferner, "Amendment 64 passes: Colorado legalizes marijuana for recreational use", *The Huffington Post*, 11.6.2012, and R. Carroll, "Big cannabis: will legal weed grow to be America's next corporate titan?", *The Guardian*, 3.1.2014.

64: use and regulation of marijuana.[54] This amendment was adopted with 55% of the votes and regulates who and under which conditions is allowed to produce, allowed to process and allowed to distribute the cannabis concerned.[55] It is based on the regulation of the production and distribution of medical cannabis and modelled after the legislation on alcoholic beverages.

The leading idea behind Amendment 64 is that for the sake of the safety and health of growers, sellers and users, recreational cannabis has to be removed from the twilight zone and transferred to the shelfs of shops where its origin and quality can be controlled.[56] The amendment concerned came into force on 1 January 2014. Apart from this, it is also obvious that the legalization of recreational cannabis has to – and will – generate quite a lot of additional tax revenue. In the state of Colorado, the new revenue stream is estimated to total 100 million dollars annually. A part of these revenues will be used to pay the inspectors who have to enforce the new legislation. Another part will be spent on information about drugs and on care for addicts. And – also important – 40 million dollars will be invested in the construction of schools. So, indisputably the broadening of the legalization of cannabis in Colorado also serves a financial purpose.[57] According to experts, it remains to be seen whether the amounts mentioned are realistic. In their opinion, the 40 million dollars for the construction of schools is definitely an overestimation. Thus, the revenues will not "close Colorado's structural budget gap".[58]

However, not only the state wants to make money from the legalization of cannabis. Municipalities also consider it an interesting source of much-needed revenues.[59] Commercial lobbyists are eager too to gain some money from it and they do: the share prices of companies that are investing in the sale of cannabis in Colorado "skyrocketed" in the beginning of 2014. There was a "real

54 For the text of this amendment, please visit the website of the state of Colorado (https://www.colorado.gov).

55 J. Healy, "Colorado stores throw open their doors to pot buyers", *The New York Times*, 1.1.2014.

56 A. Altman, "Pot's money problem", *Time*, 3.2.2014.

57 K. Wyatt, "The big story; governor: Colorado pot market exceeds tax hopes", *AP*, 19.2.2014. See also the report in the *Handelsblatt*: "Colorado verdient zwei Millionen US-dollar an Marihuana", 10.3.2014.

58 Brown and Resnick, 2014, p. 1. For the tax revenues in the first six months of 2014, see R. Baca, "202 M in pot sales?! – 10 Colorado facts from six months into 2014", *The Cannabist*, 27.6.2014.

59 For good examples, see C. Illescas, "Aurora's marijuana frontier: 57 applicants for 24 storefronts", *The Cannabist*, 3.8.2014, and N. Lofholm, "Can marijuana save this tiny Colorado town?", *The Cannabist*, 21.8.2014.

stock price explosion", the share prices of some companies increased by 200 to 300%.[60] In this context, it is noteworthy that in order to conquer the market, to increase profits and to make shareholders even happier, cannabis is offered for sale in extraordinary ways.[61] In the spring, the symphony orchestra of Denver announced that it will perform concerts for cannabis smokers.[62] At the same time another company announced that, taking inspiration from the cigarette machine, it will produce vending machines that offer cannabis for sale.[63] One of the cannabis shops adds cannabis to drinks and cakes to attract more customers.[64] And to conclude, a bus company organizes cannabis tours with visits to well-known growers and shops.[65]

Amendment 64 lists the cannabis policy objectives:

> In the interest of the efficient use of law enforcement resources, enhancing revenue for public purposes, and individual freedom, the people of the state of Colorado find and declare that the use of marijuana should be legal for persons twenty-one years of age or older and taxed in a manner similar to alcohol.

Bearing in mind these objectives, the Task Force which had to prepare the implementation of the amendment, clearly describes in its report which model its members have used when they started their task.[66] Their starting point was that the new industry should be built in line with the model of vertical integration. This means:

> that cultivation, processing and manufacturing, and retail sales must be a common enterprise under common ownership.

Related to this, the Task Force had to find a balance "between those urging state-owned and operated retail stores to sell marijuana and those endorsing a more entrepreneurial, free market model". With regard to levying taxes on the cannabis industry, the Task Force considered it necessary "to keep taxes low

60 See the report in *Het Parool*, "Wietaandelen Colorado gaan als een raket", 9.1.2014.

61 For a general description, see S. Raabe, "Manufacturers of marijuana edibles scramble to meet ravenous demand", *The Cannabist*, 17.8.2014.

62 S. Slager, "Amerikaans symfonieorkest wil meer wietrokers in de zaal", *Trouw*, 30.4.214.

63 See the report on this subject in *De Standaard*, "Eerste marihuana-automaat in de VS", 15.4.2014. See also L. Klöckner, "Schnuckertüten, pral gefült mit Hanf", *Die Zeit*, 22.11.2013.

64 J. Healy, "Snacks laced with marijuana raise concerns", *The New York Times*, 31.1.2014.

65 H. Schmidt, "Marihuana-Fahrt durch Denver", *Der Spiegel*, 14.1.2014.

66 State of Colorado, 2013.

enough so as not to encourage a persistent black market in marijuana". In this context, the Task Force argued, for instance, that a tax rate of 25% on the sale of cannabis was too high:

> encouraging the survival of the illegal market and increasing the incidence of home cultivation among private citizens.[67]

Based on the starting points mentioned, the Task Force made a number of recommendations. Some recommendations were related to the organization of the supervision of this new sector within the Taxation Division of the Department of Revenue of Colorado, other ones to the conditions under which licences could be issued. As to these conditions, it has to be emphasized that the Task Force, among other things, recommended that only Colorado residents would be eligible for licences in the cannabis industry, but that both residents and non-residents should be allowed to purchase cannabis. If only Colorado residents could legally buy cannabis, this could give rise to "a black market through straw purchases by residents and unauthorized resale to non-residents".[68]

Connected with this, it was recommended not to issue licences to people who in the past had been convicted for serious drug offences. According to a majority of the members of the Task Force, this restriction was needed to reduce the risk that licensees would sell cannabis to the black market.[69] Other recommendations were the advice to limit the number of licences a given person can receive and to restrict the size of cannabis producing companies. The Task Force also indicated that for all sorts of reasons the product information on the packaging of cannabis should meet high standards.

According to the text of *Amendment 64* and the related implementing measures, the production of cannabis is assigned to companies which, on the basis of a strict procedure, have received a licence for it. Annually, the state of Colorado, beforehand, determines the amount of cannabis the licensed plantations are allowed to cultivate. This is being done in order to avoid overproduction and the rise of an illicit market for legally cultivated cannabis – not just in Colorado, but also in the neighbouring states, where cannabis remains illicit.[70] Furthermore, every adult resident of Colorado has the right to grow up to 6 cannabis plants at home. In line with the proposals of the Task Force, certain

67 State of Colorado, 2013, p. 30.

68 *Ibid.*, p. 49.

69 *Ibid.*, p. 34.

70 *Ibid.*, p. 17.

locations have been designated where producers and sellers can dump their cannabis products and their garbage. The Task Force has much insisted on the establishment of such places, because otherwise the temptation would be strong "for both businesses and private citizens to divert these items to the illegal market".[71]

The processing of cannabis is also subject to special licences. Not everybody is allowed to process it. To do it in a legitimate manner, one not only needs to have the necessary delivery notes for the transport of cannabis, but one also has to package the cannabis or the cannabis-related products in compliance with a number of regulations and in such a way that it is always possible to detect their origins et cetera.[72]

The same is true with regard to the sale of cannabis, which is only allowed in certain licensed shops: on the one hand in shops that only (are allowed to) sell cannabis for recreational use, on the other hand in shops that (are allowed to) sell medical as well as recreational cannabis. In the latter case, both shop spaces must be separated by a wall.[73] At the moment, all the shops that exclusively sell recreational cannabis belong to companies that already have a licence for the sale of medical cannabis. This is because until October 2014 there was a transitional regulation according to which only companies that are allowed to sell medical cannabis could apply for a licence for a shop that exclusively sells recreational cannabis.[74] Since 1 January 2014 licences are issued but only since 1 October 2013 people could apply for licences. In the course of January 2014 40 "pot shops" received a licence. It is rather obvious that the decision that only licensed shops are allowed to sell cannabis will have as a result that several delivery services operating in the cannabis market will have to cease their activities.[75]

The regulation of the sale of cannabis has been modelled after the legislation on the sale of alcohol. Only people aged 21 years or older can purchase cannabis in a licensed shop. Adult residents of Colorado may purchase 1 ounce at a time, non-residents 1/4 ounce. The latter restriction has been introduced mainly to preserve Colorado's good relationships with the surrounding states and the federal authorities:

71 State of Colorado, 2013, pp. 47–48.

72 *Ibid.*, p. 46.

73 *Ibid.*, p. 44.

74 See, for instance, the report in *The Economist*, "High time; Colorado embarks on an unprecedented experiment", 11.1.2014, and J. Healy and K. Johnson, "In 2 states, corner cannabis store nears reality", *The New York Times*, 13.12.2013.

75 M. Valdes, "Weed delivery services on edge of legal pot laws", *The Cannabist*, 15.7.2014.

> In order to discourage the diversion of legally-purchased marijuana out of Colorado, reduce the likelihood of federal scrutiny of Colorado's adult-use marijuana industry, and support harmonious relationships with Colorado's neighbouring states (...).[76]

Individuals who want to purchase medical cannabis can only do that on presentation of an authorization provided by a general practitioner. They also have to be inscribed in the special register mentioned before. And cannabis can't be used in public places, but only in private.

Amendment 64 does not compel all counties or municipalities to agree with the establishment of one or more cannabis factories and/or cannabis shops in their territories. Local authorities retain broad authority to determine autonomously whether they want such establishments and, if so, how many of them and at which places. They can even prohibit this kind of facilities and shops.[77] The amendment explicitly states:

> A locality may prohibit the operation of marijuana cultivation facilities, marijuana product manufacturing facilities, marijuana testing facilities, or retail marijuana stores (...).

In 2013 R. Room estimated that in no more than about twenty municipalities and counties cannabis shops would be established.[78] The number of places where there are currently such shops or where there will be one or more of these shops in the near future, is hard to find out. It is also not known how many local authorities up to now have refused to issue cannabis-related licences.

However, in September 2013 the local authorities of more than one hundred places including the authorities of the second largest city of the state: Colorado Springs, had banned or delayed the legal sale of cannabis.[79] But apart from the numbers, the fact that over one hundred municipalities and counties do not accept – as yet – the legalization of recreational cannabis, demonstrates that the discussion about this important issue is still not over. Moreover, press reports about the developments in Colorado show that supporters and opponents make use of all sorts of incidents to prove they were, and are, right.[80]

76 State of Colorado, 2013, p. 50.

77 *Ibid.*, pp. 20–21.

78 Room, 2013, p. 346.

79 N. Flatow, "As Colorado moves toward legal pot shops, more than 100 localities ban or delay sales", *ThinkProgress*, 23.9.2013.

80 K. Wyatt, "Making marijuana edibles easily identifiable not an easy task", *The Cannabist*, 1.8.2014.

Furthermore the discussion about the therapeutic effects of cannabis is far from being settled in the state of Colorado: for which medical and/or psychic problems is it really a beneficial product?[81]

To conclude, it has to be emphasized that it is obviously too early to assess the developments in Colorado, although recently a reporter of *The New York Times* in Denver was struck by the fact "how quickly the marijuana industry has receded into normality".[82] This does not take away that we also have to be accessible – just like that reporter, fortunately, was – for the first signals about how the regulated system actually works in practice.

One of these signals is that up to now the illicit traders apparently have not surrendered.[83] In February 2014 a journalist noticed that in Denver dealers were selling cannabis for half the price charged in cannabis stores. That is not surprising, because according to his colleague of *The New York Times* it remains unclear how the legalization might eliminate the illicit trade:

> Seattle has such abundant and cheap black-market weed, pot shops may end up being only a tourist novelty.[84]

In this connection, a Seattle policeman remarked that the new legislation, paradoxically enough, could lead to an increase of the number of dealers:

> He believes the normalization of weed-smoking will increase overall demand and that users will soon turn to cheaper black-market suppliers.[85]

The second signal is that the measures that were taken to prevent Colorado from becoming a cannabis exporting state do not seem to work very well in practice. Several reports state that authorities in the neighbouring states are

81 J. Healy, "After 5 months of sales, Colorado sees the downside of a legal high", *The New York Times*, 31.5.2014; J. Healy, "Families see Colorado as new frontier on medical marijuana", *The New York Times*, 5.12.2013, and O. Devinsky and D. Friedman, "We need proof on marijuana", *The New York Times*, 12.2.2014.

82 L. Downes, "The great Colorado weed experiment", *The New York Times*, 2.8.2014.

83 See T. Griego, "Weed everywhere in Colorado, yet black market for marijuana thriving", *The Cannabist*, 30.7.2014.

84 L. Downes, "The great Colorado weed experiment", *The New York Times*, 2.8.2014.

85 J. Bindel, "Cannabis in Colorado: the ups and downs of legalizing highs", *New Statesman*, 27.2.2014. See also the report "Legal pot in Colorado hasn't stopped black market", *The Washington Post*, 3.4.2014.

complaining about "Coloradan marijuana flooding border areas" and "stoned drivers streaming out of Colorado and through their towns".[86]

These signals cannot be separated from the actual availability and the actual use of cannabis in Colorado. To apply this immediately to the second signal: recent research has demonstrated that in 2014 about 9 tons of cannabis will be sold to visitors from outside Colorado and that this sale will be concentrated in the big cities and the mountainous regions. It is not a coincidence that at this moment many of the licensed cannabis shops are located precisely in these areas.[87]

With regard to the second signal, we also cannot ignore the fact that approximately 150,000 young persons under 21 years of age are using cannabis without having access – with the exception of those who have a medical prescription – to the legal cannabis market to buy their daily, weekly or monthly portions. They have to provide themselves in the black market.

Still more important, in a sense, are the calculations that show that whereas in 2014 a total amount of 130 tons of cannabis will be needed to meet the whole demand (natives and foreigners, minors and adults) of the Colorado market, the cannabis shops will only be able to provide about 77 tons. This means that at least 53 tons of cannabis will be bought on the black or gray market. In this context, we are talking about cannabis cultivated at home, the resale of medical cannabis, and cannabis that is illicitly, or at least without a licence, produced on a large scale.[88] Only this way the inhabitants of Colorado who use cannabis once a month (393,000), less than once a month (156,000) or every day (127,000), will be able to satisfy their needs. Precisely the daily users consume proportionately the most cannabis.[89]

According to the researchers, the illicit production will probably continue to exist "if the price of regulated marijuana remains high" and, as a result, the black market stays competitive in price with the regulated market. However, if the price on the regulated market decreases, the same mechanism will probably lead to a reduction of the market share of the black market, but it may also

86 See S. Horwitz, "DEA chief says marijuana-trafficking spiking in states near Colorado", *The Washington Post*, 30.4.2014, and J. Healy, "After 5 months of sales, Colorado sees the downside of a legal high", *The New York Times*, 31.5.2014. See also the report in *The Economist*, "High time; Colorado embarks on an unprecedented experiment", 11.1.2014.

87 Light, Orens, Lewandowski and Pickton, 2013, pp. 21–26.

88 Regarding the problems the police at the moment encounters when inspecting plantations, see J. Ingold, "Growing marijuana: legalization complicates police investigations", *The Cannabist*, 14.7.2014.

89 Light, Orens, Lewandowski and Pickton, 2014, pp. 11–13, 15–16.

cause a drop in government revenues. From a federal perspective, the number of adult cannabis users in Colorado is rather large.[90]

3.4.1.3 The Situation in Washington State

On 6 November 2012, the same day on which people in Colorado voted in favour of an extension of the legalization of cannabis, also in Washington State people went to the polls to vote for or against this form of legalization. And in Washington State too the vote was the result of a campaign of years to legalize the recreational use of cannabis. A campaign that, also in this state, was not only pursued by political idealists but definitely also by commercial realists.[91]

Since 1998 the use of cannabis for medical purposes is legal in Washington State, although it was not as well regulated as in Colorado. As a consequence, the discussion about the legalization of cannabis for recreational use was a lot more complicated in Washington State than in Colorado. The sellers of medical cannabis, for example, fiercely opposed a regulation of the sale of recreational cannabis because they did not want to lose their monopoly and were afraid that many of their customers would switch to rival stores. In retrospect, this fear was quite understandable, because, unlike in Colorado, the sellers of medical cannabis did not enjoy a preferential treatment when applying for licences.[92] Up to now, attempts to integrate both regimes of regulation have failed. As a result the special shops for medical cannabis are situated in a kind of legal no man's land.[93]

On 6 November 2012 also in Washington State a majority of the voters, agreed with *Initiative Measure No. 502* and voted in favour of the legalization of

---

90 *Ibid.*, pp. 26–27.

91 See, for instance, the website of the Washington Cannabis Association: <http://washington cannabisassociation.org>.

92 See, for instance, M. Cooper, "Governors ask US to ease rules on marijuana", *The New York Times*, 30.11.2011; J. Feuer, "UCLA professor is the accidental marijuana policy expert", *UCLA Newsroom*, 3.9.2013; K. Johnson, "Marijuana referendum divides both sides", *The New York Times*, 13.10.2012; K. Johnson, "Medical marijuana bill dies in Washington State", *The New York Times*, 14.3.2014; K. Johnson, "Medical marijuana providers fear effects of wider legalization", *The New York Times*, 6.3.2014; R. Wilson, "Retail marijuana sales in Washington face regulatory delays", *The Washington Post*, 8.4.2014, and K. Johnson, "Still-divided Washington readies for start of recreational marijuana sales", *The New York Times*, 6.7.2014.

93 See, for instance, the Senate Bill Report SB 6178 (<http://apps.leg.wa.gov/documents/billdocs/2013>).

recreational cannabis.[94] By adapting the Uniform Controlled Substances Act, the proposal, according to its opening words, aimed to stop regarding adult cannabis use as a crime and to try a new approach. In section (1) of the proposal the arguments for a different approach were formulated as follows:

> 1. Allows law enforcement resources to be focused on violent and property crimes;
> 2. Generates new state and local tax revenue for education, health care, research, and substance abuse prevention;
> 3. Takes marijuana out of the hands of illegal drug organizations and brings it under a tightly regulated, state licensed system similar to that for controlling hard alcohol.

The task to work out the proposal, and the enforcement of the regulation that would result from it, was delegated to the Liquor Control Board. This commission was given until 1 December 2013 – a little bit more than a year – to design, along the lines of the alcohol legislation, a legal frame for the production and distribution of recreational cannabis.[95] And so it did. The commission has scrupulously fulfilled its task. The regulation it has designed – marijuana licences, application process, requirements, and reporting – includes dozens of sections, which in their turn are often composed of a variety of articles.[96] It is impossible to discuss it in full. In addition to what just has been said about the initial proposal, it is relevant to indicate the following.

To reach the objectives mentioned, a large number of measures has been developed. Just as in Colorado, these measures are related to the three essential components of any cannabis industry: production, processing, and sale. The measures have in common that cannabis can only be sold by private cannabis stores and these stores are only permitted to order their merchandise from licensed factories. Selling cannabis through the internet is prohibited. Whoever wants to be commercially active in the cannabis market needs a licence. In this connection it is clearly stated that whoever has a licence to

94 For the text of the proposal and the necessary explanation, see <http://weiapplets.sos.wa.gov>.

95 See the press release of the Liquor Control Board, dated 7 November 2012, about the work to be done following the approval of the proposal. A summary was published by the related Commission of the Senate of Washington State ("Summary of Initiative 502 to the Legislature").

96 See WACs, Title 314, Chapter 314–55: <http://apps.leg.wa.gov/wac/default.aspx?cite=314-55&full=true>.

produce or process cannabis is not allowed to have, directly or indirectly, any financial interests in a shop that is selling this drug. In Washington State the cannabis industry is less vertically integrated than in Colorado.

Related to this, it has been determined that anyone who applies for a licence will be subjected to a thorough background check (police record, judicial record and financial record). Applicants have to reveal the origin of the money they intend to invest in the establishment of their companies. They also must have been living in Washington State for more than three months, otherwise they will be excluded from the application procedure. Furthermore, it is not possible to receive a cannabis producer, a cannabis processor and a cannabis retailer licence together. A cannabis licensee may hold both a producer and a processor licence, but he or she cannot be at the same time a cannabis retailer. It is not permitted to export cannabis or cannabis products to other states.

Some provisions of the regulation concerned range from the layout of cannabis factories to the management of cannabis shops. Other provisions are related to the maximum permissible number of cannabis shops in a given county, to the safety in the successive stages of the production and distribution process, to the responsibilities of the above-mentioned Liquor Control Board and the powers of its inspectors, to the forms of cannabis advertising that are prohibited, to the fund that will be formed on the basis of all the tax revenues collected in the cannabis sector (the overall tax burden in the sector is set at 25%) and to the spending of these revenues – in the short and the long run – on the previously mentioned objectives: assistance, information and research. It is also remarkable that the licensees, by complying with different sorts of packaging requirements, have to ensure the trackability of each little bit of cannabis "from seed to sale", in order "to prevent diversion and to promote public safety (...)". Also relevant to the situation at the European side of the Atlantic is that, although local authorities can raise objections to the issuing of a licence, it is not clear how far their influence reaches. At this point too the regulation in Washington State differs strongly from the one in Colorado.[97]

As to the personal possession and use of cannabis, the proposal states that every person aged 21 years or older is allowed to have "one ounce of useable marijuana" (1 ounce equals 28 grams) in possession. With regard to products in which cannabis is processed, people are allowed to have 16 ounces of such

97 A. Johnson, "Washington State attorney general: cities and counties don't have to allow legal marijuana", *NBCnews*, 16.1.2014. Concerning the differences between the regulations in Washington State and Colorado in general, see B. Livingston, "Colorado and Washington State: 7 differences in state pot laws", *The Cannabist*, 7.1.2014.

products in solid form or 72 ounces in liquid form with them. An adult who has – in one of the three forms mentioned – more cannabis with him or with her, is punishable. The same is true for any person under 21 years of age who is found in the possession of cannabis in whatever form. Unlike in Colorado, home cultivation of cannabis for recreational use is strictly forbidden according to the Washington State proposal. Neither is it permitted to consume cannabis or cannabis-related products in the store(s) of purchase or at other places accessible to the public. The stores concerned are certainly not coffeeshops in the Dutch sense of the word.[98]

In this context, we have to bear in mind that in 2013, the Liquor Control Board asked Rand to conduct two studies on the size, nature and development of the cannabis market in Washington State. The reason behind the studies was that the Liquor Control Board wanted to know the size and diversity of the supply – the number of cannabis factories, cannabis processors and cannabis stores – needed to meet the demands of the market.[99] Of course, the researchers acknowledged how difficult it is to estimate the size of a market that, traditionally, to a large extent has been illicit. Nevertheless, by using various methods they succeeded in discovering that, on an annual basis, the market is probably twice as large as other institutes had previously estimated: 175 tons (the median between 135 and 225 tons) instead of 85 tons. Remarkable with regard to this finding is that 3 of Washington State's 39 counties account for about 50% of all cannabis use. For a good understanding of this result one needs to know the starting point of the study: not the number of cannabis users was counted, but the number of grams that they use. This way it was discovered that a limited group of heavy users – more precisely people who use cannabis 21 times a month or even more frequently and each time use 1.3 to 1.9 grams – accounts for an important part of the entire cannabis consumption in Washington State.

Despite the fact that the regulation and the study of the cannabis market was ready in time, the implementation of the new policy did not go smoothly. All kinds of problems put obstacles in the way. First and foremost, there was the problem of the vast amount of applications for licences to produce, process or sell cannabis – about 7,000 in March 2014; including not less than 411 applications for 21 licences in Seattle – and the time needed to handle them in a decent way. In the end it was decided to assign the licences in batches through a lottery system.

98 The Liquor Control Board of Washington State, too, has made a practical summary of the proposal. See <http://www.liq.wa.gov>.

99 Kilmer, Caulkins, Midgette et al., 2013, and Kilmer, Caulkins, Dahlkemper et al., 2013.

The very first licence to set up a plantation was issued, with some ostentation, on 6 March 2014; in July 2014 already 80 of such licences were issued. Although in April 2014 a total of 334 applications for a licence to set up a store had been selected, the applicants still had to be screened. In early July, the first cannabis shop actually opened its doors. And it was definitely not the only opening of its kind that month. "Everybody is leaping into the green rush", as a seller of medical cannabis said. The number of shops could rise to somewhere between 20 and 30.[100] In the first month the cannabis turnover amounted to 3.8 million dollars, which yielded the treasury more than 1 million dollars.[101]

To conclude, it has to be mentioned that in the literature on Washington State no attention is paid to the cross-border cannabis trade with Canada. The question whether cannabis from Canada is being smuggled into Washington State is not asked, let alone answered. Nor is anything said about the possible effects of the extension of the legalization in Washington State on the cannabis trade towards Canada. The oddness of this complete lack of attention for such matters will become evident from the following discussion of the developments in Canada and especially British Columbia. But maybe exactly these developments explain the silence at the American side of the border. Is the issue politically too delicate?

3.4.2 *The Development in Canada*

3.4.2.1 The Stance of the Federal Authorities

In the 1990s the attitude of the Canadian authorities towards drug-related offences was rather mild, in particular with regard to the cultivation and distribution of cannabis. People who were caught committing one of these crimes, mainly ran the risk of being fined. The same mildness was also shown towards migrants who were guilty of such offences. Notably some of the Vietnamese boat people who since the 1970s were accepted in Canada became involved in

100 See B. Young, "Retail pot-store openings move to early July", *The Seattle Times*, 2.4.2014; M. Adams, "Washington State stressed by recreational marijuana industry", *High Times*, 9.5.2014; the report in *The Daily Chronic* ("Washington State issues first recreational marijuana growing license"), 6.3.2014; T. McKay, "6 months since legalizing pot; Washington looks very different than Colorado", *PolicyMic*, 5.6.2014; the report in *Der Spiegel* ("US-Staat Washington erlaubt Verkauf von Marihuana"), 8.7.2014; T. Baker, "First Washington State recreational marijuana store hopes to open July 1st", *The Daily Chronic*, 6.6.2014, and J. Ellison, "Growers will have retail marijuana available for sale in early July", *SeattlePI*, 12.6.2014.

101 See the *Associated Press* report "Washington marijuana sales in first month: 3.8 million", *The Cannabist*, 8.8.2014.

the production and distribution of cannabis. These people mainly settled in and around Vancouver. There they were welcomed by Vietnamese criminal groups who used them for home cultivation of cannabis all over Canada. Whereas the Vietnamese cannabis cultivation was mainly concentrated in urban areas, the large-scale cultivation of cannabis in rural areas was dominated by the Hells Angels. The lenient attitude of police and justice towards these developments and the temptation of huge profits in the cannabis sector helped the Vietnamese gangs to become big criminal organizations that also played an important role as suppliers of the illicit cannabis market in the United States.[102]

In its turn, the gradual legalization of the medicinal cannabis market in American states has had an impact on both the production of cannabis in Canada and the cross-border distribution of the harvest in the United States.[103] In this context, it is first of all important to recall that in 2001 the Canadian government – forced by a court ruling that citizens should have "reasonable access to marijuana" for medical reasons – established a production and distribution system for medical cannabis. According to this system, not only the authorities were allowed to provide – by means of certain companies – cannabis to people who on medical grounds were qualified for the product, but also individual citizens had to some extent the right to do so: they were allowed to cultivate cannabis for medical purposes on a small scale at home or could ask someone else to do this for them. All a patient needed to get the permission from Health Canada – the Department of Health – to possess cannabis, was a written statement in which a general practitioner confirmed that the conventional medicines did not work for the patient concerned.

This form of medical regulation has resulted, on the one hand, in an enormous increase of the number of cannabis growers – 37,500 in 2014 – and, on the other hand, in an ever expanding flow of patients authorized to possess cannabis. In 2001 there were about 100 such patients, in 2014 their number had already increased to 40,000.[104] Estimates indicate that this number could rise

---

102 See, for instance, Drug Enforcement Administration, "BC bud: growth of the Canadian marijuana trade", *Drug Intelligence Brief*, December 2000, p. 3, and A. Humphreys and S. Bell, "Violence grows as marijuana profits rise", *National Post*, 19.10.2003.

103 In November 2010 in San Diego, for instance, 20 tons of marijuana were seized that had been smuggled from Mexico into the United States through tunnels. See *The Boston Globe*, "Discovery of tunnel leads to tons of pot", 27.11.2010.

104 Health Canada, press release ("Statement from Health Canada regarding the decision in Allard et al. v. Her Majesty the Queen in Right of Canada"), 21.3.2014.

to more than 450,000 in 2024. Together these people could constitute a market for medical cannabis worth 1.2 to 1.3 billion dollars.[105] Moreover, the normalization of the medical use of cannabis since the 1990s has led to the rise of "vapour lounges" in more and more cities. In these clubs not only patients but also recreational users can smoke cannabis. The authorities have not countered this development. They prefer users to smoke cannabis in such lounges rather than on streets and squares.[106]

However, parallel to this development there was a shower of complaints by citizens, police forces and local authorities about cannabis cultivation. Their complaints were not only related to security problems caused by cannabis plantations in residential areas – problems such as fire-risks or risks of water damage as well as robberies on plantations. In part the complaints were also related to the large amounts of cannabis which got dumped on the black market. The illicit supply was so big that the black market seemed to collapse due to oversupply.[107] At the same time it was alleged that criminal groups "have taken advantage of lax regulations to obtain medical production licences to protect their illegal growing operations from law enforcement".[108]

On 19 June 2014, in a press release meant to justify the introduction of a new production and distribution system, Health Canada described the problems as follows:

> The current practice of allowing individuals to grow marijuana for medical purposes poses risks to the safety and security of Canadians. The high value of marijuana on the illegal market increases the risks of violent home invasion and diversion to the black market. In addition, these production operations present fire and toxic mould hazards. These risks are not only felt by the individuals licensed to grow, but potentially also by their neighbours and community members.[109]

The new system is embedded in the Marihuana for Medical Purposes Regulations 2012 which came into force in June 2013 and implies that in the first place

105 I. Teotonio, "2014 poised to go pot", *Toronto Star*, 5.7.2014. See also W. Connors, "Canada's new marijuana laws set stage for growth", *The Wall Street Journal*, 17.4.2014.

106 I. Teotonio, "2014 poised to go pot", *Toronto Star*, 5.7.2014.

107 See the report ("How marijuana legalization hurts organized crime") in *Leaf Science*, 11.4.2014.

108 Diplock, Plecas and Garis, 2013, p. 12.

109 Health Canada, press release ("Letter to clients of Marihuana Medical Access Program"), 19 June 2014.

henceforth neither the authorities nor individual citizens are allowed to cultivate cannabis for medical purposes.[110] The possession and use of cannabis remains prohibited, unless it is, in conformity with the new regulation, permitted by a physician or a nurse.[111] In the second place, the reorganization implies that the production of cannabis for medical use is entrusted to a limited number of private companies. These companies are permitted to sell, under strict conditions, their products to patients, either directly through the internet or indirectly through call centers. In June 2014 13 (domestic and foreign/American) companies had received a licence. However, because of high profit expectations 850 companies had applied for such a licence.[112]

In view of the discussion in the Netherlands about the security of (in the future maybe) licensed companies in the sector of cannabis cultivation, it is remarkable that for security reasons – mainly the risk of robberies – the addresses of the Canadian licensees do not have to be revealed in official documents or on their products.[113] This measure is justified by the remark:

> that the illegal widespread use of marihuana for recreational purposes may increase the risk that a licensed producer would be the target of crime if the production location is more generally disclosed.

That this risk is not an imaginary one, is proven by the fact that press releases from the Royal Canadian Mounted Police, from time to time report on robberies on licensed cannabis companies.[114]

However, the security problem does not curb the licensed companies' enthusiasm for the new regulation of the legal provision of medical cannabis. Physicians, for their part, strongly disapprove of the new regulation, for the simple reason that cannabis "has not been through the testing and approval

---

110 This regulation can be found at: Government of Canada, Justice Law Website (<http://www.laws-lois.justice.gc.ca>).

111 Health Canada, press release ("Statement: changes to the reporting requirements in the Marihuana for Medical Purposes Act"), 14.3.2014.

112 J. Tilak, "Canada is primed to be a global example for medical marijuana", *Reuters*, 13.6.2014. For a list of the licensed companies, see Health Canada, press release ("List of authorized licensed producers under the Marihuana for Medical Purposes Act"), 22.4.2014. One of the licensees is Bedrocan, a company that is responsible for the production of medical cannabis in the Netherlands. See F. Kuin, "Mediwiet van Bedrocan slaat aan in Canada", *NRC-Handelsblad*, 26.8.2014.

113 Health Canada, press release ("Regulatory impact analysis statement"), 25.2.2014.

114 See, for instance, Royal Canadian Mounted Police, press release ("Home invasion at medicinal marijuana grow and attempted robbery"), 23.6.2014.

process required for other pharmaceuticals" and also because this drug is by far not as beneficial for different sorts of illnesses – for example, certain forms of rheumatism – as suggested. Without any doubt this criticism is also linked to the fact that in the coming years, as already said, the number of cannabis users in Canada might rise to 450,000.

Physicians are afraid that a large number of people do not purchase cannabis for medical reasons. These people are recreational users "with sham prescriptions". Whether or not the companies concerned expect that sooner or later also in Canada, following the example of the United States, the use of cannabis for recreational purposes will be legalized, is left an open question by the physicians. However, considering the way public opinion and some political parties are evolving, this form of legalization can be expected and may very well become a major issue in the 2015 elections.[115]

3.4.2.2 The Situation in British Columbia

With regard to the developments in Europe and especially in the Netherlands, it is relevant to add to the above-said that in the important Canadian province of British Columbia the production of cannabis, measured by any standard, far exceeds the domestic demand. Around the year 2000 the number of "grow operations" in this province was estimated at 17,500. In 2004 the cannabis market in British Columbia was valued at 4 to 7 billions on an annual basis. At that time, in any case 50 to 80% of all the cannabis cultivated over there was smuggled into the United States. The value of this illicit export was estimated at 2 to 5 billions on an annual basis.[116] These figures elicited the comment of other researchers a few years later that:

> British Columbia's considerable concentration of indoor marijuana growing operations is almost unparalleled by other Western democracies.[117]

Still in 2004 a researcher of the Fraser Institute wondered why cannabis cultivation flourished so much more in British Columbia than in other parts of the country. In his opinion, part of the answer was that in this province drug offenders were much less severely punished than elsewhere in Canada, especially in

115 I. Austen, "When cannabis goes corporate", *The New York Times*, 24.5.2014, and I. Teotonio, "2014 poised to go pot", *Toronto Star*, 5.7.2014. See also Diplock, Plecas and Garis, 2013, p. 17.

116 Ch. Chan, "B.C. pot loses market share as U.S. states ease marijuana laws", *Times Colonist*, 27.6.2014.

117 Diplock, Plecas and Garis, 2013, pp. 1–3.

proportion to the big profits cannabis can generate. Usually custodial sentences of no longer than 90 days were imposed and the average fine did not exceed 1,200 (Canadian) dollars. Unsurprisingly his conclusion was:

> While police resources are spent to destroy nearly 3,000 marijuana growing operations a year, the consequences are relatively small for those convicted.

Neither surprising was his recommendation. Viewed from a cost perspective it was obvious to legalize cannabis and to raise a tax on it comparable with the tax on cigarettes. Such a change of policy:

> would transfer the revenue from the current producers and middlemen, many of whom are associated with organized crime, to the government.

It could yield the state more than 2 billion dollars in tax revenues. To this he added that it is so easy to cultivate and export cannabis that in a democratic, constitutional state it is not possible for the police to control this industry with the usual means: "The return on investment is sufficiently great that for each marijuana growing operation demolished, another will take its place."[118]

What he did not tell in this context, has later, in 2013, been written down by other researchers. Precisely because of the great return on investment there is reason to fear that (an extension of) the legalization of cannabis in Canada will not mark the end of organized crime in this very attractive market:

> If illegal suppliers can draw a portion of these former growers toward their product and away from that of legitimate authorized producers, whether through low prices or the same stigmatization that was applied to the marijuana produced by Health Canada's growers, organized criminals may experience increased demand for their illicit marijuana as a result.[119]

Another question is what will happen with the illicit export of cannabis from Canada and in particular from British Columbia, to the United States when the

---

118 Easton, 2004, pp. 3–4. In press releases of the Royal Canadian Mounted Police regularly appear reports of demolitions of plantations of all sorts and sizes. See, for instance, the report of the Royal Canadian Mounted Police in the *Gazette* of January 2012 ("Cops and communities").

119 Diplock, Plecas and Garis, 2013, p. 16.

legalization of cannabis in Canada's southern neighbour country will continue to spread? How will this affect the prices of cannabis in Canada and the size and value of the export of (illicitly cultivated) Canadian cannabis to the United States?

Connoisseurs of the situation in British Columbia report that the prices have already declined spectacularly – as a matter of fact they have halved. The explanation is simple: the shrinking export to the United States has resulted in a big oversupply. As the legal production of cannabis in the United States will grow incrementally, it will become less and less interesting to take the risk of smuggling cannabis into the United States.

It is also important to know that for Canadian cannabis growers shifting their trade to Europe is not an option, because, as the Canadian observers report, countries such as the Netherlands and Morocco are well able to meet the needs of the European market. Moreover, in the near future the growers probably will get into even more trouble in Canada, because in Canadian politics there are calls to allow the small-scale recreational use of cannabis. Recently, a journalist astutely remarked: "Cannabis consumers have never had it so good; it's a tougher world for producers."[120]

3.4.3 *The Development in Uruguay*

The legalization of cannabis in Uruguay is not completely unique in South America.[121] Also in other South American countries the drug policy has changed over the years. However, in countries such as Argentina and Mexico the change is limited to the decriminalization of the personal use (and the associated possession) of cannabis and sometimes also other drugs.[122] It has nothing to do with the legalization of the production and distribution of cannabis or other drugs.

Bill no. 19.172 which was submitted by the Uruguayan government in December 2012 and was approved by the House of Representatives in July 2013 by a vote of 50–46 and which in December 2013 was also adopted by the Senate, did not appear out of the blue. It was not only rooted in previous attempts of members of Parliament to further decriminalize the personal use of cannabis,

120 T. Manitoba, "The grass on the other side", *The Economist*, 27.6.2014.

121 A good survey of what is happening in Uruguay can be found at the website of the Drug Law Reform Project: <http://www.druglawreform.info/en/country>.

122 See previous reports on this subject, such as the one by R. Carroll, J. Tuckman and T. Phillips, "Mexico and Argentina move towards decriminalising drugs", *The Guardian*, 31.8.2009. See also, for instance, S. Tegel, "Uruguay's neighbors now considering legalization of pot", *Global Post*, 24.12.2013.

but also the result of a campaign by all sorts of groups to legalize the production and distribution of cannabis in general. Furthermore, the bill seemed to fit in a kind of Uruguayan tradition to combine a strict state control of certain economic sectors, on the one hand, with the development of progressive solutions for social problems, on the other hand.[123]

However, the fact that the bill has been approved by only a small majority in the House of Representatives demonstrates that certainly not everybody in the country is charmed by this approach to the cannabis problem. It is understood that in the summer of 2013 still two-thirds of the population were against it. But the *Frente Amplio* pushed the bill through Parliament.[124] Nevertheless, it remains to be seen whether the decision will survive the next elections. According to a recent opinion poll the majority of the Uruguayan people still opposes the legalization of cannabis. The political opposition has announced that if it should win the elections in the autumn of 2014, it will reverse the decision. The opposition is strengthened in its intention by the fact that it appears really difficult for the current government to put the regulation into practice. To give one example, only recently the search for and selection of companies that are interested in producing cannabis has started.[125] The elections of November 30, 2014 were won, however, by the ruling Frente Amplio and the new president has promised to implement the marijuana legislation.[126]

The following aspects of the Uruguayan regulation of the production and distribution of cannabis are important:

- To establish a cannabis factory one must have a licence of the Instituto de Regulación y Control de Cannabis. A cannabis plantation that is not licensed can be demolished by order of a judge;
- Everybody is allowed to cultivate 6 cannabis plants at home for personal use. The quantity of cannabis harvested this way may not exceed 40 grams;
- Clubs with at least 15 and at most 45 members are allowed to cultivate, under the supervision of the institute mentioned, 99 cannabis plants; the

123 S. Romero, "Lawmakers in Uruguay vote to legalize marijuana", *The New York Times*, 31.7.2013.

124 G. Ramsey, "Uruguay's marijuana regulation bill passes in Lower House", *TNI Drug Law Reform*, 2.8.2013.

125 L. Haberkorn, "Uruguay: will government's pot program collapse?", *The Cannabist*, 1.8.2014.

126 See the press release of 1 December 2014 by the Drug Policy Alliance: "Uruguayan presidential election result safeguards marijuana legislation" (<http://www.drugpolicy.org/news/2014/12>).

size of the harvest has to be in proportion to the number of members and the amount of cannabis allowed for non-medical use;
- The institute mentioned can provide pharmacies licences for, on the one hand, the sale of psychoactive cannabis for therapeutic purposes on medical prescription, and, on the other hand, the sale of such cannabis for non-medical use up to a maximum of 40 grams per (registered) adult per month.

It is obvious that the International Narcotics Control Board cannot approve this regulation. In December 2013 the president of the board, Yans, accused the government of Uruguay of having a "pirate attitude" towards the drug treaties. The reply of the government – in the person of minister L. Porto – at the gathering of the board in Vienna in February 2014, was that Uruguay did not at all act contrary to the objectives of the treaties: the protection of public health and the curbing of the harmful effects of the international illicit drug trade. On the one hand, the law concerned is entirely in line with the right of freedom guaranteed by article 29 of the American Convention on Human Rights. On the other hand, this law is an outstanding tool in the fight against illicit drug trade. However, even sympathetic commentators did not hide that this defence was not so strong. They excused it by saying that for Uruguay and its government it was, politically and diplomatically, not easy "to declare publicly they are in direct violation of an international treaty they have signed".[127]

In this context it is important to indicate that the implementing legislation published in May 2014 stipulates that only inhabitants aged 18 years or older are permitted to buy cannabis and that the resale of cannabis is prohibited. There is a ban on cannabis advertising and the drug may not be consumed in public places. There is no room for "Dutch" coffeeshops in the streetscape.[128] As to the cannabis factories the authorities determine their production: how much they are allowed to produce, at what price and with which quality. This way, the creation of an open cannabis market in Uruguay is avoided: "Our production will never exceed local demand." A part of the tax revenues the cannabis sector will generate, will be spent on information about drug use and on addiction care. One should keep in mind that Uruguay is a relatively small country with a population of 3.5 million inhabitants. The number of regular

127 The above-said is mainly based on the chapter about "Cannabis reforms: the scope and limits of treaty latitude" in: Jelsma, Blickman and Bowley-Taylor, 2014, pp. 18–21.

128 See the Infographics at the website of the TNI Drug Law Reform Project: <http://www.druglawreform.info/en/publications>. See also S. Boseley, "Going to pot: legalised cannabis edges nearer in West after US states end ban", *The Guardian*, 23.5.2014.

cannabis users is estimated at 115,000 and the size of the (former) illicit market at 30 million dollars annually.[129] In April 2014 the first 6 licences for the larger-scale production of cannabis were sold.[130]

Of course it is still too early to assess the effects of the social experiment. Anyhow, there are a lot of questions. Will the authorities, unlike in British Columbia, be able to keep home cultivation under control? Will the gangs, that traditionally smuggle higher-quality cannabis from Paraguay into Uruguay, cease doing that? And in order to achieve this goal, is it enough that the official price for legally cultivated cannabis is purposely fixed at 1 dollar per gram? Does the country have the means to actually eradicate illicit plantations? How will the addiction problems evolve? Will Uruguay become the "Amsterdam of Latin America", despite the government's assertion that this is the last thing it wants? We will have to wait some time to know the answers to these questions.[131]

3.5 Conclusion

Regarding the problem of the legalization of cannabis, a lot can be learnt from the developments in the United States. The public discussion about the subject in the 1980s clearly demonstrates this. Many questions and counterquestions that are popping up in the current debate were already formulated at that time: questions about the relation between state and citizen in this context, about the (lack of) success in the war against crime, about the unintended counter-productive consequences of a criminal justice approach, about the negative effects of legalization on drug use, and about the different forms of legalization. But also questions about the Prohibition in the 1920s and 1930s as an example of the way the existing cannabis policy should or should not be changed.

The specific paragraph about this exceptional episode of American history has shown that the Prohibition must be placed in the context of its time in order to avoid totally inappropriate references to that episode in the current discussion about the legalization of cannabis. It should not be neglected, for

129 J. Davies and J. de Deken, "The architect of Uruguay's marijuana legalization speaks out", <http://reason.com/archives/2013/12/15>, and A. Serrano, "Uruguay unveils marijuana regulation details", <http://america.aljazeera.com/articles/2014>.

130 See the report of Reuters ("Uruguay to allow pot users to buy up to 20 joints a week"), 24.4.2014.

131 J. Watts, "Uruguay's likely cannabis law could set tone for war on drugs in Latin America", *The Guardian*, 18.11.2013.

instance, that the Prohibition was not an internationally agreed-upon ban on alcohol but a matter of national policy. People should also know that this ban was not at the root of organized crime in the United States, though it has certainly given a boost to that already longer existing form of crime. Such a boost, that after the abolition of the Prohibition, organized crime did not disappear at all but thrived even more and in all sorts of shapes. At least equally important for the current debate about the legalization of cannabis is the key question the Wickersham Commission, which examined the sustainability of the Prohibition, had to answer: is it possible to maintain a law that appears not to be supported by the general public? Nowadays, the same question should be asked with regard to the cannabis problem: is a total ban on the production and distribution of cannabis still tenable?

The answer of the famous Wickersham Commission with respect to alcohol is well-known. The answer of the United States with respect to cannabis is two-fold, not to say ambiguous. What in some American states has been legalized and regulated, not only for medical but also for recreational purposes, remains prohibited at federal level. This way, on federal level one is formally complying with treaty-based obligations, whereas at least some states – with the approval of the federal authorities – are increasingly evading these obligations. The principal cause of this schizophrenic situation is the problem of the enforceability of the prohibition of cannabis, given the normalized large-scale medical and recreational use of it. We should not forget that this ambiguous situation in the reality of the federal structure of the United States, has the big advantage that the space it creates at state level for the legalization of cannabis, can be kept within bounds by criminal law at federal level. It makes up a protection against, on the one hand, possible excesses in the states due to insufficient regulation and/or insufficient enforcement of the rules, and, on the other hand, illicit import of cannabis from abroad. In this respect the assignment of tasks between the federation and the states, is less bizarre than it may look at first sight.

The big question in the United States at this moment is not whether or not the federal authorities have to legalize cannabis but rather how the production and distribution of cannabis can best be regulated at state level? The regulation of recreational cannabis in Colorado and Washington State, respectively, illustrates there are very different ways to cope with this problem. When looking at the current regulations, one can easily come to the conclusion that in this connection the answers to a number of questions are of crucial importance. Major questions are for instance:

- What are the general objectives of the legalization of cannabis? Fighting large-scale illicit cultivation and, by doing so, (cross-border) organized crime which, behind the scenes, controls the cultivation and the revenues it generates? Advancing the viability and security in residential areas where, at a larger scale, the production of cannabis actually takes place? Improving public health by increasing the possibilities to perform quality checks? Expanding the free space for citizens to enjoy cannabis without too much state interference? Increasing the revenues for the state by levying taxes on the successive important activities in the entire chain of production and distribution? And how to spend the additional revenues? On information about drug use? On addiction care? On an efficient enforcement of the legislation concerned? Or may, or should, they also be used for the construction of schools, the building of roads, the financing of aged care, and other public service tasks not related to the cannabis sector?

- If small-scale home cultivation for personal use becomes legal, then how many cannabis plants should people be allowed to cultivate? How can the rules be enforced? How to restrain illicit resale? How to minimize the nuisance to the immediate neighbourhood? What are home growers supposed to do with their garbage?
- What kind of companies should be allowed to produce cannabis: state-owned or private companies? Which authorities, and under which conditions, will be qualified to issue licences? How many companies – whatever their legal shape – can or should receive a licence? No more than needed to produce enough cannabis to meet domestic consumption? Or should licensed companies also be allowed to produce for the foreign market? As to domestic consumption: does this only include cannabis use by residents or also the use by all sorts of tourists? How many companies may be run by the same person(s)? At which locations can cannabis factories be established? Do local authorities have the possibility to lodge an appeal against the issuing of a permit to establish a cannabis factory?
- Which quality requirements does the commercial cultivation of cannabis have to meet? In terms of the size of the production, the used types of plants, the way of producing and the registration of the products, the integrity of the entrepreneurs and the employees, the safety of the production process and the employees, the abatement of the nuisance to the neighbours, the processing of the garbage, et cetera. And also important: which product-oriented changes may cannabis undergo? In which foods and stimulants can it be processed?
- What kind of companies are allowed to sell cannabis? Only state-owned companies? Pharmacies, in a separate section of the store? Which authorities have the power to issue licences for the commercial sale of cannabis? With which suppliers are shopkeepers permitted to cooperate? What is the

economic and financial relationship between cannabis factories and cannabis shops? How many shops may be run by the same person(s)? Can only residents receive licences or also non-residents? Which integrity requirements have to be met by owners, managers and employees? Which management requirements have to be met in the administrative field as well as in the safety and security field? At what prices can cannabis and cannabis products be sold? At which locations can cannabis stores be established? Do local authorities have the possibility to oppose the issuing of a permit to establish a cannabis store? Will cannabis shops, one way or another, be allowed to advertise for their products? What sanctions are linked to non-compliance with the licence conditions?
- Who is allowed to purchase cannabis and cannabis products in licensed shops? Is there an age limit? And if so, which age limit? Are cannabis purchasers obliged to register and identify themselves? How much cannabis and how many cannabis products can be bought legally in a given shop or a given region in a given time span? Where should the purchased goods be consumed? In the shop where they were bought? In a private environment, or also in publicly accessible places and public places?
- Which service at which administrative level is in charge of the enforcement of the related legislation and regulation? What powers, human resources and technical instruments does the service concerned have at its disposal to do this in a conscientious and efficacious way? From the issuing of licences up to and including the supervision of the compliance with the licence conditions?

Depending on the answers to the above-mentioned questions the legalization of recreational cannabis can lead to very diverging regulatory systems. This becomes clearly visible when comparing the regulations in Colorado and Washington State with each other. Whereas home cultivation for recreational use is permitted in one state it is prohibited in the other state. The integration of production and distribution is strictly regulated in one state, while it is less rigorously regulated in the other state.

However, these and other differences do not change the fact that the legalization of cannabis in the American states concerned has, on the whole, an explicit economic dimension – although in the background several causes and purposes play an important role as well. It is no coincidence that legal cannabis is everywhere considered to be a booming business, that various observers refer to a green Gold Rush, and that in academic circles the habitual supporters of legalization are talking about a corporate takeover.

Just how much this is the case, becomes obvious when the legalization in the two American states is compared with the one in Uruguay. In that South

American country the legalization is to a much lesser degree an economic and fiscal story. Which is quite understandable, given the fact that in Uruguay the legalization is happening in a social democratic context. This major distinction, however, does not alter the fact that the Uruguayan authorities and the authorities of the American states are confronted with similar challenges. As a consequence, it is no wonder that on some points the regulations in the three states have a lot in common.

Though there are also important differences. One such difference concerns the establishment of small clubs, the members of which may grow cannabis for personal use. Another remarkable difference is the fact that pharmacies are the favoured distribution channel. Furthermore, it is clear that although the legalization of cannabis in Uruguay is a daring step towards a new drug policy in South America, up to now that step has not led to similar steps by neighbouring countries. Related to this, it also needs to be emphasized that the legalization of cannabis does not put an end to the drug wars in these countries and – by extension – other parts of the world. To date, these wars are to a large extent also centered upon the production and distribution of cocaine, heroin and synthetic drugs.[132]

Regulating something with the best intentions is one thing, but the way such a regulation works out in practice is quite another thing. Many authorities in the United States are fully aware of this and the federal government, many governors and also a large number of local authorities are therefore talking about an "experiment". They more or less want to know the practical consequences of regulation before they themselves will consider taking steps on the path of legalization. Their restraint is certainly understandable in view of what, since the 1990s, has happened in Canada and especially in British Columbia. For various reasons including unbridled home cultivation, the regulation of cannabis for medical use got completely out of hand there. As a result, British Columbia has undisputably become a "green state" the past decades. Not only as a consequence of the normalization of medical cannabis use and the related expansion of the domestic market, but also as a consequence of the very lenient investigation, prosecution and sentencing policy with regard to offenders of the regulation.

Despite the criminal justice risks, it was financially very tempting to smuggle large amounts of cannabis into the black market of the United States. This caused big problems related to organized crime and the security of neighbourhoods. So big, that recently the government of Canada felt obliged to radically reconsider the way cannabis (for medical purposes) is produced. Since that

---

132 See, for instance, the article by A. Endres, "Legales Marihuana beendet keinen Drogenkrieg", *Die Zeit*, 22.5.2013.

reconsideration, the production is entrusted to a limited number of licensed companies. There is no lack of people interested in establishing such a company. The owners are probably hoping that the production and distribution of recreational cannabis will eventually be legalized. Not everybody is happy with these (possible) developments. Medical practitioners especially fear that many users of medical cannabis will actually be recreational users in disguise.

The consequences this radical policy change will have with regard to the problem of organized crime are not clear, also because the nature and extent of these consequences depend in part on factors the Canadian government has no control over. This is true, for instance, for the reaction of organized crime to the domestic policy: will the cannabis gangs cease their activities or will they compete with the legal market? Another important factor is the spreading legalization of medical and recreational cannabis in the United States. If this process goes on, the black market for cannabis in the United States will automatically shrink and the need for illicit Canadian cannabis will continue to decrease. This thought leads us to one of the problems that are also present in the European Union: the large-scale cross-border smuggling of cannabis between states.

CHAPTER 4

Cannabis Policy in the European Union

4.1 Introduction

Since it is often said that the European drug policy was, and is, dictated by the United States and the United Nations, it is first of all important to begin in this chapter with a discussion of the origin of the drug policy pursued within the framework of the European Union. This will be done in the next paragraph by a brief discussion of the reports of the two committees of inquiry of the European Parliament that, in the early 1990s, have examined the nature of, and the approach to, drug problems, especially problems related to cannabis.

Following on from this, we shed some light upon the key provisions of the Schengen Implementation Agreement that were to serve as a workable compromise between the parties concerned and had to keep the cross-border drug traffic in the Schengen area under control.

This is followed by an examination of the extent to which the current drug policy of the European Union leaves room for the legalization of cannabis, or at least for a serious discussion on this topic. Complementary to the debate on the policy pursued, the severity of the present-day cannabis problem in the European Union is outlined.

To conclude, we look at the ongoing developments on this point in some big European member states: Spain, Germany, France and the United Kingdom. An impression of the situation in these member states is sufficient to highlight how complicated the relations between the member states are in this respect and how difficult it will be to harmonize the different drug policies within the framework of the European Union.

4.2 The Origin of the Policy Pursued: Two Committees of Inquiry

The first initiative to develop a European drug policy was not taken by the European Union, or its predecessor: the European Community, but by the Council of Europe. Under the auspices of the latter organization, and in line with policy discussions launched in 1971 by the French president G. Pompidou, in 1980 the Co-operation Group to Combat Drug Abuse and Illicit Trafficking in Drugs was established, the so-called *Groupe Pompidou*.[1] However, a few years

1 Council of Europe, *Origin, functioning and achievements of the Pompidou Group*, Strasbourg, 1998. See also Estievenart, 1995b, pp. 58–61.

 | DOI 10.1163/9789004293199_005

later, this initiative was already adopted and strengthened by the European Community. In January 1985 the European Parliament installed a committee which had to conduct an investigation "into the drugs problem in the Member States of the Community". The report of that committee was published on 1 October 1986.[2]

It was not the problem of drug addiction, however, that prompted the committee to mention a "critical situation" in its report. The reason to do so was:

> the emergence in strength of drug traffickers and their criminal organisations, operating at multinational levels, which are involved in the whole gamut of producing, processing, transporting and marketing of drugs and the laundering of 'black' money from the drugs trade.[3]

To get a grip on the situation, the committee said it was necessary "that all links in the chain of production, supply and demand for narcotic drugs must be tackled in order to deal successfully with the problem".

In line with this conclusion the committee paid much attention to the discussion about the legalization of, among other things, cannabis. The committee was not directly opposed to the legalization of cannabis, though in the end it did attach greater value to the arguments against such a change:

> Firstly, there is illogicality in making cannabis legal to consume but illegal to import. This is what the Dutch do. Secondly, the trade in cannabis is still conducted by criminal organisations. Thirdly, we know that there are stronger varieties of cannabis being grown and the possibilities of mixing this drug with chemical substances such as P.C.P. can be lethal.[4]

For the committee these counter-arguments were reason enough to "recommend that cannabis should remain an illegal drug", although the comment was added that measures should be taken "to encourage a scientific debate on this

---

2 European Parliament, *Report drawn up on behalf of the committee of enquiry into the drugs problem in the Member States of the Community*, 1986–1987, PE 106.715/B/fin.corr. (reporter: J. Stewart-Clark).

3 *Ibid.*, p. 8.

4 European Parliament, *Report drawn up on behalf of the committee of enquiry into the drugs problem in the Member States of the Community*, 1986–1987, PE 106.715/B/fin.corr. (reporter: J. Stewart-Clark), pp. 48–49.

important problem". At least, this was the opinion of the majority (8) of the committee members, all of whom belonged to right-wing parties in the European Parliament.

A minority of 4 members, representing left-wing groupings, protested and presented their own vision on parts of the report. They agreed that "the emergence in strength of multi-national criminal organisations producing and marketing drugs" was the most dangerous problem, but argued that more had to be done than "simply combating drugs". The main objective should be "to normalize society's approach to drugs, drug use and, regrettably, drug addiction".

A similar discord was expressed in the report of the committee that had been established by the European Parliament in 1990 to conduct – under the chairmanship of P. Cooney – an investigation "into the spread of organized crime linked to drugs trafficking in the Member States of the European Community".[5] The reason to set up this committee is immediately elucidated in the first sentences of the report:

> The power of the criminal organizations which control the drugs traffic is growing at an alarming rate. It is having increasingly serious effects on society and on the political institutions of the Member States.[6]

Unsurprisingly the recommendations of the committee were mainly aimed "at improving the effectiveness of control measures, in accordance with the 1988 Vienna Convention". In its report the committee established a clear and direct link between the policy of the United Nations and the policy of the European Community regarding the controlling of drug problems. No wonder that this was the primary recommendation:

> Anti-drugs efforts must concentrate not on the users and at the bottom of the trafficking hierarchy, but on organized international trafficking at the highest levels. There is a need to develop a pragmatic approach to reducing the risks associated with the use and the abuse of drugs (harm reduction) by reimbursing the costs of drugs addicts' health and social care.[7]

---

5 European Parliament, *Report drawn up by the committee of enquiry into the spread of organized crime linked to drugs trafficking in the Member States of the European Community*, 1991–1992, PE 152.380/fin. (reporter: P. Cooney). See also Estievenart, 1995b, pp. 66–67.

6 *Ibid.*, p. 4.

7 European Parliament, *Report drawn up by the committee of enquiry into the spread of organized crime linked to drugs trafficking in the Member States of the European Community*, 1991–1992, PE 152.380/fin. (reporter: P. Cooney). See also Estievenart, 1995b, p. 6.

Furthermore the committee highlighted that:

> the task of combating is an intimidating one and the most that one can say, as things stand at present, is that the war against drugs is neither being won nor is it being lost.

This finding was more or less the basis for the three-dimensional drug policy that, according to the committee, had to be pursued: "against supply, against trafficking and against demand". The latter approach was considered to be the most important: "The key to ultimate success in the war against drugs is in the area of demand." To this the committee immediately added that the drug problem was enormous and did not seem to diminish. This explained why a rather large number of people were supporting a "normalization" of the drug problem. These people considered:

> the quest for a drug-free world impossibly utopian and society should be prepared to tolerate and to provide for the use of illicit drugs, or as some would say – recognize reality.[8]

However, the committee did not want to go that far. First of all, the European Community had to endorse the position of the United Nations that drug abuse and illicit drug trade should be regarded as illegal; in the eyes of the reporter this position constituted "an insuperable constitutional impediment to a policy of legalisation". The second problem was that a "policy of legalisation" would require a broad range of controls (permitted types of drugs, age of the purchasers, fight against the black market, increasing drug use, et cetera). Precisely because of these control problems it was not recommendable to pursue such a policy:

> Control of these issues is obviously essential and will require a police response at least as substantial as that required to enforce a regime of prohibition. It is clear from experience to date that such a regime would be favoured by very few countries indeed and they would find themselves magnets for addicts from outside their borders. In 1989 in Amsterdam twice as many foreign addicts (mostly Germans) died from an overdose as did Dutch nationals, 28 as against 14.[9]

---

8 *Ibid.*, p. 48.

9 European Parliament, *Report drawn up by the committee of enquiry into the spread of organized crime linked to drugs trafficking in the Member States of the European Community*, 1991–1992, PE 152.380/fin. (reporter: P. Cooney). See also Estievenart, 1995b, p. 49.

The disunity in the Cooney committee also played an important role in the 11 May 1992 debate in the European Parliament on the content of a resolution in pursuance of the committee's report. The central point of the debate was the legalization of soft drugs and notably cannabis. It seemed that right-wing politicians would vote against it and left-wing politicians for it. Due to the disunity in socialist ranks it turned out otherwise. The resolution was passed with 171 votes in favour, 135 against, and 8 abstentions.[10]

In view of what will follow, it is important to indicate that the idea that in the previous years drug trade had gradually become a major form of organized crime and that criminals and criminal groups of all sorts had increasingly organized themselves so as to be able to operate successfully at the illicit drug market, was not an illusion of politicians in the European Parliament.

This clear change in the organization of crime has also been described in the 1980s by, for instance, researchers familiar with the developments in the United Kingdom and Italy. Not only did they notice that conventional professional criminals had gradually switched to the trade in illicit drugs and were acquiring positions in the logistics chain of the production, trade and distribution of illicit drugs. They also noticed monopolistic tendencies on this illicit market. However, because of constant collisions with counterforces, these tendencies did not give rise to factual monopolies. The market remained permanently divided between better organized but also competing criminal groups.[11]

4.3 The Schengen Agreement and Drug Policy

The Netherlands was not explicitly mentioned in the report of the Cooney committee about the adaptation of an inconsistent drug policy to a future common drug policy of the member states of the European Community. However, that part was definitely painful for the Dutch and for insiders it clearly referred to the then ongoing negotiations about the role of drug policy in the Schengen Implementation Agreement.[12]

These negotiations followed from the Schengen Agreement concluded in June 1985 by Germany, France and the Benelux countries. In the context of the unification of the market of the European Community, the Schengen Agreement not only arranged the abolition of border controls at the internal

10 For a report of this debate, see *Europa van Morgen*, 27.5.1992, p. 271.

11 Ruggiero and South, 1995, pp. 7–11, 190–205.

12 This paragraph is mainly based on Fijnaut and De Ruyver, 2008, pp. 27–30.

borders, but also provided for accompanying measures to compensate the possible decrease in safety. In article 8 of the agreement the signatory parties commit themselves to:

> combat vigorously illicit drug trafficking on their territories and to coordinate their action effectively in this area.

In article 9 it is stated that, in view of this, they will reinforce, in the short term, the cooperation between their customs and police authorities. In article 19 they commit themselves to harmonize, in the long term, laws and regulations on narcotic drugs. However, the text of the Schengen Implementation Agreement of 1990 shows that the above-mentioned was easier said than done: a whole chapter of the text is dedicated to problems related to narcotic drugs. In article 71, paragraph 1, it is announced that a permanent working party will be set up to examine common problems related to combating crime involving narcotic drugs.[13]

According to article 71, paragraph 1, the signatory parties engage to observe, also with regard to cannabis, the United Nations conventions against the illicit trafficking in narcotic drugs. Next, paragraph 2 of article 71 – and in particular this provision resulted from the deviating Dutch drug policy – compels the parties concerned to curb in all the usual ways the illicit export of narcotic drugs, including cannabis. In a joint declaration on this provision it is stated that in case the drug policy of the signatory parties departs from article 71, paragraph 2, they:

> shall adopt the necessary administrative measures and penal measures to prevent and punish the illicit import and export of such products and substances, particularly towards the territories of the other Contracting Parties.

Moreover, in paragraph 5 it is added that the signatory parties shall do everything they can:

> to prevent and combat the negative effects arising from the illicit demand (...). Each Contracting Party shall be responsible for the measures adopted to this end.

For the Netherlands this meant that, on the one hand, it was given enough room to maintain its drug policy with regard to the users of soft drugs who could still

13 With regard to the Schengen Agreement of 1985 and the Schengen Implementation Agreement of 1990, see also Van Kempen and Fedorova, 2014, pp. 105–114.

purchase their stuff in coffeeshops. On the other hand the Dutch government had to adopt all the necessary measures to prevent the import and export of drugs towards the territories of the other parties concerned. In 1989 the Dutch government wrote to the Tweede Kamer – the Dutch House of Representatives – that, as a consequence of this engagement, the sale of soft drugs to foreigners had to be curbed. In this way, the French request to control the illicit export of cannabis products purchased in coffeeshops to the territory of one or more other signatory parties could be met. When a few years later, shortly before the coming into force of the Schengen Implementation Agreement, in 1995, the French government once again sharply criticized the Dutch drug policy, the Dutch cabinet declared in the Second Chamber that the Netherlands had not committed itself to harmonize its drug policy, but:

> to identify and recognize the negative cross-border effects of the Netherlands on France and other countries, and conversely (for instance French drug runners causing lots of trouble in Rotterdam), and to look for joint solutions and to intensify cooperation.

In the neighbouring countries, the concessions of the Netherlands on this point were not always received with the same amount of confidence. A Belgian senator, for instance, stated in 1992 that, due to the freedom of movement in the Schengen area, the Schengen Agreement would enhance drug tourism instead of making it disappear. One of the practical consequences of the discussion was the start of the so-called Hazeldonk consultations with Belgium and France about drug tourism on the route Lille-Rotterdam.

More in general, the above leads to the conclusion that with regard to the development, implementation and alteration of its drug policy – including its cannabis policy – the Netherlands should take full account of the negative repercussions of that policy on the drug problems in other Schengen countries. It has to be noted that the integration of the Schengen Agreements in the legal system of the European Union, as a result of a protocol to the Treaty of Amsterdam, did not change the arrangements contained in the Schengen Implementation Agreement.[14]

4.4 The Current Drug Policy of the European Union

The debates in the above-discussed investigation committees of the European Parliament demonstrate that, despite the sharp political divisions in the

14 Council of the European Union, 2001.

European Union around 1990 with regard to the legalization of (soft) drugs, none of the parties pleaded for a one-sided, strongly repressive war on drugs such as had been propagated by the federal authorities in the United States since the 1930s and, in a sense, had reached its peak in the mainly repression-oriented United Nations Convention of 1988. On the contrary!

The first European plans to combat drugs, drawn up in 1990, show this clearly. Right from the beginning, the point of departure in the European Union was that an adequate drug policy should be based on three pillars: "demand reduction, repression of trafficking, and international action". The implementation of such a policy required, on the one hand, sufficient coordination between these pillars and, on the other hand, a monitoring centre "as a means of measuring, analysing and assisting policy decisions".[15]

The European drug policy cannot simply be compared with the American drug policy and it cannot simply be claimed that the drug policy at this side of the Atlantic is identical with the war on drugs at the other side.[16] Those who do so, have no idea what they are talking about; or they do know what they are talking about, but have political or economic motives to steer the debate in the wrong direction.

4.4.1 *Is There Room for the Legalization of Cannabis?*

In the context of this discourse it is not relevant to analyze all the regulations and plans the Council of Europe has drafted since the 1990s in order to keep the drug problem under control.[17] However, one exception has to be made: the Council's Framework Decision of 25 October 2004, laying down minimum provisions on the constituent elements of criminal acts and penalties in the field of illicit drug trafficking. The background of this framework decision was the policy developed in the previous years. The decision was based on the wish:

> to reduce the demand for and the supply of drugs and to combat illicit drug trafficking by means of a multidisciplinary and integrated approach, and to intensify and coordinate international cooperation at the national level as well as the level of the European Union.[18]

---

15 Estievenart, 1995b, pp. 68–71.

16 As to the negative consequences of the American war on drugs for the police in Belgium, see Fijnaut, 1983.

17 On this subject, and especially on the 2004 Framework Decision regarding penalties for illicit drug trafficking, see Van Kempen and Fedorova, 2014, pp. 114–138.

18 For a detailed discussion of this Framework Decision, see Van Kempen and Fedorova, 2014, pp. 118–135.

With regard to the cultivation of cannabis, article 2 of that Framework Decision makes it very clear that even the cultivation of cannabis plants that still do not have flowering and fruiting tops and do not yet contain resin is already punishable as a completed offence. This way, P. Van Kempen and M. Fedorova write:

> the Framework Decision also confirms the penalizing obligations with regard to cannabis cultivation that result from the UN Convention against Illicit Traffic (…). The penalizing obligations of the Framework Decision imply that the legalization or decriminalization of cannabis cultivation, supply and trafficking aimed at recreational use is not possible. So, this also means that such a cultivation for the provisioning of coffeeshops is excluded by the Framework Decision.[19]

For the rest, it suffices in the context of this book to look at what the current plans are telling about cannabis policy and to examine in particular whether there is room in these plans for the legalization of cannabis. The EU drugs strategy for 2013–2020 and the EU action plan on drugs 2013–2016 that ensued from it are of particular relevance.[20]

Completely in line with the policy developed in the 1990s, reducing the demand for and the supply of drugs are in the EU drugs strategy 2013–2020 considered to be the principal ways to reach – in conformity with the policy recommended at the level of the United Nations – the main targets of the drug policy: "a high level of human health protection, social stability and security". In this context it is assumed that "drug demand reduction and drug supply reduction are mutually reinforcing elements in illicit drugs policy". Complementary to these two action lines, three cross-cutting themes play a key role in the policy: coordination, international cooperation and research.

Next, these five points of departure are translated into a long series of general measures. In the case of drug demand reduction the measures are related to, for instance, the availability of efficient education programmes and good and accessible addiction care. This, for example, is one of the tasks that should be given priority:

> promote the use and exchange of best practices and develop and implement quality standards in prevention (environmental, universal,

---

19 Van Kempen and Fedorova, 2014, p.121.

20 *Official Journal*, 29.12.2012, C 402/1-402/10, and *Official Journal*, 30.11.2013, C 351/1-351/23. In this connection, see also the communication of the European Commission, "Towards a stronger European response to drugs", Brussels, 25.10.2011, COM (2011) 689 final.

> selective and indicated), early detection and intervention, risk and harm reduction, treatment, rehabilitation, social reintegration and recovery.

With regard to drug supply reduction, attention has to be paid to:

> prevention and dissuasion and disruption of drug-related, in particular, organized crime, through judicial and law enforcement cooperation, interdiction, confiscation of criminal assets, investigations and border management.

Priorities in this context are, among other things, reinforced cooperation between police services at strategic and tactical level, but also the reduction of:

> intra-EU and cross-border production, smuggling, trafficking, distribution and sale of illicit drugs and the facilitation of such activities, as well as reduce the diversion of drug precursors, pre-precursors and other essential chemicals used in the illicit manufacture of drugs.

The aim of these and other measures to reduce the supply of drugs is:

> to contribute to a disruption of the illicit drugs market and a measurable reduction of the availability of illicit drugs.

In the action plan on drugs 2013–2016 of the European Union all these measures are translated into dozens and dozens of actions. Though, for the purpose of our discourse, we can leave aside these actions. Instead it is more relevant to indicate that, in line with the letter as well as the spirit of the Treaty of Lisbon, the implementation of such measures is usually a shared responsibility of the European Union and its member states. This common responsibility for the European drug policy means that no member state can simply neglect the purposes, measures and actions laid down in the plans. We should also not forget that every member state was closely involved in the development of the drug policy. As a result no member state can suddenly disregard it. If a member state would disregard it, that member state would not only undermine its credibility but would also receive sharp criticism from the other member states.[21]

This review of the purposes, strategies and actions of the European drug policy makes it almost self-evident that this policy leaves absolutely no room

21 For a better understanding of the relations between the European Union and its member states on this point, see Chatwin, 2013.

for whatever form of legalization of whatever kind of drug, including cannabis. No exception is made in this context for cannabis clubs, let alone coffeeshops.[22] Yet, in different ways, the plans do leave plenty of room for:

> encouraging an active political discourse and analysis of developments and challenges in the field of drugs at EU and international levels.

But it stops at such general statements. Of course, this does not mean that a discussion about the legalization of drugs – given the context of the statements – would be at variance with the obvious willingness to continually call the drug policy into question. On the contrary, such a discussion perfectly fits in a debate about the starting points of the drug policy. In practice, no body or member state of the European Union can prevent that discussion, assuming any of them would want to do so.

At some places, the plans mentioned contain implicit hints to conduct the discussion on the basis of arguments, that is: in a well-founded, coherent and balanced way. This is also the way the European Union tries to develop and implement its drug policy. The report, ordered by the European Commission in 2009, about the developments in the global drug markets and the policy developments in a number of countries to keep these markets under control has to be understood in the same sense.[23]

Although that report is characterized by the wish to change the international drug policy rather drastically (the researchers had to look at the drug problem "as if it were a licit market") and although the conclusions are dominated by the unintended negative consequences of the current policy, the purport of the report has nothing in common with a plea in favour of any form of legalization of cannabis or other drugs. The authors write they had no intention to make recommendations, and in the preface also the Commissioner concerned, J. Barrot, does not show his hand on this point. However, the implicit message is clear:

> Enforcement of drug prohibitions has caused substantial unintended harms; many were predictable. The challenge for the next ten years will be to find a constructive way of building on these lessons so that the positive benefits of policy interventions are increased and the negative ones averted.[24]

22 See more specifically Van Kempen and Fedorova, 2014, pp. 134–135.

23 Reuter and Trautmann, 2009.

24 Reuter and Trautmann, 2009, p. 17.

What this "constructive way" could be, is not indicated. To date, and given the policy plans just mentioned, for the (member states of the) European Union this in any case does not seem to include the legalization of cannabis. Furthermore, it is appropriate to add that this matter has not been put on the agenda of the Italian Presidency of the Council of the European Union, nor on that of the subsequent Presidencies of Latvia and Luxembourg.[25]

4.4.2 *The Gravity of the Cannabis Problem*

One of the questions that almost automatically arise in such a discussion is: how serious is the drug problem in the European Union and its member states actually? Saying that drugs are a big problem, is one thing; but saying how big "big" is, is quite another thing. When expectations are raised that the policy pursued will be in proportion to the gravity of the problem, it is obvious to measure the magnitude of the cannabis problem as well as possible.

The bodies of the European Union rely specifically on the reports of the European Monitoring Centre for Drugs and Drug Addiction and the reports of Europol. The last three reports of the European Monitoring Centre for Drugs and Drug Addiction are the *European Drug Report – Trends and developments 2013*, the *European Drug Report – Trends and developments 2014*, and *Prevalence of daily cannabis use in the European Union* (2012). Furthermore there is the report the European Monitoring Centre for Drugs and Drug Addiction and Europol have jointly published in 2013: *EU Drug Markets Report – A strategic analysis*. Recently a research consortium headed by F. Trautmann, B. Kilmer and P. Turnbull published, at the request of the European Commission, a report about certain drug problems: *Further legal insights into aspects of the EU illicit drugs market*.[26]

According to the report the European Monitoring Centre for Drugs and Drug Addiction and Europol have jointly published, the European marijuana and hashish market is mainly supplied from North Africa, South-West Asia, the Middle East, the Balkans and South Africa. Important countries in this regard are Morocco, Lebanon, Albania and Afghanistan. In 2010 Morocco produced an estimated 760 tons of hashish, about 235 tons of which was sold and/or consumed on the European market – notably via Spain, Belgium, the Netherlands and the United Kingdom. In Albania there are places such as Lazarat where cannabis is cultivated at a very large scale and where the authorities, only by

---

25 Council of the European Union, *The future Italian, Latvian and Luxembourg Presidencies; 18 month programme of the Council (1 July 2014–31 December 2015)*, Brussels, 17.6.2014, no. 10948/1/14 REV 1, POLGEN 97.

26 Trautmann, Kilmer and Turnbull, 2013.

using military force, can put a restraint on the cultivation.[27] Afghanistan produced in 2010 somewhere between 1,200 and 3,700 tons of hashish. According to the EMCDDA report related to 2013 in particular China is a supplier of elements for the production of "cannabinoid receptor agonists (CRA's) which mimic the effects of the naturally occurring psychoactive compounds found in cannabis".

On the other hand, also in Europe and the European Union there are a lot of countries where cannabis is produced at a large scale. The Netherlands is still a major producer, but also countries such as the Czech Republic, the United Kingdom, Germany, Ireland, Poland, Belgium and Sweden have become, or are becoming, important players in this market. In many countries where cannabis is produced at a considerable scale, it is cultivated both outdoors, on the field, and indoors. However, more and more the latter way of producing seems to predominate. But no matter the way it is cultivated, most cannabis produced in European countries is destined for the domestic market or the market in adjacent countries. The United Kingdom and Germany are generally considered to be the largest markets for cannabis.

The European Monitoring Centre for Drugs and Drug Addiction and Europol note that criminal groups have increasingly taken possession of the production, trafficking and distribution of cannabis. They concentrate the cultivation in large-scale plantations, or spread it – to reduce the risks – over large numbers of small plantations. Different sorts of legal economic sectors are involved in the production, brokerages as well as technical branches. Thanks to their high level of expertise, Dutch criminal groups have become "important facilitators in the production of cannabis in the EU". Their influence is not limited to the cannabis cultivation in Belgium and Germany, but spreads to countries such as Italy, Morocco, Spain and France.

The same report shows that 24% of all EU residents aged 15–64 years (approximately 80 million people) have used cannabis at least once in their lifetime, and that 12% of young adults aged 15–34 years (about 16 million people) have used it at least once in the last 12 months. The EMCDDA report related to 2013 talks about 15.4 million young people aged 15–34 years (11.7%) and 9.2 million (14.9%) aged 15–24 years. However, we should not forget that the extent of the cannabis use can vary greatly from one country to the other. In Bulgary, for instance, the annual consumption of cannabis is only 4 tons, compared to 384 tons in Italy.[28]

27 See the report about the "Drogen-Razzia in 'Cannabis-Hauptstadt' Europas" in *Der Spiegel*, 17.6.2014. But also countries such as Turkey should not be neglected. See Akgul and Sever, 2014.

28 Trautmann, Kilmer and Turnbull, 2013, p. 23, pp. 28–29.

Since 2013, however, and after a considerable increase in the 1990s, cannabis use – generally speaking – seems to stabilize and even decrease. Though some countries, such as Bulgary, are confronted with an increase in cannabis use among young adults. When focusing on the cannabis consumption among young people (aged 15–24 years) in the European Union in the last 12 months, the Eurobarometer 2014 indicates that almost a fifth of them (17%) has used cannabis in the course of that period. That is a (substantial) rise of 3 percent compared to 2011 (14%).[29]

According to the already mentioned European Monitoring Centre for Drugs and Drug Addiction report *Prevalence of daily cannabis use in the European Union* (2012), the group of intensive cannabis users (people who use the substance on 20 or more days a month) amounts in a number of countries to about a quarter of all the people who used cannabis in the last month. In proportion to the number of people aged 15–64 years they represent 0.05 to 2.6% of that age group. We are talking about at least 3 million people in the European Union who are daily or almost daily cannabis users. This proportionately not so large group of intensive users is presumably responsible for most (in a number of countries 55 to 77%) of the annual cannabis consumption.[30]

The same European Monitoring Centre for Drugs and Drug Addiction report tells us that the prevalence of cannabis use in the last month varies considerably from country to country. In 2009 in Spain, for example, 7.6% of the 15–64 year-olds had used cannabis in the last month, whereas in 2010 the corresponding prevalence in France was 4.8% and in the United Kingdom 3.9%. In the Netherlands it was 3.3% in 2005 and in Belgium 3.1% in 2008. There are also great differences between these countries with regard to the percentages of daily users in the age group concerned: 2.6% in Spain in 2009, 1.7% in Italy in 2008, 0.9% in Belgium in 2008, 0.8% in the Netherlands in 2005, and 0.6% in the United Kingdom in 2010/11.[31]

Although the size of the cannabis market in the European Union is difficult to estimate, Caulkins and Kilmer have tried to assess it, though they make some serious reservations. In 2010, the cannabis market was worth 7 to 10 billion euros. However, it could as well be worth 8.4 to 12.1 billion euros. It all depends on the way the estimations are made.[32]

29 European Commission, *Memo: international day against drug abuse*, Brussels, 26 June 2014, no. 14/445.

30 Trautmann, Kilmer and Turnbull, 2013, p. 21, 23. See also Van Laar, Frijns, Trautmann and Lombi, 2013, pp. 118–121, 129–130.

31 In this connection, see also Van Laar, Frijns, Trautmann and Lombi, 2013.

32 Caulkins and Kilmer, 2013, pp. 308–314.

In recent years, an increasing number of cannabis users have contacted addiction centres. In 2010 approximately 108,000 people in the European Union have applied for admission to such centres, and 98,000 of them stated they used cannabis as a second drug. Not surprisingly, a lot of these frequent users are suffering from a whole series of "health, mental health and cognitive problems".

4.5 The Current Policy Developments in the Member States

Despite the fact that the drug policy pursued by the member states of the European Union at the latter level does not leave any room for the legalization of the cultivation et cetera of cannabis, it is important to look at the stances of the governments of some big member states with regard to the legalization debate.

In 2008 the European Monitoring Centre for Drugs and Drug Addiction drew a detailed "picture" of the cannabis policy and cannabis problems in a large number of European countries.[33] Obviously, the corresponding report also mentions the sometimes heated discussions that were going on at numerous places in Europe about the cannabis policy that was pursued and the policy that should be pursued. But apparently, in the previous years more had happened than debating alone. Although researchers who contributed to the report signaled again that there were still considerable policy differences between many countries as to the way the individual user was approached, they also indicated two tentative trends.[34]

On the one hand, there is a trend towards the decriminalization of the personal use of cannabis. The best-known example – apart from the Netherlands – is Portugal. In 2001 the drug policy in Portugal was adapted in an administrative-judicial direction, so as to be able to make the provision of assistance to (problematic) users more binding.[35] On the other hand, there is a trend towards restricting the room available for such use. According to the researchers, the main reasons for the latter trend are, firstly, the increasing THC concentration in cannabis, and, secondly, the demand for treatment by cannabis users. Also important was their finding that although from time to time reports pleading

33 Sznitman, Olsson and Room, 2008.

34 In this connection, see also Korf (2008) for a description of the situation at that moment in countries such as the United Kingdom, the Netherlands, Belgium, Denmark and Hungary.

35 See, among others, May and Skrine, 2013a.

for the legalization of cannabis were published, up to then not one single country had seriously considered that option, let alone realized it. Apparently, nowhere could be found a political majority for such a policy.[36]

The member state which is most explicitly exploring the limits of the drug treaties of the United Nations at this moment is Spain. New in its policy is the acceptance of the phenomenon of the social cannabis clubs. According to press reports, there are 700 of such clubs in Spain at this moment and more than 300 in Catalonia alone, with a total of about 165,000 members. These clubs count hundreds or even thousands of (registered) members, who all have their own pot with cannabis plants in the cannabis plantations.

Recently, the city of Barcelona has ceased the issuing of licences for this kind of clubs, because it wants to regulate the clubs more strictly in order to prevent this phenomenon from becoming a serious problem. These are some of the key topics in the deliberation on the further regulation of the sector:

- The maximum number of members per club will possibly be limited;
- Membership will be restricted to Spanish residents;
- Members have to be at least 21 years of age and have to belong to the club for more than 15 days before they can buy cannabis;
- Clubs have to register their plants;
- Members are allowed to buy 60 to 100 grams of cannabis a month;
- Clubs must submit to an annual inspection.[37]

Researchers signal that in several countries (for instance Portugal and Switzerland) and cities (Copenhagen) there are discussions about the establishment of similar clubs, but up till now there is clearly not yet a development comparable to the one in Spain.[38]

Recent press releases reveal that nowadays cannabis is cultivated at a large scale in Germany as well. Based on the figures, this is especially the case in the states North Rhine-Westphalia, Saarland, Baden-Württemberg, Berlin and Brandenburg.[39] No wonder, thus, that the legalization of cannabis is a rather

---

36 Ballotta, Bergeron and Hughes, 2008.

37 M. de Waal, "Een chique club, met dure jongens", *NRC Handelsblad*, 19.2.2014, and A. Kassam, "Barcelona's booming cannabis clubs turn Spain into 'Holland of the South'", *The Guardian*, 4.8.2014.

38 For background information about the developments in Spain and Portugal, see J. Ferret, 2000, pp. 21–80. About the situation in the Spanish town Rasquera, see for instance G. Tremlett, "Spanish town of Rasquera leases land for marijuana plantation", *The Guardian*, 1.3.2012.

39 M. Stolz, "Drogenküchen und Hanfplantagen", *Die Zeit*, 25.6.2014.

frequently returning subject in the German press as well as in the *Bundestag*.[40] In September 2011, for instance, the faction of *Die Linke* launched a debate about the enlargement of the quantity of cannabis people are allowed to possess for personal use (30 grams) and about permitting cannabis clubs to cultivate cannabis for their own use.[41] A year later, *Bündnis 90/Die Grünen* took the lead in the debate by presenting the proposal *Eigengebrauch von Cannabis wirksam entkriminalisieren*.[42] Together with a proposal of the SPD to curb the use of synthetic drugs, the first-mentioned proposal was at the centre of a public exchange of views in the *Gesundheitsausschuss* of the *Bundestag*. However, these parliamentary initiatives and discussions did not result in a political majority in favour of the proposed form of decriminalization of cannabis, let alone in favour of the legalization of the drug.

The latter can be deduced not only from reports on the drug problem in Germany that were published by different kinds of public authorities.[43] Similarly in the national strategic policy plan regarding drugs and addiction which was published in 2012 – and which also relates to alcohol, tobacco and gaming – not a single word was said about the legalization of cannabis as an acceptable and workable policy strategy. Reduction of demand, provision of assistance and reduction of supply remain at the core of that policy plan.

So, it is no surprise that the *Drogenbeauftragte der Bundesregierung*, whether or not under the pressure of reports on the use of cannabis, has repeatedly declared:

> Eine Legalisierung von Cannabis ist aus gesundheitlicher Sicht nicht zu verantworten. Die Freigabe wäre ein falsches Signal, denn vor allem für junge Menschen bestehen erhebliche Gesundheitsrisiken durch Cannabiskonsum. Die Bundesregierung hält diese für zu gross, als dass eine Legalisierung zu verantworten wäre. Ein regelmässiger Konsum von Cannabis führt teilweise zu erheblichen gesundheitlichen Beeinträchtigungen, bis hin zu Psychosen und einer Abhängigkeit. Daher ist nicht die Legalisierung der richtige Weg, sondern gute Aufklärungsarbeit, wie sie etwa die Bundeszentrale für gesundheitliche Aufklärung (…) in Köln betreibt.[44]

40 It would carry us too far to enumerate here the many press reports on this subject.

41 Deutscher Bundestag, 28 September 2011, Drucksache 17/7196.

42 Deutscher Bundestag, 13 June 2012, Drucksache 17/9948. See also F. Gathmann, "Abschied nehmen von der Verbotspolitik", *Der Spiegel*, 9.8.2014.

43 See, for instance, *Deutsche Beobachtungsstelle für Drogen und Drogensucht*, 2013.

44 Communication at the website of the *Drogenbeauftragte*: <http://www.drogenbeauftragte.de> (consulted on 24 March 2014). See also the reaction of her predecessor (in the period

In short, the German government is of the opinion that, for reasons of public health, it is not appropriate to legalize cannabis. In the report which we have quoted above, it is moreover emphasized that Germany and 183 other states have committed themselves by way of a treaty to allow the use of cannabis and other narcotic drugs only for medical and scientific purposes. In the case of cannabis, we are talking about the provision of cannabis to, for instance, multiple sclerosis patients. The cannabis concerned is supplied by the company in the Netherlands that has received a licence to cultivate this plant. In Germany it is distributed through pharmacies.

Also important is that on 22 July 2014 the administrative judge in Cologne decided that three patients who are suffering from severe chronic pains, who no longer can benefit from whatever regular medicine and who cannot afford to buy cannabis in a pharmacy because their health insurance company does not reimburse the associated costs, must receive a licence from the *Bundesinstitut für Arzneimittel und Medizinprodukte* to grow cannabis at home for therapeutic purposes. However, it remains to be seen whether the *Bundesinstitut* concerned will indeed issue the licences or will appeal to the *Oberverwaltungsgericht* in Münster.[45]

Without any doubt, in France the use of cannabis is still widespread and a relatively large group of people there is frequently using this narcotic drug.[46] A clear difference with a few years ago is that since 2009 cannabis social clubs are emerging in France as well (at the end of 2012 there were 150 such clubs, united in an association with the appropriate name *Les Amis du Cannabis Social Club*).[47] No wonder that also in this country the discussion about the legalization of cannabis has not ceased. On the contrary, more than ever that discussion divides France. The majority of the people (78%) is still against a form of legalization that would treat cannabis the same way as tobacco and alcohol. However, a few years ago that majority was still larger: 85%. The number of people who prefer a form of controlled use has increased correspondingly: from 15% in 2008 to 22% in 2012. The number of people who are of the opinion that in case of illness the use of cannabis, under certain

---

2005–2009) to the appeal of 120 professors to legalize cannabis: S. Bätzing-Lichtenthäler, "Kein Grundrecht aufs Kiffen", *Die Zeit*, 10.4.2014. As to cannabis use by young people, see, for instance, Bundeszentrale fur gesundheitliche Aufklärung, 2011.

45 N. Kuhrt, "Gericht erlaubt Schwerkranken Cannabis-Anbau", *Der Spiegel*, 22.7.2014.

46 Reijnaud-Maurupt, 2009. See also Costes, 2007.

47 See C. Legrand, "Les coopératives de cannabis sans but lucrative aspirant à la légalité", *Le Monde*, 25.12.2012.

conditions, should be permitted, has increased from 30% to 60%.[48] The past years, these changes in public opinion have resulted in proposals in the French parliament to legalize cannabis.

The first proposal, in June 2011, came from a working group consisting of members of the *Assemblée nationale* and chaired by D. Vaillant.[49] This proposal attracted much attention, but did not lead to a policy change. The second proposal was submitted to the Senate, amidst a lot of public uproar, on 28 January 2014 by E. Benbassa c.s.[50] In a somewhat different wording this proposal also states that the current policy, which is explicitly oriented towards a criminal justice approach, has not contributed to solving the problem of the widespread use of cannabis by young people. Additionally the proposal argues that this policy has not resulted in a restriction of "le développement de l'économie alternative mafieuse engendrée par la production et la vente illégales". And so, just as was the case with the Prohibition in the United States, that policy needs to be changed drastically: not to stimulate the use of cannabis, but to reduce the risks related to such a use. The proposal intends to permit the cultivation of cannabis by plantations that have received an official licence. The sale should take place in special shops, in conformity with the model for the sale of tobacco and alcohol. No sale would be allowed to minors, through vending machines and in the vicinity of schools, training institutes or sports facilities.

However, this kind of proposal is at odds with the policy the French government is pursuing and will continue to pursue the next years with regard to the production and distribution of cannabis. In its policy plan 2013–2017 on drugs and drug addiction, it is stipulated that in several ways the battle against the cultivation of cannabis must be intensified.[51] The new prime minister E. Valls has never made it a secret that he will implement that policy. So, the following years cannabis will certainly not be legalized in France.

In the context of the development of its next drug strategy, the British government published a green paper in 2007: *Drugs: our community, your say*.[52] In

48 See L. Clavreul, "Cannabis: les Français restent opposés à une dépénalisation, mais les lignes bougent", *Le Monde*, 2.1.2014. In this connection, see also C. Bordenet, "Traitement au cannabis; revivre normalement, sans douleurs et sans être stoned", *Le Monde*, 10.1.2014.

49 Groupe SCR, 2011. See also J. Demarthon, "Une 'marche du cannabis' pour réclamer la dépénalisation", *Le Monde*, 7.5.2011.

50 Benbassa et al., 2014. See also P. Euzen, "EELV veut autoriser l'usage contrôlé du cannabis", *Le Monde*, 5.2.2014.

51 Mission Interministérielle etc., 2013.

52 HM Government, 2007.

this consultation document the legalization of drugs, or more specifically cannabis, was not a topic. The document was completely based on the idea that the existing policy could, and therefore should, be improved, not only in so far it concerned the prevention and tackling of drug addiction, but also with regard to combating drug trafficking. It has to be noted that the then government was rather pleased with what up till that point had been achieved. Among 16–24 year-olds, for instance, cannabis use had decreased considerably (with 24%) and among 11–15 year-olds it was down by 3% (from 13 to 10% on annual basis). The number of addicted people receiving treatment had increased to 170,000.

The policy plan on how to cope with the country's drug problems that was presented in 2010 is characterized by a similar optimism.[53] In this plan it is repeated that the fight against drugs has already delivered real results, but that without question still too many people are using drugs. According to the plan, in the age group of 16–59 year-olds 9,912,000 persons ever used cannabis, 2,152,000 persons used it in the last year, and 1,250,000 persons in the last month. To reduce the use of drugs and to increase the number of people recovering from their drug addiction, three things are needed, the plan states:

- Reducing demand, by creating an environment in which people are able to resist any pressures to use drugs;
- Restricting supply, by making the United Kingdom an "unattractive destination for drug traffickers by attacking their profits and driving up their risks";
- Offering assistance on a large scale, to help people tackle and overcome their drug dependency.

Although the plan is presented as a "fundamentally different approach to tackling drugs and an entirely new ambition to reduce drug use and dependence", not a word is said about the legalization of cannabis, let alone the legalization of other drugs.

Of course, this plan has not brought the discussion about the legalization of cannabis to an end. In the United Kingdom, the debate also simply continues. This can be concluded, for instance, from the final report published by the UK Drug Policy Commission in 2012.[54] On multiple occasions that report not only hints at the discussion on this topic, but also expresses a position in the current debate.

---

53 HM Government, 2010. According to the latest reports, drug use in the United Kingdom (though not cannabis use) is increasing rather significantly. See A. Travis, "Number of drug users in England and Wales rises to 2.7m", *The Guardian*, 24.7.2014.

54 UK Drug Policy Commission, 2012.

To give an example: the commission concerned prudently pleads for the decriminalization of small-scale cultivation of cannabis (for personal use):

> We do not believe that there is sufficient evidence at the moment to support the case for removing criminal penalties for the major production or supply offences of most drugs. However, for the most ubiquitous drug, cannabis, it is worth considering whether there are alternative approaches which might be more effective at reducing harm. For example, there is an argument that amending the law relating to the growing of it, at least for personal use, might go some way to undermining the commercialization of production, with associated involvement of organized crime and the development of stronger strains of cannabis ("skunk"), that we have seen in the UK and other countries in recent years. Perhaps the most expedient course to take here would be to re-examine sentence levels and sentencing practice to ensure that those growing below a certain low volume of plants face no – or only minimal – sanctions. The impact of any such move would need to be carefully measured and evaluated so policy makers could make informed decisions about future actions.[55]

Nowhere in the report, however, does the commission make a plea for the complete legalization of the production of cannabis, although the commission repeatedly refers to the negative or dubious consequences of the existing policy, for instance when it concerns the fight of the police against drug trafficking.

A comparable prudence characterizes the debate in the British Parliament. In the report published by the Home Affairs Committee of the House of Commons in December 2012 – *Drugs: breaking the cycle* – plain language in favour of a reversal of policy is used repeatedly and in that context reference is made to the developments in North and South America. However, this does not bring the Home Affairs Committee to the conclusion that in the short or longer term the United Kingdom should legalize drugs, and in particular cannabis.[56] One of the arguments put forward against such a step is the following:

> The global nature of the drugs trade, and the potential for displacement of drug cultivation and supply routes in response to law enforcement measures, means that the international drug trade can only ever be tackled effectively by co-operative, co-ordinated international efforts. We must recognise that no one nation can do this on its own.[57]

---

55 UK Drug Policy Commission, 2012, p. 21, pp. 118–119, 150–151.

56 Home Affairs Committee, 2012.

57 *Ibid.*, no. 42.

Therefore, it is logical that the Home Affairs Committee asks the government to:

> initiate a discussion within the Commission on Narcotic Drugs of alternative ways – including the possibility of legislation and regulation – to tackle the global drugs dilemma.[58]

However, that was too much to ask for. The current British government immediately made this clear in its reaction to the report.[59] Similarly in the most recent progress report regarding the implementation of its drug policy the government does not, in any way, make mention of any initiative in that direction.[60] On the contrary, according to the government the robust fight against drug production and trafficking had to be continued, especially as far as the production of cannabis is concerned. The authorities should build further on:

> the success of the Crimestoppers 'commercial cultivation of cannabis' campaign to strengthen our efforts to identify and close down these cannabis factories and disrupt the organised crime groups behind them.[61]

It is rather obvious that this powerful language does not mark the end of the story. The think tank Transform (in full: the Transform Drug Policy Foundation), for example, is in different ways continuing its actions against the existing cannabis policy ("The war on drugs has failed") and keeps making proposals and suggestions for the legalization of cannabis. These days this lobby organization tries to gain political support for its proposals by forcing the opening of "Amsterdam-style" cafés in big English cities. Hitherto with little success, because the cafés are closed by the police as soon as their existence becomes known.[62]

The recent plea of prominent members of the Liberal Democrats to create room for the legalization of cannabis for medical use by seriously ill patients will perhaps be more successful.[63]

---

58 *Ibid.*, no. 259.

59 See R. Mason, "Cannabis will not be legalised, Home Office minister says", *The Guardian*, 10.12.2012.

60 HM Government, 2013. In this connection, see also A. Travis, "Cannabis farmers take up arms to defend crops in booming trade", *The Guardian*, 17.8.2010.

61 Home Affairs Committee, 2012, no. 17.

62 Transform, s.d., 16–17, 20, 22–24. See also C. Meredith, "Cannabis legalisation in the UK called for as Amsterdam-style café plan is proposed", *The Huffington Post*, 15.3.2014.

63 N. Watt, "Drugs minister calls for legalizing cannabis for medical use", *The Guardian*, 13.8.2014.

4.6 Conclusion

The conclusion of this chapter about the European Union can be rather short. The legalization of cannabis is at odds with the legislation as well as the drug policy of the European Union. Of course, this does not mean that such a development would be impossible because the European Union would still be entangled in a war against drugs. The latter is simply not the case. Anybody who is more or less acquainted with the origin and the development of the European drug policy knows that this policy has never been oriented that way. And therefore it is also less strange than it may appear at first sight that the European Commission, or at least one of its Commissioners, already some time ago has tried to launch, by means of research, the discussion about the legalization of cannabis.

The fact that it is not easy at the European level to start a debate on legalization, has, as such, nothing to do with the division of powers between the European Commission and the member states with regard to drugs. According to the Treaty of Lisbon they have a common responsibility in this field. However, two other reasons play an important role.

The first reason is that up to now the governments of major member states are not interested in the legalization of cannabis. This, of course, makes the dialogue about that delicate subject difficult.

The second reason is that member states want to be in control of this tricky area of policy and therefore are extremely sensitive to changes to the drug policy of other countries, because such changes can have unintended negative consequences for the policies they themselves want to pursue.

The discussion that raged in the early 1990s between the parties of the Schengen Agreement about the consequences of the Dutch drug policy for the drug problems in Belgium and France, is a case in point.

CHAPTER 5

The Dutch Cannabis Policy

5.1 Introduction

The Dutch drugs policy, and especially the production, distribution and consumption of cannabis, has never been a quiet possession. Since the 1960s, it has been called into question time and time again and for a variety of reasons. For a good understanding of the current debate on the course to be followed, it is important to highlight a few aspects of the history of that debate. These are the issues we will discuss next: the arguments of the driving forces behind the current policy of tolerance, the rise of the commercial coffeeshop system in the 1980s, the grim discussion about the coffeeshop policy in the early 1990s, followed by the step by step reconsideration of the cannabis and coffeeshop policy around the year 2000.

Subsequently, our attention will shift to the growing cannabis problem and the increasing problem of the coffeeshops since the beginning of this century. Since these problems have mainly manifested themselves – in all sizes and types – in the entire southern border area, they will be discussed separately for the Zeeland-Belgian border area, the Brabant-Belgian border area and the Limburg-Belgian-German border area. However, to avoid people from thinking that the problems only in the southern part of the Netherlands have become that big, we will also pay the necessary attention to the developments in Amsterdam, the city with the country's highest concentration of coffeeshops. An accurate outline of all these problems is needed to be able to understand the findings as well as the proposals of the Van de Donk Committee, which in 2009 was asked to reflect on the existing drug policy.

Finally, we will focus on the policy that was formulated in the wake of that committee. On the one hand, the revision of the coffeeshop policy will be discussed as well as the fight against that policy by the coffeeshop owners, left-wing political parties and a number of "their" mayors. On the other hand, we will explain how the plan to organize the combating of illicit cannabis cultivation at a wider scale is used by the political opposition within the Dutch Senate to force the minister of Security and Justice I. Opstelten to alter the cannabis and coffeeshop policy in the direction of legalization.

 | DOI 10.1163/9789004293199_006

5.2 The Naive Starting Point in the 1970s and 1980s

As in other countries, it was difficult in the Netherlands of the 1960s and 1970s to come to a drug policy which was more or less politically acceptable. Opinions were pretty divided about the way to address the problem of the larger-scale use of the different sorts of illicit drugs – cannabis as well as heroin and amphetamine. In 1976 the debate resulted in a change of the Opium Act, a change that included the acceptance of the personal use of drugs and a far-reaching decriminalization of the possession of these substances (the possession of up to 30 grams of cannabis products became an infringement punishable with a maximum custodial sentence of 1 month), while the punishments for drug trafficking became, in general, more severe. By means of two lists accompanying the act, the distinction between "drugs with an unacceptable risk" and "hemp products" was specified. This distinction was made to reduce the risk that users of marijuana and hashish would encounter dealers of hard drugs (heroin, cocaine, amphetamine). The domestic trade in cannabis products was punished less severely than the domestic trade in other types of drugs: with a maximum custodial penalty of 2 years (instead of 8 years, and sometimes even 12 years, in the case of heroin or cocaine trade). Cross-border drug trade was punishable with 4 years of imprisonment.

The more lenient treatment of cannabis use was also illustrated by the fact that in 1978 – in the directives of the Public Prosecutor's Office regarding the investigation and prosecution of infringements of the Opium Act – the possibility of appointing "house dealers" in youth centres was foreseen. Some time later, conditions were imposed on this form of cannabis sale. It was not allowed, for instance, to advertize openly for it, to offer hard drugs for sale or to create nuisance.[1] The phenomenon of the house dealer was rather short-lived, by the way. In the 1980s it disappeared due to the rapidly emerging coffeeshops, eager to gain as big a share of the cannabis market as they could. That the increase of the easy availability of cannabis through the development of a network of tolerated points of sale has encouraged the use of this narcotic drug, will be no surprise. Here, the active supply has undoubtedly stimulated demand.[2]

When examining – starting from the contemporary policy discussion – the background of this bold policy, one soon comes to the conclusion that the inventors of that policy, such as L. Hulsman, professor of criminal law at the Erasmus University of Rotterdam, did not at all foresee, and also could not

1 Blom, 2008, pp. 40–52; Korf, 1995, pp. 43–45, 69–71, and Spapens, Müller and Van de Bunt, 2014.

2 Korf, 1995, pp. 69–71, 273–274. See also Van Gemert, 1985, and Van Gemert, 1988.

entirely foresee, its possible consequences in the longer run. It is easy to illustrate this on the basis of the report *Ruimte in het drugsbeleid* (*Options in the drug policy*) that Hulsman and others wrote in 1971 for the General Central Bureau for Mental Public Health Care.[3] In the report, it is for instance stated:

- that cannabis products do not compel users to keep using them, to increase the quantities used or to switch to the use of other, heavier substances. And in case of "very effective enforcement" of the law it is imaginable "that cannabis would almost be completely squeezed out of the market", though this would not mark the end of the drug problem but would rather cause an increase of the use of heavier substances.
- that "in the Dutch context" not many people will succeed in "becoming 'rich' by the trade in cannabis". In this regard, heroin and opium offer better opportunities – provided the market is big enough.
- that in the Netherlands, unlike in larger states such as West Germany, France and England, there is no risk that an "organized drug trade" would develop, "despite rumours emerging time and again about infiltrations of gangs from abroad (...). The traders in our country originate in most cases from the circle of users, they do not operate in an organized context and sell mainly cannabis and some LSD."
- that a repressive, strongly negative attitude towards drug use would cause or increase the marginalization of certain groups. This polarization would, in turn, increase the risk that in addition to the unwanted behaviour other forms of deviant behaviour would also be developed. As a result new, stricter measures would be necessary: "Such a vicious circle does not lead to a solution of the problem, but only to the growth of violence in our society."
- that the assumption that the abolition of the punishability of drug use would incite many foreigners to come to the Netherlands "to indulge in the use of these substances" is not plausible. Moreover, that in case the amendment of the law would indeed bring about such a wave of migration, the authorities would not be powerless against it: "the authorities (have) – if production and trade remain punishable – enough possibilities to use their normal means of power with regard to unwanted foreigners".
- that in the battle against drug production and drug distribution there is "a very meaningful task for the criminal justice system", though that system should act "with the necessary prudence and nuance" and should beware of "initiating processes of escalation". Referring to the Prohibition in America,

3 Hulsman and Blok van der Velden, 1971. See also the book edited by Hulsman and Van Dijk about the drug problem in the Netherlands: Hulsman and Van Dijk, 1970.

> attention is drawn to the risk that an international drug trade (notably in opium and heroin) might be institutionalized in the Netherlands. Since such a trade wants to make bigger profits, it has to invest and, as a result, is prepared to "harshly" defend its considerable financial interests, which implies that the narcotic drug departments of the police continually have to be improved and extended in order to keep pace with "the incessant escalation".

And the commission rounded off the last statement by saying:

> The grim character the drug problem undoubtedly will have acquired in the meantime, will leave the authorities no other way to approach the problems. The trader in marijuana, the dealer of today, will have disappeared already a long time before and will then only live on in the memories of those who still remember how it all began in the romantic 1960s and 1970s.[4]

Anyone who dwells a little longer on this quote, will realize that Hulsman's prediction has largely come true: the romantic dealer of the 1960s has disappeared. However, what Hulsman did not predict – on the contrary: never thought possible – has happened as well: organized crime has become an important player in the cannabis and other drug markets in the Netherlands as well, large numbers of foreign "tourists" have travelled to the Netherlands to provide themselves with drugs in the coffeeshops and nearby illicit points of sale, and many Dutch have become exceedingly rich thanks to the production and distribution of cannabis. How did it come this far? If we follow Hulsman's reasoning, it cannot be the result of the policy the government implemented a few years after the publication of his report. From 1976 on, the government did exactly what Hulsman considered necessary to prevent serious crime from occurring: it did not criminalize drug use, it left room for tolerated sale of cannabis, and it imposed light sentences for domestic cannabis trade, et cetera.

So, the question arises: how valid were the starting points of Hulsman's discourse? Did he underestimate the impact of the widespread tolerated sale of cannabis on the numbers of users and, related to this, the strong impetus a growing market would give to the expansion and organizational reinforcement of the supply? Did he totally overlook the fact that in the end a large part of the supply of cannabis – (also) because this supply remained illicit (as Hulsman himself had wished) – would come under the control of organizations that would defend with more and more violence their ever growing interests in the

4 Hulsman and Blok van der Velden, 1971, p. 49.

market concerned? Did he not sufficiently realize that these criminal organizations would also be prepared and capable to gradually expand their selection of products with other natural or synthetic drugs? Was he not aware of the problem that the Netherlands – in case its policy of tolerance was not adopted by other countries – would act as a magnet for (potential) cannabis users in the neighbouring countries and the rest of the world? Did he really not know that it was impossible to halt such a large influx of foreign tourists by means of the Aliens Act? Was he blind to the fact that as the cannabis market would become bigger and bigger due to the increasing supply and the increasing demand, producers and traders in this market would become extremely rich?

These and related questions all can be answered affirmatively. The proposals were not sufficiently well-thought-out and the policy based on these proposals was naive. However, in defence of Hulsman and his supporters, it certainly has to be noted that at that time they could not know the European Economic Community would be transformed into the European Union, where, in principle, border checks would no longer be carried out at the internal borders of the member states and, as a consequence, immigration law would not be an efficient means to control the "domestic" movement of foreigners.[5]

The increasing interaction between demand and supply induced by the policy of tolerance in the cannabis market, and the resulting competition between drug traffickers to get hold of as large a part of this lucrative market as possible, became exceptionally manifest in Amsterdam in the 1970s and 1980s. Several criminal groups competed for hegemony over this attractive metropolitan market. Drug trader K. Bruinsma's group still serves as a model for this development, but Bruinsma was not the only one who aspired a powerful position in that market, as his liquidation in June 1991 has demonstrated; he is merely, also because of his violent death, the best-known example. The drug expert of the Dutch police in those days, R. Weijenburg, has clearly indicated in his book on drugs and drug control in the Netherlands that in the 1970s and 1980s criminal groups were competing for a share of that market all over the country which, thanks to the policy of tolerance, enabled people to gain a fortune without much penal and fiscal risks.[6]

5 See also Van de Bunt, 2006.

6 Middelburg, 1992, and Weijenburg, 1996, pp. 161–198. See also the *final report* (paragraph 4.1.) of the Fijnaut research group for the Parlementaire Enquêtecommissie Opsporingsmethoden (Van Traa Committee) about the attractiveness of the drug market for established criminals with the necessary experience, knowledge, connections and (violent) reputation (Second Chamber, 1996–1997, 24072, no. 17, pp. 7–57). In addition, see also Van Cappelle, 1989.

It was not until the middle of the 1980s that authorities began to worry about the flourishing of organized crime in the cannabis market and about the possible future consequences of this growing problem for Dutch society. These worries were for the first time clearly expressed in 1985, in the policy plan *Samenleving en criminaliteit* (*Society and crime*).[7] As a result of that concern, in 1987 the initiative was taken to combine the forces of police, justice and administration in the triangle Amsterdam-Utrecht-Haarlem by creating the Interregional Criminal Investigation Team Noord-Holland-Utrecht. A few years later, and despite the shutdown of that first interregional team due to a serious disagreement about the appropriateness of the used investigation method (uncontrolled delivery), similar teams were created all over the Netherlands in order to bring the gangsterdom, which in the meantime had infiltrated the entire drug market, as much as possible under control.[8] At the end of the 1990s, and in part under pressure from the White House, a special team was even built to reduce the production and distribution of synthetic drugs to manageable proportions.[9]

5.3 The Ratification of the Convention Against the Smuggling of Drugs

In the beginning of the 1990s, for the first time since the broad discussion that had resulted in the revision of the Opium Act in 1976, the Second Chamber – the Dutch House of Representatives – again thoroughly examined the drug problems, in particular the cannabis question and the problem of the coffeeshops. Though this is not the only and not even the main reason for us to pay attention to this second round of the political discussion.

The principal reason to do so, is the fact that in the current debate on the cannabis and coffeeshop policy, people often hint at the attitude the Netherlands supposedly had adopted during the negotiations on the 1988 convention against the smuggling of drugs. More precisely, some people suggest that the Netherlands at that occasion implicitly added a caveat regarding the cultivation of cannabis for recreational use. But is that really true? What has been said about this in the 1991–1993 drug policy discussion in the Dutch parliament?

---

7 See also Van Dijk, 1997, pp. 10–13.

8 Fijnaut, 2007, pp. 944–947. See also De Beaufort, 1989, pp. 80–84, and Blom, 2008, pp. 52–66. Some chiefs of the police doubted whether this repressive turn of the policy was a good idea. Should the emphasis not be put on a liberalization of the policy? See Wiarda, 1989, pp. 49–59.

9 Spapens, 2006, pp. 147–150. See also Snippe, Kruize and Bieleman, 2003.

Another reason to have a closer look at that discussion is related to the letter about the drug policy, and especially the note about the cultivation of the Dutch cannabis variety *nederwiet*, the minister of Justice at the time, E. Hirsch Ballin, and some of his colleagues sent to the Second Chamber on 12 March 1993. What position did they take in these policy documents with regard to the cultivation of cannabis for recreational use?

In the *Explanatory memorandum* to the bill to approve the convention concerned, the minister and his colleagues were generally positive about the convention's objectives and contents. However, as to the significance of this convention for the Netherlands the minister indicated that the paragraphs 6, 7 and 8 of article 3 belonged "to the less felicitous provisions". With regard to paragraph 6 he was of the opinion that this provision about the opportunity to prosecute persons was formulated "in a way that reveals a certain lack of understanding of the importance and function of the opportunity principle". With regard to paragraph 7 about the early release or parole of persons, he noted that the thought expressed in it did not match very well "with the starting points of our law". Similarly paragraph 8 on the statute of limitations did not fit with the starting points of Dutch criminal law. Therefore, at the ratification of the convention he and his colleagues wanted to make reservations with respect to these three paragraphs.

The reservations meant "that in the domains covered by these three paragraphs current Dutch law remains entirely applicable". Literally, the reservations were formulated as follows:

> The government of the Kingdom of the Netherlands accepts the provisions in the sixth, seventh and eighth paragraph of article 3 only in as far as the resulting obligations are in accordance with its national criminal law and its national criminal justice policy.[10]

In the context of the current discussion, the question arises: what are the practical implications of these reservations? Do they only apply to the prosecution and the judging of drug users? Or do they also apply to people who to a certain extent are involved in the production and/or distribution of narcotic drugs? In the *Explanatory memorandum* the ministers did not make this clear.[11] However, given the comments on article 14 about the eradication of the illicit cultivation of narcotic drugs and the elimination of the illicit demand for narcotic drugs, it is not obvious whether the reservations were also meant to apply to the

10 *Tractatenblad*, 1993, no. 140, p. 2.

11 Second Chamber, 1991–1992, 22080, no. 3, p. 10.

last-mentioned cases. With respect to this article, no reservations whatsoever were made for any illicit cultivation in the Netherlands. Moreover, nowhere in the *Explanatory memorandum* it was stated that this article, to a greater or lesser extent, would also apply to domestic cannabis cultivation or the domestic production of synthetic drugs.[12]

At the end of the *Explanatory memorandum* the ministers concluded that the ratification of the convention "does not require a revision of the starting points of the existing policy". To understand this clause, it is necessary to briefly recall the substance of the policy concerned. That policy was all about establishing rules for the sale of cannabis in coffeeshops and ensuring an adequate treatment of addicted or vulnerable (young) users, but had nothing to do with the promotion of cannabis cultivation. Thus, it is hard to believe that the reservations made by the then government were a way to create room for the legalization of cannabis.

Against this background, it is understandable that at the end of the discussion the Labour Party (PvdA) members of the Permanent Committee for Justice noted, to their satisfaction:

> It is clear that, thanks to the efforts of the negotiating delegation, it is ensured that also after the approval of the convention of 20 December 1988 it will be possible to continue the successful Dutch drug policy.[13]

However, this did not immediately bring the discussion about the legalization of cannabis to an end. In the spring of 1993, the debate became even more heated than ever. In a lengthy discussion about the cannabis policy, the opposition in the Second Chamber, led by the Labour Party, made it clear that it wanted to legalize the provisioning of coffeeshops by means of a system of licences. P. Stoffelen, its spokesperson, assured his opponents that this was the only way to stop organized crime, which to an ever larger extent had taken control of the trade in soft drugs, and also the only way to efficiently combat the "proliferation of the coffeeshop phenomenon, and the enormous amount of trouble and nuisance associated with it". Tougher action against illicit plantations would only increase "the joy of that part of organized crime that gets it from abroad".[14]

However, this explanation of the motion did not convince the Christian Democratic Party (CDA), nor its minister of Justice, Hirsch Ballin. Quite clearly

12 *Ibid.*, p. 21.

13 *Ibid.*, no. 7, p. 2.

14 Second Chamber, 1992–1993, *Handelingen*, no. 61, pp. 4394–4420; no. 62, pp. 4460–4487.

he stated that he was not interested in "something like legalization", if only "from the point of view of my responsibilities in the areas of law enforcement and international cooperation". It would indeed amount to "a denunciation of international treaties". In his opinion, it was above all things important to improve the provision of care, to control the coffeeshops more strictly and to tackle the cultivation of *nederwiet* more efficiently. The system of licences he had talked about previously was certainly not aimed at permitting the production of cannabis, but precisely meant as a better tool:

> to tackle the *nederwiet* plantations. So, also in this case no legalization, but a more appropriate equipment for the detection and seizure.

5.4 The Reconsideration of the Policy in 1996 and 2004

That the Dutch cannabis market really flourished in the 1990s, can be demonstrated in multiple ways.

First of all, this is clear from the large number of coffeeshops. The number of coffeeshops with an alcohol licence had risen to 1,460 in 1995. After that, and mainly as a result of a change of policy (see further) it strongly decreased, to 538 in 1999, 504 in 2001 and 483 in 2004. The highest concentrations of coffeeshops were found in the (big cities of the) Randstad, the big cities of North Brabant, the south-east of Drenthe, the south of Groningen, the Gooi, and, to a lesser extent, in Twente, the Achterhoek, the south of Zeeland and the south of Limburg. In 2004 Amsterdam counted 249, Rotterdam 62 and Maastricht 16 coffeeshops.[15]

In the second place, the flourishing of the cannabis market can be deduced from the first estimations of the extent of the use of cannabis in the Netherlands. In 1995, the consumption value of that use was estimated at 800 million Dutch guilders, an amount that also included the use of cannabis by drug tourists (300 million Dutch guilders). One half of all the cannabis consumed had been imported – mainly from Morocco, Asia and the Middle East; the other half had been cultivated in the Netherlands (*nederwiet*). At that time, the size of the production and export of cannabis/*nederwiet* was not so explicitly discussed as today. Usually, the size of the production was simply ignored.[16]

In the third place, we should not forget that in the course of the 1980s and 1990s along the axis The Netherlands-France a large-scale cross-border

---

15 Bieleman, Goeree and Naayer, 2005, pp. 17–20, 83–85. See also Korf, 2008.

16 Second Chamber, 1994–1995, 24077, nos. 2–3, pp. 36–37.

trafficking in cannabis, but also in heroin and cocaine, was set up. At that time, this trafficking was mainly studied from Rotterdam. At the time in some neighborhoods in the south of Rotterdam a sort of drug economy had already come into existence, for example in the Millinx neighbourhood'. Life in the seven streets of the latter neighborhood was completely dominated by about thirty dealing premises.[17]

5.4.1 *The Tightening of the Coffeeshop Policy*

The authorities did not let these developments take their course. We already mentioned the establishment of a network of *supra*-local investigation teams. And the readiness to intervene can also be deduced from the fact that in the course of the 1990s the Public Prosecutor's Office has tried to contain the growth and flourishing of the coffeeshops. In 1991 the College of Public Prosecutors published the first version of the so-called AHOJ-G criteria: no advertising, no sale of hard drugs, no nuisance, no sale to young people under the age of 16 years, and no sale of large quantities per transaction (that is: larger than appropriate for personal use).

In 1996 and 2000 these criteria were tightened, among other things by adding the provisions that young people under the age of 18 were not allowed to have access to coffeeshops and coffeeshops were not allowed to sell more than 5 grams cannabis per person per day. Furthermore, in 2000 it was decided that at the local level the Public Prosecutor's Office, the mayor and the police could determine the maximum size of the trade stock of coffeeshops, but that this trade stock, in any case, was not allowed to exceed 500 grams.[18]

In 1995, the tightening of the cannabis policy had been justified in a note to the Second Chamber – a note which ennumerated the achieved successes while simultaneously admitting that "also in the Netherlands the use of drugs and everything associated with it constitutes a major social and administrative problem". In this connection, there were references to "excessive nuisance" caused by drug tourists around coffeeshops, to coffeeshops that were also selling hard drugs and weapons, and to criticism from abroad about the cross-border effects of the Dutch drug policy:

---

17 Van der Torre and Hulshof, 2000, and Van der Torre and Gerz, 1996. See also, for instance, Korf, Van der Woude, Benschop and Nabben, 2001.

18 See for instance the *directives concerning the Opium Act* of the College of Attorney Generals dated 2 November 2000, which came into force on 1 January 2001, remained valid until 1 January 2005, and was then prolonged until 30 June 2011 (<http://www.om.nl/organisatie/beleidsregels/overzicht/drugs>, consulted on 28 February 2011).

> The policy will be directed at discouraging the use of drugs as much as possible, for instance by limiting the number of coffeeshops, by introducing age limits for sale, and by intensifying education about the adverse effects of cannabis.[19]

5.4.2 *The Fight Against Illicit Cannabis Cultivation*

Since the end of the 1990s a number of measures have been taken to restrict in particular the illicit cultivation of cannabis. In this context, two measures deserve special mention: the explicit criminalization in 1999 of the cultivation of cannabis and the sharp increase of the penalties for that cultivation in case the number of plants, the lighting, the heating and the irrigation indicate it is a professional occupation or a business (maximum sentence of six years in prison). In a letter entitled *Het pad naar de achterdeur* (*The path to the backdoor*), which the minister of Justice at the time, B. Korthals, on 7 April 2000 sent to the Second Chamber, it was stated straight away that part of the provisioning of the coffeeshops occurred via "the illicit, quasi-commercial cultivation of cannabis at home adresses" and that in some cities this cultivation was in the hands of:

> criminal organizations that pressurize residents to put some room at home at their disposal for illicit cultivation. In these cities such neighbourhoods are likely to deteriorate because criminal organizations have succeeded in strengthening their grip on residents.

To this, the minister added that the police and the Public Prosecutors' Office did not consider the control of the supply of the different types of cannabis to the coffeeshops as a priority: "Apparently, it suffices that coffeeshops comply with the maximum allowed stock trade (...)." According to the minister, this was in part due to the fact that the harmfulness of the product was not undisputed and the use of cannabis was gradually becoming widely tolerated in society.

However, it did not mean he agreed with the plans of municipalities such as Tilburg to transform "the complete production and sales process" into a closed system.[20] There was no room for that kind of experiments, the minister wrote: not only would they be in conflict with international treaties, but there was also no political support for such experiments in the European Union. Moreover, such experiments would only partially reduce related crime, and especially the illicit cultivation of cannabis, and they did not offer any solution to the

19 Second Chamber, 1994–1995, 24077, no. 3, pp. 11–15.

20 The detailed Tilburg proposal had been worked out by *Working Group The Backdoor* in the report *One doesn't buy at the backdoor*, Tilburg, 1 February 2000.

problem of the distribution of imported cannabis. For all these reasons, the government considered the "continuation and adequate monitoring of the current policy as most appropriate". There was "no room" for a "widening of the cannabis policy by means of local experiments". Such experiments would anyhow be regarded as "precursors of a possible legal regulation". Especially in case the experiments turned out to be successful, it would be "in the *administrative* reality no longer possible (...) to reverse things".[21]

A few years later, the fight against illicit cannabis cultivation was nevertheless intensified. In letters sent to the Second Chamber on 26 April, 27 October and 9 November 2005 the minister of Justice announced that henceforward the commercial cultivation of cannabis would be tackled in a more integrated way through a mixture of administrative, criminal law and civil law measures.[22] Both the fact that organized crime is involved in this form of cultivation and the fact that home growth of cannabis leads to the deterioration of neighbourhoods, played an important role in that decision. More specifically, in a number of districts and police regions projects were set up to get a better view not only of the role of organized crime in cannabis cultivation, but also of the companies – for instance growshops – that were one way or another facilitating cultivation.

Moreover, the so-called drug tourism caused by the "pull effect" of coffeeshops would be tackled:

> The coffeeshop policy has never been intended for foreign drug tourists.

With praise he referred to the plan of Maastricht to start – subject to approval by the city council – "with a pilot project by which access to coffeeshops will be restricted to residents". He also declared there were consultations with Belgium and Germany about strengthening cross-border cooperation to combat drug tourism. The T.M.C. Asser Instituut was asked to examine whether the treaties of the United Nations have any room for "an experiment with tolerating cannabis cultivation for the purpose of the provisioning of coffeeshops". The reply of the institute was clear: no, they did not.[23]

The aforementioned measures must be seen in the light of the findings and policy intentions the government had formulated in the so-called *Cannabis*

---

21 Second Chamber, 1999–2000, 24077, no. 75.

22 Second Chamber, 2004–2005, 24077, no. 156, and Second Chamber, 2005–2006, 24077, no. 170 and no. 171. See also Blom, 2008, pp. 72–74, and VROM-Inspectie, 2009.

23 T.M.C. Asser Instituut, 2005. In this connection, see also Second Chamber, 2008–2009, 24077, no. 232, pp. 2–3.

letter of 23 April 2004.[24] The starting point of that letter was that the coffeeshop policy was unsatisfactory from a law enforcement perspective and the fight against drug crime. In particular, it was deemed necessary, on the one hand, to further reduce "the coffeeshop phenomenon" and, on the other hand, to tackle "street trading, drug tourism and cannabis cultivation" more strictly. To achieve these goals, the importance of an integrated approach to the problems was emphasized once again. By means of administrative measures as well as criminal proceedings the cultivation had to be combated efficaciously, because it led to "the highly unwanted deterioration of especially residential areas" and was moreover facilitated by organized crime.

The offensive against cannabis cultivation got even sharper traits by the letter the minister of the Interior sent to the Second Chamber on 16 June 2006.[25] In that letter the importance of an integrated approach to the problem of cannabis cultivation – an approach involving the Public Prosecutor's Office, the police and the local authorities as well as the tax authorities, the housing corporations and the energy companies – was stressed yet again. The administrative approach would be directed against the immediate nuisance caused by cultivation; the criminal justice approach would target the criminal organizations concerned. To stimulate the cooperation between the different parties under the guidances of the municipalities, a model covenant would be developed.

Moreover, in July 2008 – equally in the context of a strengthened approach to organized crime – a Task Force on Tackling Organized Cannabis Cultivation was installed, which had to ensure a noticeable reduction of this kind of cultivation by 2011 and had to put an end to the "process of normalization" of cannabis cultivation.[26] The accompanying action plan developed by the police and the Public Prosecutor's Office contained several measures we have already mentioned: an integrated approach to the problems, charging the costs of the closing down of plantations to the cultivators, et cetera.[27]

5.4.3 *The Legalization of Cannabis for Medical Use*

The great efforts to prevent the cannabis and coffeeshop policy from derailing could almost make us forget that the Dutch government proceeded to the legalization of

24 Second Chamber, 2003–2004, 24077, no. 125. See also Second Chamber, 2005–2006, 24077, no. 170, and Second Chamber, 2005–2006, 24077, annex to no. 184.

25 Second Chamber, 2005–2006, 24077, no. 184 (with annex).

26 <http://www.justitie.nl/actueel/persberichten> (consulted on 10 July 2008).

27 See the (unpublished) document *Programma georganiseerde hennepteelt* (*Program organized cannabis cultivation*), January 2008.

cannabis as a means to ease the suffering of seriously ill people. The initiative to do this was taken by the minister of Public Health E. Borst in 2000. On 14 December 2000 she informed the Second Chamber that on the basis of article 28 of the Single Convention on Narcotic Drugs of 1961 she had established the Office for Medicinal Cannabis.

In the first place, this office was established to conduct (commissioned) studies on the medicinal effects of cannabis, and to cultivate, in this context, cannabis for medical purposes. The office would select qualified and reliable cultivators who could deliver the needed cannabis. These cultivators had, and have, to sell the entire yield of the cultivated cannabis to the office, in particular to avoid that part of the crop would be diverted to illicit networks. So, right from the start a sharp distinction was made between the cultivation of cannabis for medical use and the cultivation of cannabis for recreational use.

In the second place, the Office for Medicinal Cannabis was tasked with providing "cannabis of pharmaceutical quality", which seriously ill people (AIDS patients, MS patients) would be able to obtain, on prescription by a physician, through pharmacies. In September 2003 medical cannabis was provided for the first time to patients this way.[28] Over the years, according to reports in the *Pharmaceutisch Weekblad* (*Pharmaceutical Magazine*), the dispensation of cannabis by pharmacies has increased substantially. From almost 6,000 transactions in 2004 to approximately 13,000 in 2013.[29] The office presumes that today 1,200 to 1,400 patients in the Netherlands provide themselves (at their own expense) with cannabis this way.[30]

These numbers show that in the Netherlands – unlike in North America – the legalization of cannabis for medical use has not got out of hand. This is likely thanks to the careful and excellent procedure seriously ill people have to follow to obtain cannabis.[31]

5.5 The Development, Organization and Functioning of the Illicit Cannabis Cultivation

It is not the proper place here to examine whether and – at least equally important – how all the measures that were announced in the course of the years

28 Second Chamber, 2000–2001, 27400 XVI, no. 60; Second Chamber, 2000–2001, 27874, no. 3, pp. 2–3, 7–8 and no. 6, pp. 2–6; and Senate, 2001–2002, 27847, no. 316b, p. 3.

29 See the report "Apotheken verstrekken meer cannabis" in *Pharmaceutisch Weekblad*, 2013, no. 37, pp. 1–4.

30 Written declaration of the head of the office on 20.8.2014.

31 In this connection, see also the brochures of the Office for Medicinal Cannabis.

have actually been more or less implemented.[32] And, of course, not all these measures are relevant in the context of this book. Important here are mainly the reports that have been written about the development, organization and functioning of illicit cannabis cultivation.

First of all, it is worth to note that, generally speaking, the reports about the size, development and organization of the cannabis cultivation that date from the first decade of this century point to a market that has become rather large. As such, that is not really strange. We can repeat here what we already wrote about the developments in the 1970s and 1980s: criminal groups then could gain fortunes without much penal (and fiscal) risks. And so they did! This is why the report of the study on cannabis cultivation conducted by the National Police Force in 2008 was entitled *Het groene goud* (*The green gold*).[33] However, at the time the actual size of the cannabis production and the cannabis market were not exactly known.

In their report of 2003 on cannabis cultivation in the Netherlands F. Bovenkerk and W. Hogewind noted a wide discrepancy between, on the one hand, the size of the cannabis cultivation calculated by D. Korf on the basis of the domestic use by Dutch young persons and foreign tourists, and, on the other hand, their own estimations on the basis of the number of cannabis plantations that were demolished at that time in the police region Utrecht. The difference was "that big that we may assume a considerable part is cultivated for export". How big that part can be or must be, they did not calculate. Though in their opinion it is "probably more, or much more, than one half", perhaps even up to 80%.[34]

In 2006, after all possible estimations made by others, A. Van der Heijden tried to estimate the development of the cannabis production in a more systematic way. Making use of, among other things, the then available data on the number and size of plantations and the yield per hemp plant, he first estimated the national production to be 315 to 755 tons, the production by amateur growers (7,5 to 10 tons) not included. However, in the same report he seriously questioned this estimation and thought it possible – based on other assumptions about, for instance, the size of the plantations – that the actual minimum amounts to 133 tons annually.[35]

32 In this connection, see for instance the annex to the letter of 9 November 2005 to the Second Chamber (24077, no. 171). In that letter the implementation of the measures of the *Cannabisbrief* is discussed.

33 Dienst IPOL, 2008b.

34 Bovenkerk and Hogewind, 2003, p. 73, 143.

35 Van der Heijden, 2006.

The report *Het groene goud* also describes how cannabis cultivation has developed into a big, professional but illicit branch of business. In that report, the size of the industry is chiefly measured by the number of plantations and their size. It was estimated that in 2008 the Netherlands counted 12,000 to 20,000 plantations of all shapes and sizes, which together produced 61 to 142 tons of cannabis. Of this volume, 37 to 54 tons would be consumed domestically, whereas 7 to 104 tons, that is: 10 to 74% of the national cannabis production, would be exported. With an average wholesale price of 3,000 euros per kilogram *nederwiet*, in 2006, the national production accounted for a turnover of 182 to 424 million euros. According to the authors of the report, in 2008 only a limited amount of cannabis was imported from abroad. The criminal organizations that imported hashish, stored it in companies, offices and sheds. From there, it was distributed domestically and abroad.

Next, the authors of *Het groene goud* distinguished – following the example of A. Spapens, H. Van de Bunt and L. Rastovac, who in 2007 published *De wereld achter de wietteelt* (*The world behind the cultivation of cannabis*) – several categories of producers, traffickers and smugglers active in this branch.[36] Besides home growers and independent growers there are operators and also – at least according to Spapens, Van de Bunt and Rastovac – criminal cooperatives.[37] The key figures of these cooperatives have the right contacts at home and abroad to be able to sell large amounts of cannabis. Turnovers of 100 to 200 kilograms a week are not unusual for them. In addition, Spapens, Van de Bunt and Rastovac – just as Van der Heijden – indicate that the international dimension of the Dutch cultivation of cannabis comprises more than this type of rather large-scale export. On the one hand, there are also the foreign drug tourists and drug couriers who travel to the Netherlands to provide themselves with a few grams or kilograms of cannabis, and, on the other hand, there are Dutch people who, one way or another, are involved in cannabis plantations in the neighbouring countries.

Furthermore, both reports indicate that the key figures – be they independent operators or key figures of criminal cooperatives – usually have been, or still are, involved in other forms of serious crime, such as armed robbery, production of synthetic drugs and illegal contracting. In this connection, the *Nationaal dreigingsbeeld 2008* (*National threat assessment 2008*) notably refers to Turkish criminal cooperatives and criminal cooperatives consisting of caravan dwellers.[38]

36 Spapens, Van de Bunt and Rastovac, 2007. See also Van Nimwegen, 2009.

37 For a study on the home growers, see Siesling, Smeets and Spapens, 2011.

38 Dienst Ipol, 2008a, pp. 63–64.

In this respect, it should not be neglected what Bovenkerk and Hogewind, in conjunction with the results of a previous study on cannabis cultivation in the city of Utrecht, already in 2003 wrote about key figures in the large-scale cannabis cultivation in the Utrecht region.[39] At the time, at least a part of that cultivation – how big that part was, they could not tell – was in the hands of organized crime:

> There are persons with a criminal background and also newcomers without a crooked past, who together control the local market. These people know each other well and do all sorts of things in varying small groups. Among them, there is no misunderstanding about the destination of the marijuana. A part of it goes to the eighteen coffeeshops in Utrecht, though here too, as a rule, eighty percent of the production is intended for export (…). There cannot be any confusion about who is the boss. They are least concerned about checks by the police. The situation of all the other of the nine growshops and seven wholesale traders in the province would not be different. The researchers note that the people involved are tough business people, lacking any ideological inspiration with regard to our national soft drug policy.

In order to get a clear picture of the current situation, it is also important to state that according to the *Nationaal dreigingsbeeld 2012* the size of the production of *nederwiet* in 2011 amounted to 187 to 1,196 tons. A comparison with the figures of the domestic consumption of cannabis in the period 2008–2011 (32 to 92 tons) leads to the conclusion that a large part of Dutch cannabis – for hefty sums (5,000 euros per kilogram) – is exported:

> The major part of the Dutch cannabis production is destined for export to other European states.

The latter refers in particular to Great Britain, Germany and Italy. For 2011, the part of the production that crossed borders is estimated at somewhere between 96 and 1,164 tons, which corresponds to 51 to 97% of the total production. A few criminal cooperatives are exporting "300 kilos or more" a week.[40] The

39 Bovenkerk and Hogewind, 2003, p. 79. See also pp. 92–97, 112–118, 119–129, 137–139.

40 An example of a drug gang that around 2010 not only on a large scale exported Dutch cannabis to Great Britain and Italy, but also on a large scale imported hashish from Pakistan and then transited it to other countries, was the gang of the assassinated A. de J. His business in Eindhoven was brought to light by the "Maskerbij" inquiry. On the basis

total turnover on an annual basis is estimated at 2.4 billion euros, 0.5 billion of which is realized on the domestic market and 1.9 billion on foreign markets. In all, it is a relatively large market where the parties concerned can make a lot of money.[41] This probably explains why there appears to be no competition between the different cooperatives: demand exceeds supply. "When it is beneficial, they work together."

According to this threat assessment, the cultivation of cannabis is still mainly in the hands of Dutch gangs – whether or not mixed with persons from communities of caravan dwellers or members of one of the well-known motorcycle clubs: the Hells Angels or Satudarah – and Turkish cooperatives. Within these flat and hierarchical "family companies" every member plays a certain role. It is striking, by the way, how well their illicit activities are protected:

> Locations are guarded by cameras, mobile phone alarms and sometimes also by armed watchmen. Real estate and cars are registered in the name of family members, close friends or others. In many cases drugs are transported hidden in other loads. People communicate with each other disguisedly. Telephones and SIM cards are regularly exchanged.[42]

Since a large part of the domestic cannabis consumption is enabled by coffeeshops, it is, finally, also appropriate to indicate that in 2004 a special study has shown that coffeeshops are a crime-related sector. Many entrepreneurs in this branch – notably in Venlo and Amsterdam (about 80%) – had criminal records, which covered a wide range of offences: infringements of the Opium Act, of course, also in the area of hard drugs, but also illegal possession of weapons, road traffic offences and (serious) violent crimes.

---

of the results of that inquiry, M. Steenberghe wrote a very informative reportage in a *Spectrum* annex to the *Eindhovens Dagblad* ("Dossier Maskerbij", Saturday 9 March 2013). See also the decisions of the Court of Justice and the Court of 's-Hertogenbosch on Rechtspraak.nl (for instance: ECLI:NL:GHSHE:2014:956 and BZ3427). That still large quantities of hashish are imported into the Netherlands is illustrated by the report in the *Volkskrant* of 22 April 2014 about the discovery of a freight of five tons of hashish from Thailand in the port of Zeebrugge that was destined for the Netherlands.

41 See also the estimate made in 2014 by the Centraal Bureau voor de Statistiek (p. 13) of the added value of the cannabis sector in 2010: 1,039 million euros (with the production 1,417 million euros was involved and with the consumption 378 million euros). Kazemier, Bruil, Van de Steeg and Rensman (2012, p. 13) suppose that the added value of the production and sale of *nederwiet* corresponds with 0.0 to 0.2% of the gross domestic product.

42 Dienst IPOL, 2012, pp. 56–65, 225, 255.

It is remarkable that the authors of the report from 2004 could not pass judgment on the role of organized crime in the cannabis sector of that time. The reason was simple: "the low priority that was given to the investigation of soft drugs-related Opium Act offences in the Netherlands". There were just not enough data available on the role of this form of crime. However, in line with Bovenkerk and Hogewind, the researchers were convinced organized crime did indeed play a role in the cannabis sector: at the time of their study, both in Amsterdam and Venlo, there were entrepreneurs at work who had been convicted for involvement in a criminal organization.[43]

In sum, if we combine, in light of this finding, the results of the screening of the coffeeshop sector with the results of later studies on the organization behind the cannabis cultivation, it is difficult to avoid the conclusion that this sector is at its core largely dominated by criminals: they are the key figures in the production as well as the distribution of weed. This conclusion raises the question whether in a number of cases both the production and the tolerated distribution of weed are in the hands of the same criminal cooperatives. In other words: have key figures in these circles in the course of the years (at a number of places?) largely integrated the cannabis sector, from weed plantation to coffeeshop?

5.6 The Cannabis Problem and the Problem of the Coffeeshops

In the Netherlands, the discussion about the legalization of cannabis is closely linked to the coffeeshop phenomenon. Coffeeshops are the tolerated points of sale for, among other things, cannabis that is illicitly cultivated on Dutch (and foreign) soil. It should be clear that the booming of this business over the past decades is without any doubt in part connected with the way many coffeeshops have developed during that period: from small-scale local facilities to large-scale sales organizations for Dutch people and foreigners. Due to this transformation, the coffeeshops undeniably have largely stimulated the expansion of the illicit weed cultivation. If the coffeeshops had remained the small-scale local facilities about which Hulsman and his supporters talked in the early 1970s, then domestic demand for cannabis would certainly have remained much smaller than it actually is today, and consequently much less cannabis would have been cultivated for these shops.

Conversely, it can be stated that those who were involved in the expansion of the illicit cannabis cultivation had every interest in an increase of domestic

43 Snippe, Bieleman, Naayer and Ogier, 2004.

demand and therefore also in an expansion of the coffeeshop business. This way they were ensured of a permanent distribution network for large volumes of cannabis. In other words, the problem of large-scale illicit cannabis cultivation, and the problem of organized crime which is so closely related to it, cannot be separated from the fact that until recently the coffeeshop business could almost unhindered be expanded, both at its "front door" and its "back door", by the entrepreneurs concerned. The coffeeshops became, so to speak, the portal of organized crime to the illicit cannabis cultivation.

Clearly, there is much to say about the coffeeshop problem in the Netherlands, but not everything has to be said here. Here it is in the first place important to look at the problem as far as it is relevant for the debate on legalization. Since that relevance can best be elucidated by means of the struggle that in a number of municipalities has been waged for the (continued) existence of the existing coffeeshops, on the following pages we will briefly focus on the best-known examples of that struggle. The starting point of our discussion is Terneuzen, a municipality in the south of the province of Zeeland. The terminal point are the case of the Euregio Meuse-Rhine and Amsterdam, the urban conglomerations at the extremities of the A2 motorway.[44]

5.6.1 *The Zeeland Border Area: Terneuzen*

In recent years, the problem of the coffeeshops in this border area has manifested itself in particular in the city of Terneuzen. In other Zeeland municipalities there were also problems with coffeeshops, but especially the coffeeshop Checkpoint and, to a lesser extent, the coffeeshop Miami in Terneuzen still serve as a kind of test case for the Dutch coffeeshop policy.

In the 1990s, and with the approval of the mayor, these coffeeshops were developed to halt as much as possible the widespread (soft) drugs trade, which was scattered over seventy "addresses" in town and caused a lot of trouble in the public domain.[45] At the start of this century, the town has, to a certain degree, facilitated the expansion of Checkpoint by issuing a licence for an extensive new building and by constructing a large parking lot. However, it should be

44 It is rather obvious that also in the more north-eastern part of the Netherlands there are problems with cross-border drug tourism. However, also because of the lesser degree of urbanization on the German side of that border area, these problems are smaller than in the south-eastern part of the Netherlands. See for instance Bieleman, Nijkamp and De Haan, 2011 (about the situation in Groningen) and Afdeling Onderzoek en Statistiek, 2008 (about the situation in Nijmegen).

45 Mein and Van Ooyen-Houben, 2013, pp. 39–47.

noted that in the tolerance statement issued in 2005 two important conditions were laid down:

1. In the preamble of the letter concerned it is explicitly stated that the trade in soft drugs will only be tolerated "in view of the local need";
2. The statement itself stipulates: "Prohibited is the sale or supply of cannabis products to persons of whom one can reasonably assume they will export these drugs abroad."[46]

In the course of 2006, the coffeeshops mentioned above increasingly became the object of criticism. A major reason for this were the large numbers of Belgian and French drug tourists who provided themselves in the shops: 3,500 a day, 25,000 a week, about 1 million a year. That flood of visitors caused all sorts of problems in the centre of the town: from traffic nuisance up to and including urinating in public. In the context of the project *Houdgreep* ("Grapple hold") the town of Terneuzen, in cooperation with the municipalities of Sluis and Hulst, tried to combat these forms of nuisance. However, also other problems raised concern. The fact, for instance, that "an increasing shift is noted towards illicit plantations, in the context of which the cultivation (laboratories), the provisioning (coffeeshops) and the black market come into the picture". Moreover, the town of Terneuzen played with the idea of allowing the establishment of a third coffeeshop, close to the border. The mayors of the neighbouring Belgian municipalities were absolutely opposed to that idea, however.

In 2007, the developments in and around Terneuzen took a different turn. On 1 June 2007 the police and the Public Prosecutor's Office raided both Checkpoint and the home of the owner of that coffeeshop. They detected 4,489.8 grams of soft drugs, including 3,610 joints – much and much more than the permitted quantity. About a year later, on 28 May 2008, a second raid was carried out. On that occasion, the police and the Public Prosecutor's Office detected 130 kilograms of soft drugs in (the vicinity of) the coffeeshop. As a result of the first raid, the mayor decided to close Checkpoint from 21 July 2008 to 20 January 2009. However, even before that period had expired, on 17 December 2008, the mayor decided to revoke the license to sell soft drugs per 1 January 2009. In September 2008, the other coffeeshop, Miami, had to close for about three months

46 These conditions are cited in the judgment of the Court of 's-Gravenhage: ECLI:NL:HR:2013:7, pp. 10–11.

and from 1 December 2008 onwards its permission to sell soft drugs was restricted to maximum 3 grams per customer.[47]

In June 2009, the criminal case against Checkpoint commenced at the Court of Justice in Middelburg. Among other things, the coffeeshop was accused of infringement of the Opium Act.[48] The suspect immediately argued that the claim brought by the Public Prosecutor's Office had to be declared inadmissible. The court rejected this defence: the principles of due process had not been violated. The circumstances in which Checkpoint had been able to prosper and expand were nevertheless "very relevant" for the assessment of the case and would be taken into consideration in the determination of the penalty. The court also noted that in this case it was faced with a criminal organization which, though it was not linked "to a more extreme criminal organization", had been running, at variance with important license conditions but in line with its objectives, an "all-encompassing trade in soft drugs" in a commercial and professional way. Moreover, at the "back door" several sorts of offences had been committed. The suspect and his accomplices:

> however, have taken over the management of the 'back door': the large quantities of purchased soft drugs were processed and stored in other places than the coffeeshop.

Given, for instance, the disguished language they used in phone calls, they were very well aware that what they did was punishable. Or, as later researchers have written: at the "back door" a (necessarily) large-scale illicit provisioning had been set up to enable the above-mentioned growth.[49] In the period 2006–2008 the net operating result amounted to 27,650,996 euros.

On 2 February 2012, the Court of 's-Gravenhage, on appeal, nevertheless decided to dismiss the claim against the suspect because of a violation of the principles of due process. In the opinion of the court, the owner of the coffeeshop (in particular) might have been confident that the public prosecutor when assessing whether or not to prosecute, would take the suspect's specific interests into account in a reasonable and fair manner.

On 2 July 2013, however, the Supreme Court annulled this judgment and referred the case to the Court of Amsterdam. The Supreme Court argued that the Court of The Hague had failed to recognize that:

---

47 See some of the contributions to De Ruyver and Surmont, 2007. See also Fijnaut and De Ruyver, 2008, pp. 79–81; Bieleman and Naayer, 2007, and Werkgroep Drugsoverlast, 2007.

48 As to the verdict, see the Court of Middelburg: ECLI:NL:RBMID:2010:BL8815.

49 Mein and Van Ooyen-Houben, 2013, p. 60.

> such a lack of enforcement activities cannot be put on a par with a statement by, or attributable to, the Public Prosecutor's Office that has given the suspect the justified confidence that he will not be (or no longer will be) prosecuted.

Moreover, the Supreme Court recalled once again that with regard to the admissibility of the case, the criminal judge is:

> not permitted to fully assess in this way the public prosecutor's decision to prosecute (...). (...) The criminal judge only has to examine whether there is a situation in which no reasonably judging member of the Public Prosecutor's Office could have decided to initiate or continue the prosecution concerned.[50]

On 16 July 2014, the Court of Amsterdam decided that in the Checkpoint case the conditions under which this coffeeshop was allowed to sell soft drugs – that is: the conditions such as the coffeeshop could reasonably understand them – had not been breached, and thus that the shop could not be prosecuted for this sale. On this point, the court decided the case was inadmissible.

However, the court did condemn the owner and the collaborators for the stocking of large quantities of soft drugs, but it saw no reason to punish them for this offence because for years, Checkpoint had been facilitated and stimulated by the authorities, which therefore should have known that the coffeeshop purchased and stored huge amounts of soft drugs.

Finally, the court also dismissed the claim that the owner and the collaborators of the coffeeshop constituted a criminal organization. The preliminary investigation had not revealed the existence of such an organization. According to the court, and having regard to all the circumstances, prosecuting them would be at variance with a reasonable and fair balancing of interests.[51]

For a good understanding of the judgments of both courts, it is important to emphasize that they do not imply a condemnation of the lenient policy the authorities had pursued in the previous years with regard to the coffeeshops concerned, nor a condemnation of the policy of tolerance the authorities, in general, have pursued with respect to cannabis. The whole point is that authorities that have pursued such a policy cannot all of a sudden radically

---

50 For the decisions of the Court and the Supreme Court, see: ECLI:NL:HR:2013:7.

51 This account is based on the press release published by the Court of Amsterdam on 16 July 2014 (see the website rechtspraak.nl). Recently, the text of the judgment has been made public: ECLI:NL:GHAMS:2014:2840.

change that policy. If they want to reconsider that policy, they have to reasonably balance the interests of all parties involved. It also explains why, as we shall see later, the Administrative Court of Amsterdam does not have a problem with the fact that many coffeeshops in the centre of Amsterdam have to close down: years ago already, the city has warned the owners and the people who run the shops that this would happen.

An administrative evaluation of the events in Terneuzen has shown that in the case of an illicit market such as the cannabis market a reasonable and fair balancing of interests, as asked for by the courts of justice, is no easy feat. For years the town had not intervened, out of fear "that a restriction of the tolerated supply would, by definition, imply the re-emergence of the illicit trade". However, nothing was less true. It remained quiet in Terneuzen after the closing down of Checkpoint: within a few months the flood of foreign visitors had, for the most part, came to a standstill and thanks to a strengthened enforcement capacity a return of the illicit trade was largely avoided. In the autumn of 2009 the total number of drug tourists in Terneuzen had decreased by 82% in comparison to 2007. In other words, due to its fears the town had "shut itself off from alternative solutions and lost control over the policy of tolerance".[52]

5.6.2 *The Brabant Border Area: Task Force B5*

In the Brabant border area, unlike in the Zeeland border area, the cannabis problem manifests itself in several large municipalities: Roosendaal and Bergen op Zoom, Breda and Tilburg, and, finally, Eindhoven. This has not only to do with unequal urbanization of the province, but also with its location with regard to Flemish and French urban agglomerations and the fact that it is – at least partially – connected to the European motorway network.

In 2003 the drug problems in Roosendaal and Bergen op Zoom worsened to such an extent that the administrations concerned, in an effort to get a grip on the situation, were forced to launch a comprehensive project: the *Courage* project.[53] An analysis of the situation in 2005 showed that both municipalities had to contend with a market for hard drugs and a much bigger soft drug market. For traders in soft drugs, the situation was very favourable. Especially from Belgium and France, there was a huge demand. Traders had used their gains to purchase real estate, which enabled them to further facilitate and expand their businesses.[54] Because the eight existing coffeeshops were not

52 Mein and Van Ooyen-Houben, 2013, pp. 55–57, p. 65. See also Bieleman, Nijkamp and Buit-Minnema, 2009, p. 1.

53 The following description is mainly based on Rovers and Fijnaut, 2011, pp. 47–52.

54 To get a picture of the situation, read the judgment of the Court of Breda, dated 4.12.2009, against one of the families concerned: ECLI:NL:RBBRE:2009:BK5301, no. 02-811158-06.

able to cope with the notable foreign demand, a large illicit parallel market had also emerged. The latter was supplied from drug houses and by drug couriers and stray dealers. In 2003, each week about 10,000 drug tourists travelled to Roosendaal and about 12,000 to Bergen op Zoom.

In 2008, it became clear that despite all the efforts to get the situation under control, the problems had not really decreased. Research revealed that both cities attracted 1.3 million drug tourists on an annual basis, and that about 90% of them visited the coffeeshops. This led to a drastic change of course: it was decided that, as from 16 September 2009, all eight coffeeshops would be closed down. Although this measure was not a panacea, it accomplished what could have been expected. In no time – and partly thanks to several supportive measures, such as media campaigns in Belgium and France – the number of foreign drug tourists decreased by 90%, and the street trade and the nuisance declined considerably. Of course, they did not completely disappear like snow before the sun. For the simple reason that, on the one hand, the illicit local market continued to function, and, on the other hand, the illicit parallel market continued to exert some attraction on foreigners.

In the first decade of this century, two reports were written on the security issues in Tilburg and Eindhoven.[55] Both reports emphasized the drug problems the cities were suffering from – not only in terms of organized crime, but also in terms of social insecurity. In the report on the (in)security in Tilburg it was stated that, although at the time no systematic analysis of the problems was made, there was reason enough to be worried:

> In this regard the committee wants to refer to accounts of intimidation – in (parts of) a neighbourhood – by the organizers of the weed cultivation, and to accounts of the (intermediate) trade in prohibited drugs.

What already was a problem in Tilburg at that time, was definitely also an issue in Breda. In 2009, this became evident from two reports on drug scenes in and around this city.[56] In both reports it is clearly stated that:

> The drug trade is characterized by a high degree of organization, in the sense that there is a lot of money at stake and that networks of traders often succeed in evading the police and the judiciary.

So, it is no surprise that in the documents of the city of Eindhoven on the promotion of integral security in the period 2014–2017 much attention is paid to

---

55 Fijnaut and Zaat, 2003, p. 15, pp. 60–61. For Eindhoven, see Fijnaut and Van Riessen, 2008.

56 See Dobbelaar, Van der Torre and Besselink, 2009a and 2009b.

the cultivation of cannabis.[57] The documents not only indicate how this cultivation will be combated by clearing plantations and by tracing the criminal cooperatives behind them, but they also draw a pretty alarming picture of the cannabis problem. An excerpt from the *Policy paper on public security for the years, 2014–2017* illustrates this:

> Criminal organizations are making huge profits from the illicit cultivation of cannabis. In this context, they do not eschew violence, extortion, corruption and assassinations. (...) It concerns criminal cooperatives that are engaged in the (large-scale) production of cannabis and are often managing several plantations. This means they organize the cultivation process, appoint supervisors, instruct assistants and in a number of cases process and sell the harvested cannabis. (...) Often cannabis operators are also engaged in other criminal activities such as handling stolen goods, burglary, production and trade of hard drugs, trade and smuggling of firearms, VAT fraud, human trafficking and money laundering. (...) Only a part of the cultivated cannabis is intended for the internal Dutch market. Within the Netherlands, specially prepared cars, buses or trucks are used for the transport of cannabis to distribution points, storage points, trading points or points of sale. A large part of the cannabis is intended for export. Prior to its exportation, cannabis is stashed in storehouses. Cannabis transports are often combined with the transportation of hashish, ecstasy and/or cocaine. Apart from the criminal organizations there are also home growers who cultivate cannabis at a small scale and are, or become, increasingly (financially) dependent on criminal organizations. The risks associated with cannabis plantations in districts and neighbourhoods are big – especially the risks of leakages and fires caused by short-circuiting. Theft of energy by illegal tapping often occurs, since much light and heat is required to make cannabis grow fast. The damage caused by cannabis cultivation is great. Housing corporations and energy companies have to bear the costs of leakages, fire damages and illegally tapped energy.

Of course, such descriptions of the situation nourish the idea that the drug problems in and around the big cities of Brabant have gotten completely out of hand. In 2011, that idea was once again reaffirmed by a scan of the region,

57 More specifically, it concerns the *Beleidskader integrale veiligheid, 2014–2017*, and the *Actieplan integrale veiligheid, 2014–2017*. Both documents can be consulted on the website of the city of Eindhoven.

which indicated that in Brabant the circumstances for criminal groupings to develop themselves on the local, the national and the cross-border drug market were splendid, not least because the police, the Public Prosecutor's Office and the local authorities mainly focused their attention on "*reported crime*" and nuisance. Thus, the groupings concerned remained largely off the screen.[58]

Strangely enough, the fact that for years the large-scale cannabis cultivation in the province had already regularly been accompanied by brute violence, had done little or nothing to change their approach. The scan mentioned and a number of serious incidents – such as the attack on the town hall in Waalre and the threat to the mayor of Helmond – ultimately created a sense of urgency. Brabant, the message was now, was really and in several respects suffering from the drug problems. It was necessary to intervene vigorously, otherwise it would, over time, become even more difficult to solve the problems. This new perspective, in any case, formed the basis for the initiative taken by minister of Security and Justice Opstelten to establish a Task Force on Tackling Organized Crime in Brabant, also called Task Force B5.[59]

For a better understanding of this new approach, one should know that Task Force B5 in its recent report *Integraal appèl* (*Integral appeal*) estimates that in Brabant about 6,000 cannabis plantations are in operation, that these plantations produce 343 tons of dry weed annually and that they generate an annual turnover of more than 1 billion euros. Eye-opening too are the following data on Tilburg, a city of about 200,000 inhabitants. According to Task Force B5, approximately 2,500 people in Tilburg are working in the business of cannabis cultivation. In that business, 60 criminal organizations are operating. Their annual cannabis sales amount to about 800 million euros. A large part of the production is exported.[60]

No wonder that in the public opinion increasingly the feeling prevails that in Brabant, with the currently available resources, it is impossible to curb organized crime in cannabis cultivation.[61]

5.6.3 *The Limburg Border Area: Maastricht*

In three municipalities in the Limburg border area: Maastricht, Heerlen and Venlo, the drug problems and, consequently, also the discussions about the

---

58 Beke, Van der Torre and Van Duin, 2011, and Van Dijk, 2010.

59 See his letter to the Second Chamber on this subject (2010–2011, 29911, no. 49)

60 This document was issued by, among other institutions, the Regional Information and Expertise Centre, in which police, administration, tax services, justice et cetera closely work together.

61 See recent reports on this subject in the *Brabants Dagblad* (30.4.2014), and *NRC Handelsblad* (28.5.2014).

drug policy to be pursued flare up from time to time. Per municipality, one could easily write a book about everything that has occurred related to this topic area the past decades. But that is not what we intend to do here. We will confine ourselves to the events in Maastricht, because to a large extent they are indicative of the general development of the cannabis and coffeeshop policy in the Netherlands.

As early as 1993, cross-border drug tourism was noted in Maastricht. That was not entirely surprising: the city is located in the centre of one of the most urbanized Euregions of the European Union and counted 28 coffeeshops. The number of coffeeshop tourists who, at the time, traveled to Maastricht in the weekend, was estimated by the police and the municipality to be at 400 to 600 persons. On one day of the weekend they spent 25,000 guilders. Most of them were Belgians and French. The Belgian tourists usually lived 50 kilometers and the French tourists up to 550 kilometers from Maastricht. Apparently, their presence in the city was not regarded as a problem.[62]

Over the years, the picture changed substantially. Understandably. Although in the period 2008–2011 the number of coffeeshops had been halved (to 14), the number of customers – a large part of them still coming from Belgium and France – had increased to 2.5 million, who paid a total of 4 to 4.5 million visits to these coffeeshops. No wonder that in 2010 25% of the inhabitants of this medium-sized city (120,000 inhabitants) declared they often experienced drug-related nuisance – a much higher percentage than in the country as a whole (5%), and also much higher than in the rest of South Limburg (15%).

More specifically, from 2007 onwards, it was signaled that an important part of the nuisance was caused by drug couriers who, in an aggressive way, were acquiring clients for drug houses in a large number of city districts. In 2009, a police team that had been established in 2008 to combat drug couriers made 400 arrests (dealers and buyers), raided 74 premises (37 of which were closed down) and seized – besides weapons and the like – 100 kilograms of hard drugs and 40 kilograms of soft drugs.[63]

5.6.3.1 The Fundamental Backing by the Luxembourg Court of Justice

Given the (increasing) "touristic" problems in municipalities such as Maastricht (and Terneuzen), it is obvious that reducing drug tourism has become an important objective of the policy plans that have been developed since the start of this century to restrict the cannabis sector. The idea to stop the sale of

62 Korf, Müller, Freeman and Lettink, 1993, pp. 42–44.

63 Rovers and Fijnaut, 2011, pp. 23–31.

cannabis to non-residents through coffeeshops, suggested in the previously discussed *Cannabis letter* of 2004, was followed by an experiment in Maastricht in 2006. By means of an annex to the General Municipal Code Maastricht introduced the country of residence principle, which prohibits the admission of non-residents to coffeeshops. In this context, residents are people who are actually domiciled in the Netherlands.

On the basis of the provisions concerned, the mayor of Maastricht G. Leers decided on 7 September 2006 to close the coffeeshop Easy Going for a period of three months, after it had been established on two occasions that citizens of the European Union, who were not domiciled in the Netherlands, had been admitted to the shop. The owner of the coffeeshop objected to that decision, but his protest was declared unfounded by decision of the mayor on 28 March 2007. Next, the person involved appealed against this decision before the Court of Maastricht. That court declared the appeal well-founded: the distinction on the basis of residency came down to an indirect distinction on the basis of nationality, and since such a distinction could not be justified in this case, it was a violation of the principle of non-discrimination as set out in article 1 of the Constitution.[64]

In May 2008, both the owner of the coffeeshop and the mayor of Maastricht lodged an appeal with the Council of State. The Council, by decision of 8 April 2009, decided to request the Court of Justice in Luxembourg to give a preliminary ruling on four questions related to the country of residence principle and its application in the context of the coffeeshop policy and therefore also the cannabis policy.[65] In sum, the leitmotif in the questions was whether the regulation concerned fell, in whole or in part, within the scope of the European Community Treaty, "in particular the free movement of goods and/or services, or the principle of non-discrimination", and, if so, whether the prohibition concerned "(was) an appropriate and proportional means to reduce drug tourism and the nuisance associated with it", including the indirect distinction that in this connection was made between residents and non-residents.

Advocate General Y. Bot, in his conclusion of 15 July 2010, advised the Court of Justice in Luxembourg to answer the questions of the Council of State in the sense that both the European Community Treaty and the Schengen Agreements:

> do not preclude such a measure when it is the expression of the right conferred on the local public authority to preserve internal public order

64 Second Chamber, 2008–2009, 24077, no. 232, p. 6.

65 Council of State, 8 April 2008, case number 200803357/1. In this connection, see Klip, 2009, pp. 185–196.

> from the problems caused by drug tourism and/or the fulfilment of its duty to contribute to the maintenance of European public order.[66]

In its arrest of 16 December 2010 the Court of Justice followed this advice.[67] It stated in plain terms that, with regard to the sale of narcotic drugs, a coffeeshop proprietor could not object "to municipal rules such as those at issue in the main proceedings, which prohibit the admission of persons who are non-resident in the Netherlands to such establishments". In addition, the court declared that although the regulation concerned indeed constituted a restriction on the freedom to provide services laid down by the European Community Treaty, that restriction was justified "by the objective of combating drug tourism and the accompanying public nuisance".

The Council of State continued the handling of the case. After a hearing on 5 April 2011, it passed its judgment on 29 June 2011.[68] Obviously, the Council first of all repeated that although the Maastricht regulation constituted a restriction on the freedom to provide services laid down by the European Community Treaty, this restriction was justified "by the objective of combating drug tourism and the accompanying public nuisance". In the second place, it repeated that although the country of residence principle without any doubt implied an indirect distinction between people on the basis of their nationality, there were "objective and reasonable grounds" to make this distinction, namely "combating the increasing coffeeshop tourism and the negative effects on public order associated with it". Nevertheless, the Council – surprisingly enough – ruled that, although the regulation concerned violated neither the European law nor the Dutch Constitution, it was incompatible with the Opium Act, and thus the mayor of Maastricht should not have closed the controversial coffeeshop for a period of three months in 2006.

5.6.3.2 The Rejection of the Maastricht Resolution

In this regard, we have to bear in mind that long before the court in Luxembourg in 2009 was asked to decide on the conformity of the Maastricht regulation with European law, a few other policy initiatives had already been taken in Maastricht to efficiently tackle the cannabis and more specifically the coffeeshop problem.

---

66 Court of Justice, case C-137/09 (Marc Michel Josemans versus the Mayor of Maastricht), Conclusion of Advocate General Y. Bot, 15 July 2010.

67 Court of Justice, case C-137/09 (Marc Michel Josemans versus the Mayor of Maastricht), Arrest, 16 December 2010.

68 Council of State, case no. 200803357/1/H3-A, 29 June 2011.

In March 2005, for instance, the mayor of Maastricht had published an open letter in which he stated that the cannabis and coffeeshop problems had become so big that new drug policy choices had to be made:

> Either you slam the back door – and then you can also close the coffee-shops because they will no longer be supplied – or you regulate the back door just like you regulated the front door. But stop the leniency policy.[69]

The mayor clearly showed a preference for regulation since it provided the opportunity to get a grip on the cultivation, trade and sale of cannabis. Though this needed to happen in cooperation with the neighbouring regions, which were also struggling with the question of how they could avoid that "the trade and the often young customers would fall into the hands of criminals". In this regard, the mayor was thinking of:

> creating a closed system of regulated cannabis cultivation, distribution, sale and consumption. Removing it from the criminal circuit and being tough on remaining offenders.

However, in reply to a question of a member of Parliament, the minister of Justice P.-H. Donner immediately made clear he did not like the idea.[70] The regulation or legalization of the production of cannabis, he stated in his answer, was at odds with Dutch law. Moreover, such a policy would not lead to a reduction of the cannabis production at all. For the sake of exports it was even expected the production would increase: "This way the Netherlands could become an international cannabis producer, which we consider undesirable."

Furthermore, he was afraid that such a development would make the Netherlands more attractive to foreign criminal organizations and that it would result in a shift from one form of crime to the other. He also remarked that illicitly produced cannabis will probably always be cheaper than regulated cannabis. Although it was not explicitly said, the purpose of this remark was evident: maybe the regulated cultivation would be outcompeted by the illicit cultivation. Later, combating the illicit market would be one of the reasons

69 See the open letter mayor G. Leers published on 18 March 2005 in *De Limburger* and which was attached as annex to Minister of Justice P.-H. Donner's reply to a question about this document: Second Chamber, Annex Proceedings, 2004–2005, no. 1290.

70 See the reference to this reply in the previous footnote (Annex Proceedings, 2004–2005, no. 1290).

why the authorities of some American states proceeded with the legalization of cannabis.

In May 2005, the open letter of Leers was followed by the *Resolutie van Maastricht* ("Maastricht Resolution"), which was signed by the mayors of Aachen, Hasselt, Heerlen, Liège, Sittard-Geleen, Kerkrade, and, of course, Maastricht. It almost goes without saying that this was a very remarkable resolution: for the first time (local) authorities from three states pleaded for a common approach to the problem of soft drugs, in the context of which the governments of the Netherlands, Germany and Belgium were not only asked to take better account of the negative effects of the drug policy and to increase the available resources to neutralize these effects, but also:

> to examine new scenarios to solve the so-called back door problem (...) and to include in these scenarios the possibility (in particular in the border area) of small-scale experiments, in conformity with the adopted motion of the member of the Dutch Parliament, Mr Van der Ham c.s.

In the letter Donner sent to the Second Chamber on 8 February 2006 in response to this Maastricht Resolution, he elaborated on a number of his objections to such a development. He stressed once again that the illicit cultivation and trade considerably exceeded the demand in the coffeeshops, and that a large part of the sale of cannabis still took place outside the coffeeshops. Consequently:

> the problems mentioned in connection with the cultivation and trade of cannabis: nuisance, endangerment of people living nearby, increase of organized crime, poor consumer protection, will not disappear by allowing, under certain conditions, a limited part of it. Tolerating the supply to coffeeshops may solve a problem for the coffeeshop owners, but it is in no way a remedy for the problems mentioned, which are the result of illicit cultivation and trade. (...) Combating the problems mentioned in the manifesto requires, above all, that the illicit cultivation and trade of cannabis is systematically addressed.

In addition, the minister emphasized that the authors of the Maastricht Resolution apparently thought a further step could be taken in the existing coffeeshop policy. What they wanted, he wrote, was not the regulation or legalization (which are not compatible with the obligations of the State, because they are contrary to current legislation and international obligations), but an extension of the policy of tolerance. Such an extension, however, was not "imaginable in a constitutional state that takes itself seriously":

> In that case it would be accepted that the legislator categorically prohibits certain activities, but nevertheless allows that the enforcement comes down to the opposite.

In conjunction with these remarks, he focused on the statement of the authors of the Maastricht Resolution that a further development of the policy should happen in close consultation with the neighbouring countries. Donner called this a legitimate condition, but there was no indication that the neighbouring states:

> have sympathy for the first steps taken by the Netherlands in this field, let alone for possible further steps. It is stated that, on this point, the way of thinking in other states is changing. We have not noticed such a change. But when the surrounding states reach the point where they decide to adopt and implement the Dutch coffeeshop policy, the time may come for the Netherlands to start thinking about experimenting with the next step.

In short, there was no other possibility than to implement the policy as it was described in the *Cannabis letter* of April 2004: by efficaciously combating the illicit cultivation of cannabis.

5.6.3.3 The Relocation of the Coffeeshops to the Border

Another initiative to relieve the pressure of the drug problems in the centre and a number of districts of Maastricht was the plan to move (some of) the coffeeshops to the Maastricht border and thus inevitably to the border with Belgium.[71]

This plan was conceived in 2005. However, The Hague did not like the initiative. Donner wrote, it is permitted to move coffeeshops in order to combat nuisance, but "not in the direction of the border". Nevertheless, the municipality of Maastricht sticked to its plan. On 28 November 2005, the project presented to the Municipal Council. Their justification was to a large extent based on the argument that the serious deterioration of the living conditions in parts of the city could no longer sufficiently be countered by means of closing drug premises, combating cannabis cultivation, screening persons and companies, et cetera.

The idea was to move the coffeeshops – at the expense of the owners, but with the guarantee that they could continue their business – to three locations at the border of the city. On 20 December 2005, the Town Council commissioned the Municipal Executive to develop a relocation plan. That plan was

71 This subparagraph derives mainly from Fijnaut and De Ruyver, 2008, pp. 93–98.

made public on 3 April 2007. On 17 April the Municipal Council agreed to the plan and on 26 June 2007 it also agreed to the further proposals. According to these proposals 8 of the 15 coffeeshops would be moved to three specified locations.

In the affected border municipalities in Belgium concerned and in the Dutch municipality of Eijsden the opposition to the proposals was enormous. In particular on Belgian territory the implementation of the proposals would lead to an increase in insecurity and nuisance because the sale of soft drugs would be moved to the "source", the purchasers from Belgium and France. The opposition culminated in an attempt of the municipalities to obtain a preliminary injunction from the Court of Maastricht to suspend the building permit of one of the planned coffeeshops. On 12 March 2008, the judge agreed with that request. Not only because Maastricht itself had pointed out the security problems around the coffeeshops, but also because the city had not demonstrated that the nuisance would remain within acceptable limits. The immediate response of the city was twofold: a call to The Hague to provide additional resources for the enforcement of the drug policy in the border areas and an invitation to the Belgian border municipalities to work together to find a solution.

On 11 June 2008, the mayor of Maastricht informed the General Affairs Committee of the Town Council about the situation that had arisen.[72] The committee unanimously stated that the relocation policy had to be implemented in full, that permanent locations for the coffee corners were needed, and that the dialogue with the municipalities concerned had to be continued in full. Of course, this statement could not hide the fact that also this solution had led to a kind of deadlock. Immediately thereafter, in terms of policy not much more happened than further research into the nuisance connected to the drug problems in the city. Not until the Cabinet decided to support the idea to introduce, on a pilot basis, a weed pass system in the coffeeshops, the drug policy got a new impetus. In August 2009, the minister of the Interior granted Maastricht a subsidy of 150,000 euros to try out such a system.

Yet, that was not all. On 27 September 2011, the Municipal Council adopted the zoning plan *Relocation of Maastricht coffeeshops: Köbbesweg*. The plan left room for the relocation of three coffeeshops to the business park Eijsden-Maastricht. It was to be expected that the municipalities mentioned above and the private parties concerned would oppose the plan. And indeed, they went to the Council of State with the request to issue a preliminary injunction. On 22 March 2012, the president of the Administrative Law Division approved that

72 What follows is based on information from the Auditor's Office Maastricht, 2010, pp. 31–35.

request and suspended the related decision of the Municipal Council. His principal argument was that the Municipal Council, when adopting the zoning plan, was acquainted with the intention of the Minister of Security and Justice to introduce on 1 May 2012 a "closed club criterion" and a "resident criterion", and that the Municipal Council itself at the session in question had stated that thanks to the introduction of these criteria the number of people who visited the coffeeshops in Maastricht would decrease by more than 50%. However, as the Municipal Council had not examined the impact of the introduction of these criteria in the context of the adoption of the zoning plan, the president found, therefore, that it had not carefully prepared the plan in this regard.[73]

Following this decision, the municipalities and parties mentioned lodged an appeal with the Council of State. On 10 October 2012, the Council made its ruling.[74] The Municipal Council was given twenty weeks to show on solid grounds that the controversial zoning plan "is still feasible now that the so-called weed pass has been introduced". According to the Council of State, the inadequacy of the justification was more specifically due to the fact that the Municipal Council had not demonstrated "that the coffeeshops will be able to move to the Köbbesweg at their own expense". It was indeed plausible that not only the number of visitors would decline, but that, as a result, the revenues of the coffeeshops would also be considerably smaller than prior to the introduction of the weed pass. In the opinion of the Council of State, the Municipal Council had also not provided any factual evidence for the assertion that the coffeeshops were willing to participate voluntarily in the relocation process. Furthermore, the Council of State dismissed the appeal of the Belgian municipalities (Blegny, Lanaken, Riemst, Visé and Voeren) as being inadmissible since these municipalities had no direct interest in the procedure: they were located too far away from the new location of the coffeeshops.

5.6.3.4 The Reports Fijnaut-De Ruyver and Rovers-Fijnaut

Over the years the tensions between the Netherlands, Belgium and Germany with regard to the drug problems in the Euregion Meuse-Rhine had accumulated considerably. The main reason was that Maastricht persistently stuck to its plan to move a number of coffeeshops to the border of the municipality, that is: in the direction of Belgium. In the spring of 2008, feelings were running so high that the governor of the Dutch province of Limburg at the time L. Frissen, supported by the governors of Belgian Limburg and the province of

73 Council of State, case no. 201112936/2/R1, 22.3.2012.

74 Council of State, case no. 201112936/1/T1/R1, 10.10.2012. The quotes are from the press release of the Council of State.

Liège, as well as the *Regierungspräsident* of Köln, felt compelled to ask the authors of this book to identify the problems in the Euregio Meuse-Rhine and to make recommendations to tackle these problems.

In the resulting report published in the autumn of 2008, for obvious reasons not only the international normative framework of the drug policy was outlined, but also the way the drug problem manifests itself both at the Dutch side and at the German, French and Belgian sides of the border. The main point of this outline that is also relevant in the context of the present study, is the fact that despite the increasingly converging drug policies of the four states concerned, there was still one important difference, which has substantial negative consequences, in the first place for the Dutch: the acceptance of coffeeshops in the Netherlands. Indeed, due to the presence of these shops:

- large numbers of (so-called) tourists have found their way to these points of sale, where they could buy a limited amount of soft drugs in a rather safe environment. These tourists are a gift from heaven for criminal groups, which are eager to sell them all sorts of prohibited drugs, with all the consequences that this entails: drug couriers, drug premises, and so on;
- a large-scale and fine-meshed commercialization of the consumption of soft drugs had been realized, with the result that a part of the production of these drugs was being organized at an ever larger scale and had increasingly fallen into the hands of organized crime, with all the nasty effects associated with it: the flourishing of an illicit economy in cities and municipalities, the use of (threatening with) violence within the own ranks and beyond, huge illicit gains that had to be laundered, and active, secret and open, opposition to administrative policy;
- the coffeeshops had not only developed – at variance with the Schengen Agreements – into real export companies, but were also the link par excellence between cannabis users and organized crime. Often, the latter was supplying at the "back door" what the users were purchasing at the "front door";
- decreasing the number of coffeeshops in the border areas and subjecting the coffeeshops to stricter rules (for instance by limiting the trade stock to 500 grams) in order to reduce the problems, would not induce a revival of the underground market for the simple reason that the (so-called) drug tourists from the neighbouring countries could also buy domestically, and without much risk, everything they could get today in (and around) the coffeeshops;
- there were good reasons to investigate what people – that is: which criminal groups – are operating at the "back door" of the coffeeshops and to tackle

> these groups. As a result of the policy of tolerance, the police and the judicial system had disregarded the "back door" way too much.[75]

On the basis of these findings – though also because of the rejection of the Maastricht Resolution – it was obvious that our report contained a large number of recommendations aimed at making and keeping the serious drug problems within this important Euregion manageable; the latter objective was of course not attainable by means of all the daydreaming and flights of fancy at that time about the legalization of cannabis. The recommendations included, on the one hand, several measures to significantly reinforce the supervision, tracing and prosecution in this Euregion, and especially in the Dutch part of it, and, on the other hand, a call to substantially reduce, certainly in Maastricht, the number of coffeeshops. A further reduction of the supply, the report states, could greatly contribute to a decrease of the serious nuisance the drug tourism and the problems associated with it: large-scale cannabis cultivation, deterioration of housing estates, etc.[76]

A few years later, the municipality of Maastricht, anticipating the judgment of the Council of State in June 2011 on the appropriateness of the resident criterion, ordered some investigations into the drug-related nuisance in Maastricht and the neighbouring (Dutch and Belgian) municipalities. The findings of these investigations were integrated in a report by B. Rovers and C. Fijnaut about the drug nuisance in Maastricht and neighbouring municipalities, in which, as specified in the request, "also the possible effects of the proposed policy (such as the dispersal of the coffeeshops, the resident criterion and the weed pass) on the state of affairs are included".

In this report, first of all the results are summarized of all the research done until then on the restriction or combating of nuisance caused by coffeeshops, drug tourism and cross-border drug trade. These results lead to the conclusion that:

> measures to combat drug nuisance in border municipalities are mainly successful if they are (primarily) directed towards the reduction of foreign demand for cannabis on Dutch territory. In this regard, the measure that will have the biggest impact is to render coffeeshops inaccessible to foreigners, since that will lead to a drop in demand and will also hit, in its wake, the illicit market. The available research demonstrates without exception that the coffeeshops are the principal reason for foreigners

75 Fijnaut and De Ruyver, 2008, pp. 85–89, 136–140.

76 Fijnaut and De Ruyver, 2008, pp. 164–167.

> to travel to the Netherlands because there they can make legitimate purchases. Only a marginal part of this group buys on the illicit market.

The reduction of foreign demand is indeed a necessary, but most probably not a sufficient, condition to combat drug nuisance in a municipality. In the longer term, curbing the nuisance requires, on the one hand, targeted communication with potential foreign purchasers, and, on the other hand, the immediate and structural combating of the illicit market.[77]

In connection with these and other findings, the report secondly examines a number of possibilities to thoroughly combat the drug nuisance in Maastricht and elsewhere. The first two – radical – possibilities that are considered, are the normalization of the cannabis market and the closure of all coffeeshops. The first of these two options is called the unrealistic option, partly because of the treaties of the United Nations and the policy of the European Union and its member states. The second option is called the realistic option – for several reasons, but especially as a result of the positive consequences of the closure of the coffeeshops in Terneuzen, Roosendaal and Bergen op Zoom and the accompanying relocation of the drug tourism to cities and regions in the countries of origin of the drug tourists.

Next, two less far-reaching options are considered: the relocation of coffeeshops to the border and the exclusion of drug tourists by applying the resident criterion. In the first case, a relocation of the nuisance may be expected but not a reduction of it, since the tourism as such will not decrease. In the second case, it is "predicted" that not admitting foreigners to coffeeshops will lead to a sharp decline in the number of tourists, and thus to a shrinking of the illicit market and a substantial decrease of the drug nuisance and all the problems associated with it. Therefore, it is obvious to recommend the second option.

This recommendation was also prompted by the argument that by applying this measure, there would no longer be a reason to move the coffeeshops to the border of the municipality. The drug nuisance in the centre of the city would decrease so drastically that the nuisance as such would no longer justify their relocation. Moreover, it was a way to ease the conflict with the neighbouring municipalities. That would already be a very important positive consequence.[78]

Hereafter, we shall see that the minister of Security and Justice, when the decision of the Council of State in June 2011 made it clear that there were no legal obstacles to do this, has actually implemented the resident criterion for the coffeeshops in the southern part of the country.

---

77 Rovers and Fijnaut, 2011, pp. 61–66.

78 Rovers and Fijnaut, 2011, pp. 86–93.

5.6.4 *The Problems in the Inner City of Amsterdam*

Finally, in the context of this outline of the drug problems in (the southern part of) the Netherlands, it is for various reasons also appropriate to describe in short the situation in (the inner city of) Amsterdam, such as it has been portrayed a few years ago by Projectgroep Emergo.[79]

One of these reasons is that this is (the part of) the city in the Netherlands with by far the largest number of coffeeshops: in 2012 there were still 208 such shops in Amsterdam and (about) 76 of them were located in the inner city. A second reason, closely related to the first, is that in this state it is of course not easy to develop a cannabis and coffeeshop policy that is not only appropriate for the 102 "average" municipalities with one or a few coffeeshops, but also for the capital, for Amsterdam. A third important reason is that a description of the situation in Amsterdam very well illustrates the extent to which the cannabis sector in the Netherlands has become a dubious "big business". That, in any case, is the qualification many citizens of Amsterdam attribute to the sector. In 2009, 31% of the inhabitants of the inner city, interviewed about the coffeeshops in the context of a survey, believed the coffeeshops were not exactly beneficial to Amsterdam's image. On the other hand, 44% of them did believe they were beneficial in this respect.[80]

In the past years, the municipality of Amsterdam has pursued a firm coffeeshop policy, in the sense that the shopkeepers, to prevent their licences from being revoked, must strictly comply with the imposed conditions. All the stranger it is that, by definition, there was and still is little clarity on the turnovers of the coffeeshops in the city. The problem is that the Internal Revenue Service, in principle, does not have the possibility to check with reliable suppliers the size of the drug purchases by coffeeshops or the purchase prices they have paid. Estimates on the basis of the turnover data in 2007 enabled Projectgroep Emergo to calculate, more or less, the average turnover of a coffeeshop in the inner city that year: 51.515.040 euros. Taking into account the presence of 76 coffeeshops, this meant that the cannabis turnover in the inner city of Amsterdam that year probably amounted to about 38.121.130 euros. Starting from the average selling price of cannabis per gram, it could also be calculated that, together, the coffeeshops concerned must have sold 52.221 kilos of cannabis in 2007.

In addition, and in part on the basis of the latter number, the number of cannabis plants that must have been cultivated in 2007 to ensure the supply to the coffeeshops in the inner city has been calculated: an estimated 138.884

---

79 Projectgroep Emergo, 2011, pp. 187–202.

80 Benschop, Buijs, Engelfriet et al., 2009, pp. 9–10.

plants. The successful growth of these plants required a surface of 9,259 square meters. To produce all this weed, 380 operational plantations (with an average surface of 24 square meters) were needed. Around the same time, an estimation by the police of the total number of weed plantations in the Amsterdam region suggested that there were 3,880 small, medium-sized and large plantations. Even today, many of these plantations are concentrated in certain poor neighbourhoods of the city. So, instead of relying on social assistance or debt assistance, a number of – sometimes young – inhabitants of these neighbourhoods are trying their luck in the drug economy. However, large-scale cannabis cultivation also exists in and around the centre of the city. Even the P.C. Hooftstraat is not free of it.[81]

Also in Amsterdam mainly the cultivators themselves are arrested. The people who organize the plantations remain largely unaffected, due to a lack of capacity to investigate them. Not only can these people, without much risk, earn a lot of money with cannabis cultivation, they can also rather easily reinvest their revenues in the legal economy. With the result that the structural intertwining of the world of organized crime and legitimate society increases with impunity. The fact that with regard to the financing of the purchase and the operation of the coffeeshops in the inner city, private cash loans and remissions of debts are not at all exceptional, gives much food for thought in this connection. How real are these loans and are they really repaid? Or are we actually talking about money-laundering constructions?

In this context, we should of course not forget that a thorough investigation of the criminal records of the shopkeepers and the people employed in the coffeeshops in the inner city has pointed out that a large majority of them has pretty serious antecedents not only in the area of, obviously, drug trade, but also in the area of traffic legislation (speeding offences, no valid documents, drink-driving) and arms legislation. According to this investigation, which was also carried out as part of the Emergo Project, a number of them have ever committed serious violent offences or participated in a criminal organization. The people who supply the needed cannabis at the "back door" of the Amsterdam coffeeshops, have never been systematically investigated. As a result of the policy of tolerance, the large number of coffeeshops and the priorities set by the Public Prosecutor's Office, the investigation capacity is not focused on these suppliers. For the same reason it is more than plausible that criminals in Amsterdam are concentrating on the cultivation of cannabis in an organized context. The proceeds of this illicit business are very big and the risks of being caught very small.

81 See the reports in *Het Parool*, 8.8.2014 and 21.8.2014.

So, the Municipal Council of Amsterdam rightly considers, for years already, the coffeeshop sector to be a criminogenic sector, and, in part for that reason, rightly wants to substantially reduce that sector, notably in the inner city. As early as in 2009, the shopkeepers of 26 coffeeshops in this area were given notice that from 1 July 2014 they would no longer be allowed to sell soft drugs in their shops and therefore had to look out for another trade. It is rather self-evident that the shopkeepers concerned did not agree with this. After they had, already regularly expressed their dissatisfaction with this decision through the media and had, through their lawyer, even presented themselves as supporters of the legalization of cannabis, or at least of the legalization of the supply of cannabis at the "back door" of their shops, they filed a civil suit against the Municipal Council.[82] In vain, however. On 23 April 2014, the Court of Amsterdam decided that the mayor of this city, on the basis of article 13b of the Opium Act:

> in principle has the freedom, with a view to the protection of public order, to pursue the policy which he, under the circumstances, considers to be reasonable and desirable, and that a judge has only the power to minimally assess it. In this context, attention must also be paid to general principles of government.

The court then continues with an explanation of the policy the municipality is already pursuing for years to set things straight in the inner city, and hereby refers also very specifically to the report *Grenzen aan de handhaving* (*Limits to enforcement*) from 2007, which was the starting point for the Emergo Project. In particular, the court repeats the remarkable conclusion of this report:

> that coffeeshops also constitute an outlet for organized crime and that for the 1012-area improved enforcement is not only not sufficient, but that criminogenic functions have to be reduced.

Equally important is the conclusion that:

> coffeeshop keepers (must) take into account that as a result of changed administrative or social insights with regard to (for instance) public order the policy of tolerance will be revised, even if this means that a tolerance declaration will no longer be issued. This is especially true now that the sale of soft drugs is prohibited. The exceptional position granted to coffeeshop

82 See for instance the report in *Het Parool* "Legale wiet kan coffeeshops redden" (<http://www.parool.nl/parool/article>, consulted on 25.9.2009).

> keepers implies that they have to accept the ending of the tolerance for the sale of soft drugs as a normal business risk. As a matter of fact, by depriving them of their special status, the coffeeshop keepers, or at least the coffeeshops run in their premises, are treated on an equal footing with common entrepreneurs or companies in the catering business. Important is also that the loss of this status was foreseeable by the coffeeshop keepers, since in the letter of 10 July 2009 they were already told that they could only qualify for an extension of the operating licence with a declaration of tolerance for running a coffeeshop just one more time.

The claims of the coffeeshop keepers – in short: that the municipality of Amsterdam acted unlawfully towards them and should be obliged to issue new tolerance certificates – were rejected on the basis of these and other arguments.[83]

5.7 The Tolerated Sale and the Use of Cannabis Around 2010

Before discussing the current development of the coffeeshop policy, it is appropriate to shortly describe the general state of affairs around 2010 with regard to the tolerated sale and the use of cannabis. This way, one gets a picture of the background against which that policy is pursued.

At the end of 2012, the total number of coffeeshops in the Netherlands amounted to 617; they were located in 103 out of 415 municipalities.[84] In April 2013, the number of shops had slightly decreased to 614. That decrease was not entirely accidental. In the past period coffeeshops have been closed definitively on the basis of a negative BIBOB advice or because one of the tolerance criteria had been infringed. In this context, account should be taken of the fact that in 13 municipalities there are more coffeeshops than the officially allowed number (32 shops).

Furthermore, it has to be mentioned that in 31 municipalities (one or more) infringements of the tolerance criteria have been noted, more specifically concerning the trade stock, the youth criterion and the resident criterion. Because of such infringements, in 16 municipalities coffeeshops were temporarily closed; the "closing time" ranged from a period of 4 weeks to a period of 6 months.

83 See ECLI:NL:RBAMS:2014:2151. This sentence has on 25 February 2015 been confirmed by the Council of State (nr. 201306110/1/R1).

84 What follows is borrowed from Bieleman, Nijkamp, Reimer and Haaijer, 2013.

On the other hand, in 64 municipalities there was no problem at all with the enforcement of the (municipal) coffeeshop policy. And if a problem is mentioned, it is the lack of policy regarding the provisioning of the coffeeshops.

The latter is, if only because of the extent of the use of cannabis in the Netherlands, quite understandable. The report *Evaluatie van het Nederlandse drugsbeleid* ("Evaluation of the Dutch drug policy"), published in 2009, is still one of the best sources for an estimation of the cannabis consumption.[85] The finding in this report is that the prevalence of the use of drugs, cannabis included, in the general population is below the European average and moreover lower than the prevalence in the United States. Though it is emphasized in the report that this does not apply to cannabis use among 15- and 16-year-old school-goers in the Netherlands, which, from an international perspective, is high – both in terms of "current users" and in terms of "frequent users". Additionally, the awareness in this group of users of the risks associated with cannabis consumption is the lowest, internationally speaking. However, the researchers are reluctant to attribute these findings to the (perceived) availability of cannabis; this should be investigated further. The same is true for the highly increased number of cannabis users who are seeking help from addiction care. Is there a link with an increase of problematic cannabis use?

The *Jaarbericht 2012* ("Annual review 2012") of the *Nationale drug monitor* more or less confirms this picture.[86] In this review it is stressed once again that the number of users among 15- and 16-year-old school-goers is high in comparison with the numbers in the other European countries: 14%, whereas the European average is 7%. However, according to this review, the use of cannabis among the general population in the Netherlands (people aged 15–64 years) is not below the European average but coincides with it: 7%. Of these people, 4% is a "current user" and almost 1/3 are daily users (141,000 persons). Given the number of joints smoked on average, the total annual cannabis consumption is estimated to amount to 44 to 69 tons (the consumption by drug tourists not included).

As to cannabis dependence, it is stated in the *Jaarbericht 2012* that in 2007–2009 almost 30,000 people of the age group 18–64 years were dependent on this drug. They are suffering from disorders such as anxiety, depression, ADHD and behavioural disorders more often than the general population. In 2012, the number of people requesting help stagnated. Whereas in the period 2002–2011 the number of (registered) primary cannabis clients tripled from 3,251 to

85 Van Laar and Van Ooyen, 2009, pp. 14–15, 69–108.

86 Van Laar, Cruts, Van Ooyen-Houben et al., 2013 (summary).

10,637, this number decreased with 4% from 2011 to 2012. Both the increase and the decrease can have various causes. The increase could be related to, among other things, the increase of the THC content; the decrease to, for instance, the introduction of a personal contribution for addiction care. From 2010 to 2013, the average THC content of *nederwiet* diminished from 17.8% to 13.5%. In imported hashish, the THC content was 16.8% in 2013.

How much cannabis is consumed in the Netherlands, whether or not distributed by the coffeeshops, is one question. Another question is: how much cannabis is produced, for domestic and for foreign use? Equally in 2012–2013 this could only be estimated. Much clearer information was available about the number of cannabis plantations that were demolished. In 2013, it concerned 5,294 plantations (1.2% more than in 2012). In 2012, 168 million kilowatt-hours of energy were stolen; in 2013, the amount of stolen energy was a lot smaller: 140 million kilowatt-hours. The explanation for this decrease could be the fact that cannabis growers opt for risk reduction and make their cannabis plantations smaller and house them more often than before in ordinary family homes instead of large sheds. To avoid any misunderstanding in this context, it must be noted that the mentioned 140 million kilowatt-hours are only:

> a fraction of the estimated one billion kilowatt-hours that cannabis plantations illicitly use each year. This is as much energy as all households of The Hague together consume on an annual basis.[87]

5.8 The Proposals of the Van de Donk Committee

Considering the above, it is not so strange that the Dutch drug policy with regard to soft drugs and the coffeeshops is not yet a quiet area today. In view of a good understanding of that policy, we shall first elucidate the proposals presented in 2009 by the *Adviescommissie drugsbeleid* ("Advisory committee drug policy"). Next, we shall focus on the revision of the drug policy that was carried out in part on the basis of these proposals. The two main points of the new policy are, on the one hand, the revision of the coffeeshop policy, and, on the other hand, the criminalization of the preparation or facilitation of illicit cannabis cultivation.

The *Adviescommissie drugsbeleid* was established in 2009 in order to create new benchmarks for the drug policy as a whole, that is: for the policy as it had

87 See the press release of Netbeheer Nederland of 14 February 2014 on this subject, <http://www.hwtccv.nl/nieuws/2014/02>.

been developed since the 1970s.[88] Not only because scientific knowledge about the possible negative consequences of drug use had increased, but also because the social context of drug use had considerably changed – for instance through the involvement of organized crime in the production and distribution of drugs and the growing role of the Internet.

The actual starting points of this committee were fully consistent with the research that had been done in the previous years. As to the domestic consumption of cannabis, the committee noted that among young people this consumption exceeded the average in Western countries. Problematic use of cannabis appeared to occur mainly among young people who, given their background and/or situation, anyway did not belong to the most privileged ones. In line with the increasing demand over the past decades the drug trade had expanded and was professionalized and commercialized: professional criminals could earn more money and their risk to be arrested and severely punished was smaller when they opted for drug trade instead of traditional forms of crime.

> The production of cannabis has developed strongly with the aid of modern cultivation techniques, which enable the large-scale creation of high-quality supply for domestic consumption and for exportation. In the mean time, the production of cannabis is no longer only concentrated in our country, but is also often organized by enterprising criminal organizations, transferred to other European countries.

In this regard, the committee noted that these organizations focus on everything they can easily make money with (from export of cannabis to trafficking of women). Moreover, the presence of emphatically organized criminal gangs leads to a lot of violence (assassinations, batterings, threats in poor neighbourhoods and against vulnerable groups), creates a very high integrity risk (of employees, of business service providers such as notaries and lawyers), and involves investments of criminal money in dominant positions in parts of cities and the formal economy. Also, it should not be neglected that the development of the coffeeshops, "mainly due to their attractiveness to foreigners, but also due to the connection of a number of them with organized cannabis cultivation in our country", poses a serious problem.

According to the committee, the response to these and other problems had to be based on the restriction of personal and social damage. This goal was not attainable by means of one single measure, but required a mix of measures. Just like a "war on drugs", the legalization of drugs is not a panacea:

88 Adviescommissie drugsbeleid, 2009.

> that way the personal and social problems resulting from 'normalized use' do not necessarily disappear from society (compare with the effect of alcohol) and a legalized supply does not by definition take away the illicit market and can make it even more difficult to combat it. But there are also advantages to legalization.

In line with these starting points and findings, the committee dedicated a whole chapter to the coffeeshops (Chapter 4). Departing from a profound description of the connection between cannabis cultivation and organized crime and the entirely changed position of the coffeeshops – their transformation from small shops run by idealists into "at a large scale and often also *supra*-local operating commercial enterprises who are, whether or not directly, linked to the world of organized crime" – the committee stated that the coffeeshop policy needed to be adjusted in the knowledge that "the coffeeshop policy (can) only have a modest effect on addressing the production of cannabis and organized crime associated with it".

The adjustment of the coffeeshop policy as recommended by the committee comprised in the first place the formulation of a national policy framework that – given the existing local differences in circumstances and wishes – left enough room for local adaptation. Secondly, it included that – regardless of the way in which the possible regulation of the coffeeshops would be given shape – both the criminal and the administrative enforcement of the policy had to be tightened "to make the coffeeshops be what we want them to be". In the third place, the committee discerned a number of directions in which the coffeeshop policy could be developed further.

The starting point in this context was that neither a ban on coffeeshops nor the legalization of cannabis is obvious. Legalization is not obvious because it does not solve the problems related to the use of cannabis. It would strengthen the "pull factor" of the Netherlands for foreigners and it would allow cannabis growers to freely produce for exportation in that case:

> The discussion about whether or not to prohibit cannabis must be conducted internationally. The committee considers it to be unrealistic and therefore undesirable for our country to follow its own course (through the unilateral denunciation of the treaties concerned).

The committee worked out the following possible policy directions:

- no further development towards a "back door" regulation as such;
- a development towards a more private coffeeshop;

– a development towards a more private coffeeshop with a "back door" regulation.

The committee preferred the third direction, that is: the transformation of the coffeeshops into clubs "with a sharply delineated and relatively stable member base", each member of which is allowed to cultivate a few plants for personal use; this way, the "front door" and the "back door" would be connected to each other. The possibility to become a member must be restricted to residents of the region concerned. This would create the kind of situation that was initially intended: "the coffeeshop is a local facility for the local or regional consumer". Such an approach would also reduce the problems in the border areas.

In all clarity the committee added that it was recommendable to conduct small-scale experiments with this model to check whether it was also "in terms of enforceability and possible unwanted side effects" a realistic model. Before proceeding to such experiments, it had to be examined under which legal conditions they could be carried out and how the organization of the cultivation and the consumption as well as the supervision of these two aspects could take place.

For the rest, the committee made a number of recommendations with regard to the categorization of drugs and the functioning of addiction care.[89] As to the approach to the illicit market, the committee unequivocally stated that the combating of organized crime in cannabis cultivation was "still insufficient". The authorities concerned had to cooperate more with each other and also with the business sector, for instance with energy and insurance companies, to be able to combat this cultivation efficiently and to curb the "related phenomena of violence, corruption and power formation through investments of criminal money". The *Programma Aanpak Georganiseerde Hennepteelt* ("Programme on Tackling Organized Cannabis Cultivation") went in the right direction, but had to be executed consistently and with adequate support: "it is still more a promise than a fact". The committee noted, for instance, that the programme appeared to have been reduced to "pilot projects", which still had to be translated into the regular performance of the related tasks.

5.8.1 *The Revision of the Coffeeshop Policy*

As we have already indicated, the recommendations of the Van de Donk Committee have been converted into policy on two major points. The first point concerns the revision of the coffeeshop policy. The plans of the Cabinet on this point, as

89 In this connection, see Coördinatiepunt Assessment en Monitoring Nieuwe Drugs, 2008; Van Amsterdam, Opperhuizen, Koeter et al., 2009, and Expertcommissie Lijstensystematiek Opiumwet, 2010.

well as the implementation of these plans and the opposition to them, will be discussed immediately hereafter. The second point concerns the criminalization of the preparation and facilitation of illicit cannabis cultivation. The plans of the Cabinet on this point will be discussed later in this chapter, up to and including the stagnation of the debate on them in the First Chamber, mainly as a result of the political discussion about the coffeeshop policy.

5.8.1.1 The Plans of the Cabinet

The response of the Cabinet to these recommendations was unanimously positive. In a detailed letter concerning its drug policy sent to the Second Chamber on 11 September 2009, the Cabinet stated that it would largely adopt the recommendations.

With regard to the coffeeshop policy this meant, on the one hand, that the coffeeshops through a phased implementation of the resident criterion – first in the southern part of the country – would actually be reduced to small businesses, directed at local users. On the other hand, it stressed once again that it opposed "any experiment with regulated cultivation", among others because experiments with regulated cultivation directly compromise the international obligations the Netherlands has entered into: "Therefore a policy-related exploration of this topic is not opportune."[90]

The Rutte I government, which took office in the autumn of 2010, continued – in the person of Opstelten – on the path chosen by the preceding governments. On 15 May 2011, it announced that it would put an end to "the present open door policy" of the coffeeshops and that, by means of a number of measures, the coffeeshops would be transformed into "private clubs for the local market".[91] One of these measures was the concretization of the existing resident criterion (admission to coffeeshops only on presentation of a valid proof of identity): the so-called *I-criterium* ("I criterion").

Another, and new, measure was the decision to limit admission to coffeeshops to people who had a club pass (*wietpas*). This pass would only be granted on presentation of a valid proof of identity and after the applicant had proven to be a Dutch resident: the so-called *B-criterium* ("B criterion"). At a later date, the maximum number of members of a coffeeshop was restricted to 2,000 people. All this would be regulated by adjusting the existing criteria for running a coffeeshop, as they were laid down by the *Aanwijzing Opiumwet* (Directive Opium Act) of the College of Attorneys General.

---

90 Second Chamber, 2009–2010, 24077, no. 239.

91 Second Chamber, 2010–2011, 24077, no. 259, pp. 2–4.

The introduction of the new policy was postponed until after the decision of the Council of State on the lawfulness of the resident criterion.[92] We already indicated that in June 2011 the Council of State – in part on the basis of preliminary rulings by the European Court of Justice – came to the conclusion that this criterion withstood the test of criticism. Then, on 15 December 2011, Opstelten announced that the tightened policy – in the form of the B and I criteria – would be introduced in phases. In May 2012 this would happen in the provinces of Limburg, North Brabant and Zeeland (apart from the maximum number of 2,000 members per club; this criterion would be introduced on 1 January 2013). From 1 January 2013, the criteria would be applied all over the country.[93]

No wonder this new policy caused a lot of political discussion. That discussion was strongly reminiscent of the debate as it had been conducted in the 1990s. With the government parties VVD, CDA and PVV on the side of the supporters of the policy and PvdA, D66, SP and GroenLinks on the side of the opponents. In March 2012, all these parties defended, with a strong sense of being right, twice their positions in the Second Chamber.[94]

The I criterion and even more so the B criterion were the main targets of the critics. According to the representatives of the opposition, these measures would only lead to more drug nuisance and thus be totally ineffective. A lot of people would not be prepared to register themselves as members of a cannabis club and, as a consequence, would turn to the black market to obtain cannabis. Therefore, a change of course was needed, a radical change of course. The only real solution was the legalization of cannabis cultivation, which would enable the establishment of a "closed system, reaching from production to consumer". The coffeeshops had to become normal businesses. That way, we would get a clear view of the flows of money and it would be possible to impose quality requirements on both cannabis as such and the sellers of it. Additionally tax evasion could be prevented, et cetera. Criminals who still would continue to cultivate cannabis, should be dealt with hard.

The government parties did of course agree with the measures. Only by doing so the pressing problems in the area of crime and nuisance – mainly caused by drug tourism – could be combated efficiently. Moreover, the new policy was completely in line with the initial objective of the policy of tolerance. The CDA even went a step further. Its spokesperson emphasized that the policy of

92 Second Chamber, 2011–2012, 24077, no. 265.

93 Second Chamber, 2011–2012, 24077, no. 267.

94 Second Chamber, Handelingen, 2012, nos. 58 and 69.

tolerance was the "odd one out" in Europe and the source of a lot of trouble. For this political party it was very obvious what had to happen: "towards zero coffeeshops".

Of course, the minister also stood firm. On the one hand, he was opposed to the regulation of the "back door" and therefore saw no room for local experiments – such as they had been proposed in for instance Utrecht – with this form of legalization. On the other hand, he advocated the implementation of the measures discussed, among others because the experiences in Roosendaal and Bergen op Zoom showed that ever since the closure of the coffeeshops in these places – and in part thanks to the accompanying measures – the large majority of the foreign drug tourists had stayed away. He was not afraid that people would "turn in large numbers to the illicit circuit". A month later, in a letter to the Second Chamber, he explained for the umpteenth time the goal of the tightened coffeeshop policy: reducing the attractiveness of the Dutch drug policy to foreign drug users by transforming the coffeeshops into facilities for the local market. Concomitantly the fight against organized (drug) crime had to be intensified.[95]

In June 2012, he announced that in the southern part of the country the measures were already having a large impact: "The implementation has already resulted in a strong decrease of the number of drug tourists." In the beginning, street trade had increased, but that phenomenon was controllable by means of sufficient police deployment.[96] The application of the resident criterion did what it was supposed to do and therefore would be implemented nationally from 1 January 2013. A few months later, in November 2012, the achieved success was one of the minister's main reasons to drop the club pass. Another important reason was the resistance of many residents to membership of a coffeeshop, a resistance that stimulated them to turn to the illicit circuit. Henceforth, adult residents could be admitted to coffeeshops on presentation of valid proof of identity (or a residence permit with an extract from the Municipal Basic Administration).[97]

It was to be expected that the opposition in the Second Chamber would use this adjustment of the pursued policy as an opportunity to call the policy into question.[98] Equally predictable was the content of the debate. Very peculiar, nevertheless, was the attitude of the PvdA, now in its role as a

95 Second Chamber, 2011–2012, 24077, no. 286.

96 *Ibid.*, no. 287.

97 Second Chamber, 2012–2013, 24077, no. 293 (with an annex concerning the experiences in the southern provinces). See also the May 2013 report on this subject: Second Chamber, 2012–2013, 24077, no. 309.

98 See for instance Second Chamber, Handelingen, 2013, no. 41.

government party. Its spokesperson acknowledged that the PvdA in the run-up to the elections had been campaigning in favour of the weed pass and that therefore the party's present position in the new coalition was far from simple on this point. However, he stated that there should be no mistake: "in the end, our ideal (is) regulation and legalization". If the PvdA group has its way, one day:

> and maybe this can happen under the banner of a Samsom I cabinet, we will completely legalize and regulate this drug.

In this debate, Opstelten obviously sticked steadfastly to his policy. Though he announced that he was prepared to arrange for an inventory of municipal initiatives to regulate the "back door" of the coffeeshops.[99] In June 2013, he confirmed this promise, which was certainly not a concession.[100] For the minority in the Second Chamber this was once again a reason to start a debate with Opstelten about his soft drug policy. That debate took place on 3 July 2013, but amounted – again – to little more than a repetition of arguments. This time, the opposition, and in particular D66, tried to undermine the policy on the basis of a report of the Research and Documentation Centre on the implementation of the I and the B criterion. Even for the PvdA, this action was over the top. The party's spokesperson indicated that the data in the report were related to a situation in which the B criterion was still relevant.[101]

In December 2013, Opstelten informed the Second Chamber about the plans and discussions in 25 municipalities regarding the regulation of the cultivation of cannabis. He was very understanding of the worries of the municipalities about the fact that "cannabis cultivation (has), in the broad sense, got a grip on society", but at the same time he emphasized that a powerful tackling of this illicit cultivation should be the answer to the locally experienced nuisance. "Regulation really cannot solve this", because the larger part of the cannabis cultivated in the Netherlands is destined for export:

> Neither the illicit plantations nor the (organized) criminals behind them will disappear through the regulation of the cultivation for the coffeeshops.

In addition, he indicated that municipalities that expected financial gains from the regulation of cannabis cultivation, made a mistake. One cannot levy excise duties on a prohibited product such as cannabis, the enforcement of

---

99 Second Chamber, 2012–2013, 24077, no. 307, p. 13, 25.

100 *Ibid.*, no. 310.

101 *Ibid.*, no. 312, p. 5, 16.

a regulated system costs a certain amount of money, and the tackling of illicit cultivation equally is a costly affair. And those who believed that the regulation of cannabis cultivation was possible within the existing treaty framework, were given a lesson in international law. To summarize: critics who were of the opinion that the reservations made by the Netherlands with regard to certain paragraphs of article 3 of the 1988 Convention made such an approach possible, were sorely mistaken: the reservations had nothing to do with this subject.[102]

In connection with the discussion about this letter, Opstelten at a given moment pointed out that he had taken the initiative to further examine the foundations of his point of view.

In the first place, he had asked the Research and Documentation Centre of his ministry to take a closer look at the informed estimate by the police that 80% of all the produced cannabis is destined for export. The results of this examination would be revealed after the summer of 2014.

In the second place, he had asked researchers of the Radboud Universiteit Nijmegen to assess the conformity of the municipal and foreign opinions in favour of the regulation of cannabis cultivation with the drug treaties of the United Nations and the European Union drugs legislation.

In the meantime, these researchers have completed their research. As the minister told the Second Chamber on 21 March 2014, their general conclusion is that:

> in view of the international obligations concerning the fight against drugs there is no room for the regulation of cannabis cultivation to supply the coffeeshops, in the context of cannabis social clubs or through other modalities that serve the recreational use by third parties.

In the sentence preceding the latter sentence they wrote:

> In other words: none of the arguments advanced and modalities suggested by Dutch municipalities and foreign jurisdictions can legitimate allowing cannabis cultivation for the recreational users market under the UN drug treaties and relevant European law.[103]

To this conclusion Opstelten then added the final conclusion that it:

---

102 Second Chamber, 2013–2014, 24077, no. 314.

103 Van Kempen and Fedorova, 2014, p. 233.

> corresponds with the line that I, in conformity with the position of former cabinets, have consistently propagated: legally there is no room for the regulation of cannabis cultivation to supply coffeeshops or in the context of cannabis social clubs.[104]

It was obvious that a number of groups in the Second Chamber would not accept these conclusions. For that reason, the Security and Justice Committee organized on 15 May 2014 with a group of academics, administrators and pamphleteers a round-table discussion about the report.

Actually, the members of this committee would do well to read the texts of the debate that was conducted in the early 1990s about the 1988 Convention. That way they would see with their own eyes that – as already explained in paragraph 5.3. – even the opposition at the time did not realize that the Netherlands should have made a reservation to this convention in view of the legalization of the cultivation of cannabis.

5.8.1.2 The Opposition of a Number of Coffeeshop Keepers

The tightening of the policy of tolerance announced by Opstelten in 2010–2011, did not only meet with opposition in the Second Chamber and from the local equivalents of the parties concerned in cities such as Maastricht. Obviously, also the owners/keepers of the coffeeshops were fiercely opposed to it. Via the media they stated in every possible way that the adjustment of the policy would be a complete fiasco. They even tried to buy scientific research.

The main form of resistance was the initiation of legal proceedings. The most important proceedings that have to be discussed in this context, are the proceedings initiated by the coffeeshop owners in Maastricht and in Tilburg against the plans of the minister.[105] The origin of that case was the decision of the mayor of Maastricht on 8 May 2012 – on the basis of article 13b of the Opium Act (and not, as in the earlier proceedings against the resident criterion, on the basis of the General Municipal Regulation) – that from 11 May 2012 the manager of the coffeeshop Easy Going had to close his shop for a period of one month.

The reason was that checks in the beginning of May had shown that the manager had acted in violation of the I criterion, after having previously infringed the B criterion. The manager objected, but the mayor declared the objection unfounded by decision of 16 July 2012. That same month of July, the mayor of Tilburg closed the coffeeshop Tourmalijn for 24 hours,

---

104 Second Chamber, 2013–2014, 24077, no. 316.

105 We do not take into consideration indirect proceedings such as have been conducted in for instance Breda and The Hague.

because it was ascertained twice that the company De Cirkel had not complied with the two new criteria. Next, both coffeeshop owners went to court – respectively in Maastricht and Breda – in the hope of being proved right after all.

On 25 April 2013, the Court of Maastricht declared the appeal for various reasons (partially) founded (on 17 January 2013, the Court of Breda had already ruled in the Tilburg case).[106] Subsequently, all parties concerned turned to the Council of State. The Administrative Law Division subsequently asked one of the Councillors of State, L. Keus, to draw a conclusion on the divergent judgments of courts regarding the resident criterion. On 24 December 2013, the latter published a more than 40 pages long advice, in which he comes to the conclusion that – not really surprising given the earlier "Maastricht" proceedings – neither from a national nor from a European legal perspective there is anything wrong with the I criterion and the (in the meantime withdrawn) B criterion. The Court of Justice, he concludes, considers the I criterion justified because of the – under EU law obligatory – objective to combat drug tourism, and the Court considers this criterion also to be appropriate and proportional in this context. And national courts cannot ignore this judgment of the Court.[107] Of course, this advice raised an outcry among the coffeeshop keepers.

However, the verdict of 18 June 2014 showed that in both the Maastricht and the Tilburg case the Council of State followed the advice of the Councillor of State.[108] After again having described the existing legislation and regulation at the national and the European level, the Council decided in favour of the mayor of Maastricht with regard to the application of the I criterion. The mayor had sufficiently stated the grounds for the introduction of this criterion to curb drug tourism. Furthermore, he was not obliged to demonstrate "that without this introduction drug-related nuisance cannot be reduced and that therefore less far-reaching measures to avoid that nuisance are not possible". In particular, he had rightly taken the view that the intended relocation policy with respect to a number of coffeeshops "is not an adequate alternative to combat drug tourism".

The owner of the coffeeshop, on the other hand, was told that he had not in any way made his allegations about the negative consequences of the new policy "plausible through factual data", nor had he substantiated these

106 As to the text of this judgment, see: ECLI:NL:RBLIM:2013:BZ8548.

107 As to this conclusion, see: ECLI:NL-RVS:2013:2532.

108 It concerns the verdicts numbered 201304752/1/A3 (Maastricht) and 201301818/1/A3 (Tilburg).

allegations. This reproach was addressed to him both for his claim that the mayor, by applying the I criterion, was endangering the health of non-residents by making them "dependent on illicit street trade", and for the claim:

> that the I criterion is hardly enforced, that the coffeeshop visits are shifting from the southern provinces to the northern provinces and that in the southern provinces a considerable increase of the street trade can be perceived.

5.8.1.3 Empirical Research Into the Actual Effects

It is quite understandable why the coffeeshop owners did not present any figures about the alleged negative consequences of Opstelten's policy. As a matter of fact, serious research into these consequences points out that the measures, and notably the application of the I criterion with the accompanying implementing measures, to a high extent produce the intended effects.

Nevertheless, the results of the extensive study carried out in 2013 at the request of Opstelten on the intended and unintended consequences of the introduction in 2012 of the two supplementary criteria (I and B) did indeed, in some respects, cast doubts on the workability of the policy pursued.[109] In particular, mention has to be made of the fact that it was not that easy to put the new policy into practice everywhere and the fact that many cannabis using Dutch residents no longer went to a coffeeshop, but bought their stuff at illicit places (in the southern part of the Netherlands three fifths of the younger customers).

On the other hand, most of the foreign visitors shunned the coffeeshops, without being present in large numbers outside the coffeeshops. So, there was indeed a growth of the illicit market in the southern part of the country, but mainly due to Dutch buyers, not due to foreign drug tourists. As a result the nuisance experienced in the neighbourhood of the coffeeshops accordingly changed: whereas in the past that nuisance was mainly caused by foreign coffeeshop visitors, it is now caused by street drug dealing. Therefore, it was a wise decision, at the end of 2013, to drop the B criterion. This is also shown by the few assessments of the policy that since then have been made "on location".

The assessment of the situation in Maastricht completely refuted the allegation of mainly the coffeeshop keepers that in the city a gigantic black cannabis market would develop.[110] The contrary is the case. Foreign customers

109 Van Ooyen-Houben, Bieleman and Korf, 2013.

110 Van der Torre, Holvast, Keijzer et al., 2013.

no longer visit the coffeeshops and the "drug traffic" on the streets has decreased spectacularly. Everyone can see this, because the traffic jams on the drug routes have disappeared. The inhabitants of the coffeeshop area say that since 1 May 2012 the general nuisance and the nuisance around the coffeeshops is in almost all respects much less than before. Of course, as a result of this development the coffeeshop owners now earn a lot less money than in the past (the loss of turnover could amount to 54 million euros). This is beneficial, the researchers write, to the city and the region, since these millions of euros no longer end up – through the "back door" of the coffeeshops – in the circles of drug criminals. That way, the risk of criminal investments by the "underworld" decreases.

Obviously, the Maastricht coffeeshop owners saw, and see, things differently. The collective closure of their coffeeshops they organized in the spring of 2012, was clearly meant as a tactical move to artificially raise drug nuisance in order to compel the authorities to abandon the intended policy. Before May 2012, they expected that, through the relocation of a number of shops to the border of Maastricht, they would be allowed to sell – causing much less nuisance – very large quantities of soft drugs to foreign drug customers. That perspective of a multimillion euro market disappeared after May 2012. It remains to be seen whether they still want to move if they can. In this context, it has to be noted that since a year or two there are indications that the nuisance that currently exists in Maastricht is partly organized by coffeeshop owners/managers: they would pay little boys to act as dealers.[111]

The assessment of the situation in Tilburg happened in two steps.[112] In November 2012, it was found that the stream of foreign drug tourists to the city had almost completely dried up. As a result of the new tolerance criteria the number of local and regional customers of the coffeeshops was also declining heavily, whereas the illicit soft drug market was growing rather substantially, although the related nuisance remained within bounds. The sale of soft drugs to teenagers by some criminal (youth) groups was worrying, but provided a basis for targeted interventions by the authorities. A year later, in December 2013, that is: one year after the revocation of the B criterion, it was found that the "residing" soft drug customers had returned to the Tilburg coffeeshops, but that the foreign drug customers still stayed away:

> This reduces the criminalized purchase of soft drugs at the back door (...) and has a favourable effect on drug nuisance in Tilburg.

111 See the report on this subject in *Dagblad de Limburger*, 27.6.2014.

112 Van der Torre, Schaap, Beke et al., 2012, and Van der Torre, Beke, Goering et al., 2013.

Although the increased Dutch clientele of the coffeeshops implies more nuisance for the people living in the neighbourhood of these shops. This does not alter the fact, however, that there are still self-reliant users and traffickers who, because of their shared interest, try to sell soft drugs in a clandestine and little or no nuisance causing way. Some traffickers even seem to try to set up a sales organization as an alternative for a coffeeshop. Probably they do this in view of the possible reduction of the THC content of the soft drugs that are allowed to be sold in a coffeeshop.

Finally, there is also the assessment of the situation in a large region: Middle and West Brabant & Zeeland. This study from 2013 covers the developments in the area of the (illicit) sale of cannabis in the municipalities of Tilburg, Etten-Leur, Goes, Vlissingen and Terneuzen. The main conclusions of this empirical research are:

- The number of foreign drug tourists who visit the (coffeeshops of the) examined municipalities because of the retail trade in soft drugs has dropped to almost zero. This is an important improvement: less nuisance and a very serious reduction of the flows of criminal money via the coffeeshops to the drug underworld in Middle and West Brabant and Zeeland.
- The I criterion has for the most part favourable effects and is therefore broadly supported by the police and the authorities.
- The decline of the number of coffeeshop visitors led to a growth of the illicit soft drug market (in the spring of 2012 because of the B criterion, CF). Since that time, this effect is diminishing as a result of: a. the ever larger number of foreign drug customers who are staying away, b. the increasing number of local coffeeshop customers, and c. the alertness of the police for the illicit street trade.
- The nuisance caused by the illicit soft drug market remains within bounds because of the shrinking of the market since August and September 2012 and because of the clandestine nature of important forms of illicit soft drug trade, such as mobile trade and resale.
- Over the past five years, the annual turnover of the coffeeshops in Middle and West Brabant and Zeeland has very probably decreased with more than 75 million euros as a result of the policy adjustments (not only the I criterion, but also the closure of the eight coffeeshops in Roosendaal and Bergen op Zoom, and the closure of the giant coffeeshop Checkpoint). Over a period of one decade, this would correspond with a loss of turnover of more than 0.75 billion euros. The researchers suppose this is a conservative estimate.
- The coffeeshop keepers had an ambivalent attitude towards the B criterion, and they are also ambivalent towards the I criterion. They cooperated

> against their will and wished the "weed pass" would be a failure. A number of coffeeshops made the best of it and hoped for a policy change and "better times". Other coffeeshops tried to thwart the policy or are evading policy and regulation.

These findings clearly show that it was quite feasible to reduce, within the existing policy frameworks, the coffeeshops to relatively small local or regional facilities for Dutch residents and to keep, at the same time, the nuisance caused by the illicit sale of cannabis under control. Anyway, the worst-case scenarios from coffeeshop keepers and other people who predicted the development of an enormous illicit market as a result of the closure of the "front door" for non-residents did not come true. Furthermore, one should bear in mind that also in the period when the coffeeshops, without any restraints, could develop into export companies, there was already an illicit market for soft drugs. The question whether and, if so, to what extent this illicit market has increased as a result of the new policy has not been answered yet.

5.8.1.4 The Manifest Counteraction of a Number of Mayors

The proposal of the Van de Donk Committee to venture on an experiment with an enclosed coffeeshop of which the "back door" would also be regulated, was particularly embraced by the municipality of Utrecht. This municipality asked the research institute IVO to investigate – also by following the example of cannabis clubs in Belgium and Spain – what such an experiment in the Netherlands might look like. Until now, the proposal developed by IVO has not been executed.[113]

However, the idea that the "back door" of the coffeeshops should be regulated has not been abandoned. Both inside and outside the Second Chamber this idea is still as alive and kicking as it was at the end of the 1990s. The point of view of the supporters crystallized, so to speak, into the *Manifest Joint Regulation*, which was presented on 31 January 2014 in Utrecht by a few dozen Dutch mayors. The initiators were the mayor of Heerlen, P. Depla, the mayor of Eindhoven, R. van Gijzel, and an alderman of Utrecht, V. Everhardt. Given the political nature of the discussion about the cannabis and coffeeshop policy, it is relevant to add that the first two initiators belong to the PvdA and that the third signatory is a member of D66.[114]

---

113 Barendrecht, Meerkerk and Van de Mheen, 2011.

114 We do not mention here other contributions to the discussion about a different approach to drugs. See, for instance, Stichting Maatschappij en Veiligheid, 2014.

The manifesto contains the proposal to introduce a national system of "certified and regulated cannabis cultivation". This proposal is mainly based on the following premisses:

- The pursued, strongly repressive policy does not offer a solution to three longstanding problems with which the big cities have had to cope: the health of cannabis users is not protected; security in the districts is under pressure; and the current policy makes it almost impossible to successfully combat (organized) crime related to soft drugs.
- The consequences of this policy are enormous: the composition and the quality of the cannabis are not known because there is no supervision of the production process. In thousands of attic rooms cannabis is illicitly cultivated. This leads to fires in housing estates all over the Netherlands. An extensive criminal black circuit has emerged, with all its consequences: assassinations, briberies and the intermingling of the world of crime and the legitimate society.
- The minister states that international treaties would not allow the development of such a system, but that is a one-sided and negative reading of the treaties. Such an interpretation seems to be mainly politically inspired; initiatives in the United States and Uruguay, but also in Belgium and Spain, prove the opposite.
- Of course, it would also be good and effective to tackle the cannabis problem in the European context. However, a large number of cities in the Netherlands cannot wait for that. The problems are too big.
- The national introduction of regulated cannabis cultivation implies that the detection of, and the punishment for, illicit cannabis cultivation should considerably be intensified. Only then will it be possible to tackle organized crime to the bitter end.
- If a national introduction of regulated cannabis cultivation would not be possible in the short run, one should start – in line with the proposals of the Van de Donk Committee – with regulated cannabis cultivation at the local level. That way, the problems of public health and security in the areas concerned can be tackled more effectively. It will be a first important step towards an improved approach and a better grip on the domestic cannabis market, though in the knowledge that it will not suffice to entirely solve the problem of organized crime.
- As a first step, and preferably as soon as possible, the cities and the government together should work out the objectives and preconditions of the new policy and a fitting administrative-judicial framework for it.

This manifesto was obviously intended as a preparation for the debate on the cannabis and coffeeshop policy of Opstelten that took place in the Second Chamber on 19 February 2014. In a letter to the Second Chamber, dated 19 December 2013, the latter VVD minister had, at the request of the Second Chamber, once again clearly explained the coffeeshop and cannabis policy he was pursuing and wanted to continue to pursue.[115] In short, it came down to this:

- The minister understands the problems the mayors of a number of municipalities are facing, therefore a vigorous tackling of illicit cannabis cultivation is necessary and must address the locally experienced nuisance. "However, regulation is not the solution in this case." Most of the cannabis cultivated in the Netherlands is intended for export. Neither the illicit plantations nor the (organized) criminal groups behind it will disappear if the cultivation for coffeeshops is regulated.
- A number of municipalities refer to the possible financial gains associated with the regulation of cannabis cultivation, but they are mistaken. Under European law it is impossible to levy taxes on cannabis, because it is a prohibited product. Moreover, there still will be costs, resulting from law enforcement with regard to regulated coffeeshops and the fight against illicit cultivation.
- Since cannabis is not a legal product, there can be no question of regulating the production chain, not even for the purpose of promoting public health. However, different tools are already used now to avoid harm to health that is related to cannabis consumption, such as the age limit of eighteen years for visiting a coffeeshop.
- The argumentation of some professors and, in their wake, a number of municipalities that an extension of the policy of tolerance is possible on the basis of the reservation the Netherlands has made with regard to (the first paragraph of) article 3 of the 1988 Convention against Illicit Traffic in Narcotic Drugs and Psychotropic Substances "lacks a legal foundation and neglects the rationale concerned".[116]
- An exemption, on the basis of the treaties and the Opium Act, for cultivating and supplying cannabis for the benefit of coffeeshops is not possible within the existing legal framework of international and European obligations.

---

115 Second Chamber, 2013–2014, 24077, no. 314.

116 This paragraph refers to the paper by Brouwer and Schilder, 2012. In this connection, see also Groenhuijsen, 2013.

- It is true that in the United States and Uruguay there are developments going on towards allowing the cultivation et cetera of cannabis for other than medical or scientific purposes, but these developments are considerably less clear and unambiguous than they are described in several discussions and publications in the Netherlands.

The comparison between the manifesto of a number of mayors and the letter of the minister leaves no doubt about it that these mayors and the minister agreed on at least one point: in many respects the Netherlands are contending with a serious problem of illicit cannabis cultivation. For the rest, they completely disagreed – on all essential points – on the cannabis and coffeeshop policy that should be pursued. They disagreed on the direction of the pursued policy or the policy to be pursued, on the room international treaties whether or not leave for the commercial cultivation of cannabis in view of the sale of such cannabis in coffeeshops, on the relevance or irrelevance of certain foreign examples for the discussion in the Netherlands, and on the financial gains for the government.

Given these opposing views, it will be no surprise that the debate concerning the manifesto on 19 February 2014 in the Second Chamber was the umpteenth repetition of arguments. Two days earlier, Opstelten had told in a letter that he agreed with the writers of the manifesto on the seriousness of the problems (insecurity in neighbourhoods, organized crime), but that regulating cannabis cultivation was not the right way to tackle these problems. The right way was "to persevere a vigorous approach".[117] The debate in the Second Chamber on this letter did not provide the participating political groups with new insights. D66, SP and GroenLinks once more expressed their strong support for (experiments with) regulation. CDA and VVD supported the minister *con amore*. The PvdA remained a little bit vague, but showed once again sympathy for the views of the opposition.[118]

For the framers of the manifesto, this stalemate was no reason to accept Opstelten's point of view. In particular their front man Depla, the mayor of Heerlen, made it clear in many ways in the press that according to him that point of view was untenable. So, it is not really astonishing that this mayor, together with the mayors of the other (seven) coffeeshop municipalities in the province of Limburg, is determined to suit the action to the word.[119] Also the

117 Second Chamber, 2013–2014, 24077, no. 315.

118 *Ibid.*, no. 317.

119 Besides Heerlen the municipalities of Venray, Venlo, Weert, Roermond, Sittard-Geleen, Maastricht and Kerkrade are involved.

announcement by the management of the National Police Force that it expects no good from the plans, has not stopped the campaign of the mayors to regulate the "back door" of the coffeeshops.[120] Yet, the content of that announcement is revealing:

> The National Police Force does not expect a decrease of organized crime in case the cultivation and the sale of cannabis to coffeeshops is regulated. Criminality is not tackled by regulation. It is imaginable that organized crime will be focusing on the 'ripping' of the 'legal' cannabis plantations. The ripping of harvestable plants is a phenomenon that already now regularly occurs and often involves – extreme – violence and high security risks for the persons in or nearby the plantation concerned (battering; hostage-taking; assassination). In order to achieve the security objective, legal cannabis plantations have to be guarded 24 hours a day. In addition, provisions have to be made to ensure the safe delivery of cannabis to the coffeeshops. In short: with regard to surveillance and detection, rather more efforts are required, such as deployment of guards and (private) laboratories (determination of THC content). (...) This makes tackling criminality extra complex. The number of illicit plantations will not immediately decline; probably there will only be a shift of the market, from the Netherlands to abroad.

In September 2013, the Limburg mayors made a proposal, entitled *De voor- en achterdeur open* (*The front and back door open*), for (a pilot project regarding) the regulation of the cannabis cultivation in Limburg. After Opstelten's rejection of the manifesto, Depla repeatedly said he would not resign himself to that decision. In June 2014, he announced that they were busy with the preparations for the issuing of a licence to a company to cultivate cannabis. In this context, he noted that he would not mind if this licence would be challenged via the Administrative Court or if the Public Prosecutor's Office would prosecute the company for infringing the drug legislation. In that case a new situation would emerge, in which not the minister but a judge would determine whether regulated cannabis cultivation is allowed.[121]

In this point of view, he is apparently supported by a member of his party in the First Chamber. At the end of June, namely, G. Ter Horst announced that she

120 This internal communication can be found on, for instance, the following website: <http://www.voc-nederland.org/2014/02>.

121 P. de Graaf, "Limburg lokt proces gedoogde wietteelt uit", *De Volkskrant*, 19.6.2014. See also P. de Graaf, "Je lijkt bijna gek als je geen wiet teelt", *De Volkskrant*, 7.7.2014.

would ask the minister to start a test in which certified companies are allowed to deliver cannabis to coffeeshops.[122] How much cannabis these companies will be allowed or will have to produce to supply certain coffeeshops, is one of the many questions that are not included in this request. Recently, Depla indicated that the Limburg coffeeshops need 10,000 kilograms of cannabis to meet demand. However, a little bit of journalistic investigation revealed that this estimate of the needed quantity is unreliable. So, the journalist concerned assessed the allegation as "unfounded".[123]

5.8.2 *The Struggle Against Illicit Cannabis Cultivation*

The other pillar of the revision of the cannabis policy concerns the plans of the Cabinet to criminalize the preparation or facilitation of illicit cannabis cultivation. The bill that should make this possible has already been discussed in the Second Chamber and is now for consideration in the First Chamber. With regard to this political battle, we will briefly elucidate which parties are using which arguments to underpin their approval or rejection.

5.8.2.1 The Step by Step Discussion in the Second Chamber

Already in the spring of 2010 the minister of Justice, Hirsch Ballin, sent the draft of a bill to change the Opium Act "on the subject of preparation and facilitation of illicit cannabis cultivation" for advice to, among other addressees, the Public Prosecutor's Office and the Council for the Judiciary. Unlike the bill that was sent to the Second Chamber in July 2011 by his successor Opstelten, the draft mainly focused on tackling the growshops, which were the hubs of that illicit cultivation. The bill as such (on the insertion of a new article 11a) was about all possible practices (the preparation, processing, offering for sale et cetera of substances or objects) of which the person involved "is aware or has serious reason to presume that they are intended for committing" certain offences mentioned in the Opium Act.[124]

In the *Explanatory Memorandum* it was explicitly stated that the submission of this bill should also be seen in the context of the Task Force that shortly before had been established to combat organized crime in Brabant. This partly explains why the bill was directed against the whole "conglomerate of activities related to illicit cannabis cultivation" and no longer especially

---

122 She announced this in the television programme *Nieuwsuur* on Thursday 26 June 2014. See the related report in *Dagblad de Limburger*, 26.6.2014.

123 L. Boon, "10.000 kilo wiet nodig om Limburgse coffeeshops te bevoorraden", NRC-*Next*, 14.7.2014.

124 Second Chamber, 2011–2012, 32842, nos. 1–2.

against the growshops. The separate criminalization of all these activities was considered necessary, because experience had learnt that existing legal concepts such as inchoate offences were not sufficiently applicable to them.

In October 2011, the Permanent Committee for Security and Justice showed – as could be expected – that it was divided in its opinion on this bill.[125] VVD, CDA and SGP did have some questions regarding the legal necessity of the bill, the practical feasibility of its enforcement, the risk that people who – or companies which – have nothing to do with cannabis cultivation would fall within the reach of the new article, and the displacement problems that could result from a strict enforcement of the law on this point. However, as such they agreed to the bill: the enormous industry behind cannabis cultivation had to be tackled.

But in the opinion of notably the PvdA and the SP the bill was the wrong solution to what they too regarded as a big problem. According to these political groups, illicit cannabis cultivation was the result of a contradictory policy. A policy that accepted coffeeshops that, under conditions, were allowed to sell cannabis, but also a policy that did not want to know where these shops got their stuff from. Thus, the only real solution to the problem was "to allow the controlled cultivation of cannabis on behalf of the supply to coffeeshops". For the rest, also in their circles there were questions about the limits and effects of the criminalization of the related activites.

Opstelten's response in December 2011 was strongly focused on the numerous legal questions that had been raised about the limits and effects of the criminalization of the activities concerned in relation to the punishability of inchoate offences and the professional approach to the current cannabis cultivation. But he did not sidestep the strategic countermove of the PvdA and the SP. He told them plainly "that the wishes of the coffeeshop keepers for a regulation of the supply to coffeeshops are not endorsed by the Cabinet".[126]

After the Rutte II Cabinet was installed, Opstelten resumed his work and wrote, in December 2012, a rather long letter to the Second Chamber about a number of issues that were relevant with regard to the bill: the illicit cannabis cultivation, the way to tackle the growshops and the risk of relocation to do-it-yourself centres and horticulture centres, the relation to the existing tools of criminal law, and the capacity to enforce the new provision at a given moment.[127] The letter did not contain much new information. So, it was not at all strange that the bill, on 2 April 2013, was adopted by the Second Chamber, that is: by

125 *Ibid.*, no. 5.

126 Second Chamber, 2011–2012, 32842, no. 6.

127 Second Chamber, 2012–2013, 32842, no. 13.

VVD, CDA, SGP, ChristenUnie and PVV. PvdA, SP and D66 abstained from voting in favour of the bill.

5.8.2.2 The Stagnation of the Discussion in the First Chamber

Two months later, in June 2013, the Permanent Committee for Security and Justice of the First Chamber examined the bill.[128] VVD and CDA immediately stated that, in principle, they supported this proposal. For the simple reason that illicit cannabis cultivation, due to its extent and professionalism, had become a real security risk for society. From the side of PvdA, SP and D66 it was, of course, once again put forward that regulating cannabis cultivation was preferable to the current approach: "Is it not precisely the current policy of tolerance that sustains crime in this area?", the PvdA wondered.

D66 said it shared the analysis of the problem (nowadays, unlike before, "the production, the transport and the trade are almost completely controlled (…) by criminal organizations"), but not the answer to it: "As long as the cultivation for the supply to coffeeshops is not, under conditions, legalized or regulated, the situation will, by definition, remain the same." Experience shows "that actually a further criminalization does not lead to improved security, but to the further development of the degree of organization of crime and to higher criminal proceeds". D66, together with VVD and CDA, also still had some questions concerning the legal and operational issues that had already been amply discussed in the Second Chamber.

A month later, in July 2013, Opstelten responded by means of a rather lengthy *Memorandum of Reply*. All previously mentioned issues passed in review.[129] As to the separate criminalization of the activities concerned, he clarified this time the rationale of their criminalization, and particularly emphasized the social impact of illicit cannabis cultivation:

> With regard to this bill, the seriousness and the extent of illicit cannabis cultivation in greenhouses, barns and other spaces, but also in housing estates where not just attics but complete houses are arranged as illicit cannabis plantations with all the related risks for the living environment, are the direct reason for the criminalization of acts that promote or facilitate that illicit cultivation. There is also political and social support for this.

The latter is, to some extent, certainly true, but at the beginning of his response Opstelten nevertheless had to do his utmost to (try to) convince PvdA, SP, D66

128 First Chamber, 2012–2013, 32842, A.

129 *Ibid.*, B.

and GroenLinks that they were mistaken: regulating the cultivation of cannabis is no solution. Notably not "because the illicit cannabis cultivation and the facilitation of it have an extent and an intensity that far exceeds the needs of the coffeeshops". Moreover, he repeated once again, the cultivation of cannabis for coffeeshops is incompatible with the commitments we have made in the context of the drug treaties of the United Nations and in conflict with European Union law. He strongly doubted whether the "further criminalization" would lead to a higher degree of organization of crime and higher criminal proceeds: "the illicit cannabis cultivation and the facilitation of it are already highly organized in the Netherlands and also now the facilitation is already lucrative (...)".

In their response to this memorandum on 15 October 2013, in particular the members of SP and GroenLinks clearly showed what, in the end, they were working towards: the rejection of this bill, and the regulation of cannabis cultivation following the example of some states in North and South America.[130] This point of view led Opstelten to the position that the issue of the criminalization of activities with regard to the large-scale and professional cannabis cultivation should be distinguished from the issue of the provisioning of the coffeeshops. In line with this starting point he repeated yet another time the reasons why, in his opinion, a regulation or decriminalization of cannabis cultivation was out of the question.[131] Hereupon, the committee concerned decided on 28 January 2014 that the public discussion of the bill had sufficiently been prepared.[132]

But until now, there has not been a public discussion of the bill. Why did it not take place on 1 April 2014, as initially intended? According to the so-called "short notes" about the meetings of the forementioned committee, this was in part due to procedural and personal obstacles. However, for another part it was also due to reasons related to the content. This is evidenced by the initiative of PvdA-member Ter Horst in March 2014. She then asked to postpone the discussion until the Second Chamber in a General Consultation with the minister would have debated on the coffeeshop policy.[133] Since in the meantime that consultation had been postponed to an unknown date, the committee subsequently decided to postpone the plenary discussion of the bill to 1 July 2014, and later to 8 July 2014. And when it became known that the consultation with the Second

130 First Chamber, 2013–2014, 32842, C.

131 *Ibid.*, D.

132 *Ibid.*, G.

133 See on the website of the First Chamber the short note about the meeting of the committee concerned on 25 March 2014.

Chamber on the coffeeshop policy was postponed to 10 September 2014, the committee decided to move the plenary discussion of the bill to 7 October 2014.

The extent to which this repeated postponing was related to the discussion about the coffeeshop policy and in particular to the action of a number of mayors, with the PvdA members among them leading the pack, to force Opstelten to regulate cannabis cultivation in the Netherlands, is reflected in the "short note" about the meeting on 8 July 2014. In that note it is announced that the committee has decided to address a letter to the minister of Security and Justice and the minister of the Interior and Kingdom Relations:

> about the administrative relations in the Netherlands with regard to the coffeeshop policy, and to invite both ministers for oral consultations on this subject on 9 September 2014. The member Ter Horst (PvdA) will provide input to the letter, the draft of which will subsequently be submitted to the committee.

The draft of the letter was not disclosed, but the final version, written by the president of the committee, was. In this letter, which, by the way, was only addressed to Opstelten and not to the minister of the Interior, it was stated that within the committee there was:

> a sense of urgency regarding the problems associated with the production of cannabis in the Netherlands. A large number of mayors see with regret that ever more inhabitants get involved in the production of cannabis and, as a consequence, fall into the hands of criminal organizations. The plea that was made to you by these mayors, did not make you change your mind. The committee is of the opinion that it belongs to proper administrative relations that the government is attentive to municipalities in the Netherlands. It emphatically asks you and your colleague of the Interior and Kingdom Relations to take the problems outlined by the mayors seriously and to enter into contact with them in order to find a solution for the problems. Furthermore, the committee invites you and your colleague for oral consultations on 9 September 2014, in order to hear from both of you what you already have done to solve the problems experienced by the municipalities in the context of the soft drug policy and what you, practically speaking, intend to do in this area, both in terms of process and content.

This is one of the most remarkable writings on the cannabis and coffeeshop policy in the Netherlands that have been published since the 1970s. That should be clear to anybody who has read this chapter up to this point. Not only because the style of this letter suggests a political display of power, but also because the content of the letter attests to great naivety. As if the problems concerned can be solved – in a flash, so to speak – through consultations at the ministerial level with a number of activistic mayors.

5.9 Conclusion

This chapter about the cannabis and coffeeshop policy in the Netherlands lends itself to manifold observations. When we limit the contemplations to the main theme of this book: the legalization of cannabis in the national and international context, we can, to begin with, conclude that the cannabis and coffeeshop policy has clearly become the plaything, if not the victim, of the irony of history. The policy of tolerance that was advocated – with good intentions – by progressive people in the 1960s and 1970s, is now stigmatized as the source of great evil by the progressives of our time. Whereas in the past the supporters of that policy considered it to be an appropriate method to curb organized crime in the area of soft drugs, it is nowadays by the supporters of the legalization of cannabis regarded as the big booster of crime in that field.

Anyone who accepts this definition of the development, is immediately and irrevocably faced with the question: how could this happen? The given description of the history of the policy of tolerance provides, by way of a starting point, an answer that encompasses three closely connected partial explanations.

The first partial explanation is that the inventors of this policy completely underestimated the entrepreneurship of, in the first place, the coffeeshop owners, and, in the second place, the cannabis cultivators, and as a consequence did not sufficiently realize that a lenient policy of tolerance with respect to such a profitable, although still illicit, market as the cannabis market inevitably would lead to large-scale organized crime, and everything that goes with it in terms of violence, intimidation and corruption. The signs in the 1980s and 1990s that clearly foreshadowed this development were not, or not sufficiently, understood. It is true that the reports on drug-related organized crime in the Netherlands that were written in the middle of the 1990s for the Van Traa Committee opened the eyes of many people, but they did not lead to the development of a vigorous strategy to eliminate this hazard as much as possible. Only from the year 2000 onwards, the huge crime problems that had matured within the cannabis sector were step by step publicly acknowledged, but at the same time it became increasingly clear that it was not easy to reduce these problems.

The second partial explanation is that not only the inventors but also the later implementors of this policy did not pay sufficient attention to the dynamics of the European Community and more specifically to the transformation of this economic alliance into a European Union with a gigantic "borderless" internal market, reaching from the Mediterranean to the North Pole. Thus, they have much too late discerned that the policy of tolerance, and the coffeeshop policy that is part of it, due to their "apartheid" not only exerted a magnetic attraction on numerous drug users from all over Western Europe and the wide world around it, but was partly for that reason also a powerful incentive for the development of an extensive cannabis industry, that could both ensure the supply to the increasingly flourishing coffeeshops and meet the cannabis needs far beyond the Netherlands. The problems that manifested themselves at an ever larger scale and in an ever more devastating way in Terneuzen, Bergen op Zoom, Roosendaal, Venlo and Maastricht are obviously striking illustrations of the very negative consequences of this development.

The third partial explanation is that for many years the policy of tolerance – with the exception of the tolerance criteria for coffeeshops – has not, or not adequately, been enforced in a consistent way. The transformation of the coffeeshops into export companies – a clear violation of international agreements – has been tolerated for so long at the "front doors" of the shops that eventually the administrators in many municipalities in the southern part of the country were faced with so much trouble that in a number of cases they had to take the drastic decision to close the shops to prevent even much worse things from happening. And when finally an appropriate countermeasure (the resident criterion) was placed in position, it took, due to different sorts of obstinate opposition of the coffeeshop owners – in particular the ones in Maastricht – against this fully justified restriction of their economic power position, and also due to the active and passive support the coffeeshop owners got from several political parties at the national and the local level, many years before this measure could generate its beneficial effects. As to the illicit cannabis cultivation, also in its relation to the coffeeshops, it was time and time again, until today, and both at the national and the local level, found that – notwithstanding the successive policy plans – the actual fight against this cultivation was not a real, coherent and consistent priority of the police, the judicial authorities and the administration. The past years, in some regions of the Netherlands that fight has, forced by necessity, finally taken shape, though in large areas of the southern, eastern and western part of the Netherlands combating illicit cannabis cultivation is still limited to clearing big and small cannabis plantations. At these places, in-depth investigations remain the exception to the rule.

Together, these three partial explanations make it easy to understand why at this moment the public debate on the policy of tolerance – which is essentially the issue at stake here – is pushed to extremes and why, in the First Chamber, the debate got stuck on the question whether, one way or another, the provisioning of the coffeeshops, as far as the supply of Dutch cannabis is concerned, could or should be legalized.[134]

Obviously, given the current state of affairs one should ask oneself whether the latter question is as acute as it appears to be now. Is it really impossible to combat illicit cannabis cultivation – during a long period of time and all over the Netherlands, though first and foremost in the southern part of the country – much more vigorously than it has been combated in the past years? If that would actually happen, then it is very well imaginable that the arguments that are now, with a lot of aplomb, put forward in favour of the legalization of cannabis for coffeeshops – in particular the deterioration of poor neighbourhoods – would lose a lot of their strength, and thus of their urgency. This way, room would be created for a more thoughtful and in this sense also more reasonable debate on what could or should be done in the short or the long run. That room could also be used for the necessary reflection on the recent decisions of the Courts of The Hague and Amsterdam with regard to the criminal law approach to important coffeeshops. Some people will view these decisions as a death blow to the policy of tolerance, or at least to the incoherent and inconsistent way this policy has been applied for so many years. Others will say that this is a totally wrong interpretation of the decisions concerned, and that these decisions only demonstrate that important changes of the cannabis and coffeeshop policy must be put in practice with the necessary carefulness. Conversely, for the judiciary the decisions could also be a reason to reflect on its own role in controlling the so complicated cannabis problem in our society. Is the sentencing policy of the courts still in proportion to the seriousness of this problem? Or does it suffice for the judiciary to be critical of the role of local administrations, the police and the Public Prosecutor's Office in the implementation of the cannabis and coffeeshop policy?

But those who do not opt for this way out of the conflict, have to realize that people can think differently about the answer to the question whether the question that is posed so concisely in the First Chamber is the right question. Like the minister of Security and Justice Opstelten, we do not think it is, because the cultivation of cannabis on behalf of the coffeeshops is indeed only

---

134 See also the informative report on the deadlock written by M. van de Wier, "Verslaafd aan het eigen gelijk; hoe het cannabisdebat een loopgravenoorlog werd", *De Groene Amsterdammer*, 30.7.2014.

a part of the whole problem of hemp cultivation and coffeeshops in the Netherlands. Not only because a large part of the domestic cannabis cultivation is not at all destined for the coffeeshops, but also because coffeeshops equally (want to) sell – in one form or the other – cannabis that has not been cultivated in the Netherlands, for instance cannabis from surrounding countries or from Morocco, Lebanon or Thailand. This means that the problem of the provisioning of the coffeeshops – unless these shops or other points of sale would be forced to purchase from specific domestic cannabis factories – can only be solved in case a solution is found for a much bigger and also much more international problem: the legalization of cannabis as part of an international movement to legalize this drug. Moreover, in this regard the question arises whether it would be wise to treat the coffeeshops as the most suitable distribution channel in case recreational cannabis would be legalized. The current data on the criminal nature of this sector clearly indicate that this would certainly not be a lucky choice.

In addition, those who nevertheless only want to legalize the cannabis cultivation on behalf of the coffeeshops, should ask themselves what must happen with the illicit cannabis cultivation in the Netherlands that is not directly related to the licensed coffeeshops. Will it, unlike in the past, efficiently be combated? Not only to curb unfair competition with the coffeeshops and to limit the size of the illicit market for persons who, for very good reasons – their age, for example – have no access to coffeeshops, but also to avoid that the criminal groups concerned can keep supplying cannabis to black markets in countries that do not want to legalize cannabis. There is no guarantee for such an efficient strategy, and therefore a limited, rather nationalistic legalization of the cannabis cultivation is almost impossible. This is a bogus solution, a solution that is not a solution. The assertion in the manifesto of the mayors that the problems in the Netherlands are so big that it is no option to wait until also the other countries will be prepared to legalize recreational cannabis, bears witness to little insight and much rashness. Apparently, the authors do not realize that it is no longer possible to successfully combat the illicit cannabis production and distribution on Dutch soil without close cooperation with at least the surrounding countries. And they are clearly not well-informed about the serious political conflicts with the neighbouring countries that the wayward Dutch drug policy has repeatedly caused.

Finally, there is still the key question: the legalization of the production and distribution of cannabis in the Netherlands may be desirable, or may seem desirable, but is it also possible? In principle, the answer to this question is: no, it is not. The drug treaties of the United Nations and the policy of the European Union are hindering this. They leave no room for the legalization of the cannabis cultivation such as it is taking place at this moment in some American states and in Uruguay. The suggestion in the manifesto of the mayors that these examples precisely demonstrate that the legalization of cannabis is not at variance with the treaties, is in any case completely wrong and testifies furthermore to a lack of knowledge about what is actually and legally going on in the United States. Should the Netherlands nevertheless neglect the obligations it has entered into in the context of these treaties? We do not think so: a civilized country complies with the treaties it has signed. If it would act the other way, the Netherlands would have to pay the world a high price in terms of unreliability and incredibility.

The royal road to follow here is to work diligently and together with other countries towards the official adjustment of the treaties and of the policy on this point. A choice for the latter option does not mean the illicit cannabis cultivation should be left in peace during the years that will be needed to adjust the drug treaties. Certainly not! The criminal groups that have acquired dominant positions in this industry and thus have earned lots of money must as yet be tackled severely, so that in the future they cannot play any significant role in the illicit cannabis sector, let alone in a possible legal cannabis market or in the legal economy in general.

CHAPTER 6

General Conclusion: Towards a Third Way

6.1 The Reformulation of the Question

At the beginning of the foreword of this book we submitted the old question: what is sensible when it comes to developing and implementing a policy with regard to products which, certainly in the case of regular use, are harmful, even very harmful, to the well-being of people, but which at the same time exert a strong attraction, even so strong that people may become dependent on or addicted to them?

This question, albeit in more general terms, had been posed by the Wickersham Commission, which produced the report that heralded the end of the Prohibition Era in the United States. At the end of its inquiry, the Commission wondered if it was possible, to maintain a law which, as the facts showed, was infringed more and more and which increasingly met with indifference and hostility among the public? The Commission's answer to that question is well-known: no, such a law cannot be maintained.

In our opinion, the authorities in the Americas as well as in Belgium, the Netherlands and the other member states of the European Union are nowadays confronted with a similar question concerning the existing cannabis legislation: is this legislation still tenable in a time in which there is not only an extensive illicit production and distribution of cannabis, but also a fairly large-scale consumption of the drug? In other words, shouldn't we legalize and regulate (the production and distribution of) cannabis for medical as well as recreational use?

We think that, over time, the current legislation is not entirely tenable and we believe that at different levels – from the level of states to that of the United Nations – the authorities need to provide clear information about the directions in which they intend to adapt their cannabis policies in the future. However, what we discussed in the previous chapters demonstrates that reconsidering the present cannabis policy is in several respects a complex and for that reason difficult task. The essence of the discussion on the cannabis policy has little to do with the simple as well as radical choice between criminalization and legalization of the drug. On the contrary, it has to do with the question whether a possible legalization and associated regulation of this drug will enhance public health and public safety, and also whether it will contribute to a better command of the related social, economic and political problems.

 | DOI 10.1163/9789004293199_007

In this chapter, using the insights and data we presented and discussed before, we aim to outline the direction in which the discussion about a well-balanced reconsideration of the cannabis policy could go.

In the next paragraph we will focus on the preliminary question about the impact of the legalization of cannabis on the drug treaties of the United Nations and, as a result, on the cannabis policy pursued in North America, the European Union and therefore also in Belgium and in the Netherlands. Generally speaking, this policy is indeed deduced from what is agreed upon in the drug treaties.

Immediately, and closely connected to this, the question that will be considered in the third paragraph arises: how do we have to regulate this drug if ever in the future there would be sufficient political support to legalize it? And since in the United States the regulation of cannabis is mainly based on the regulation of alcohol and tobacco, we will examine in this paragraph whether the last-mentioned regulation is really a good example for the regulation of cannabis. Another reason to do so, is the fact that equally in the European Union a number of supporters of legalization recommend cannabis to be treated in a similar way as alcohol and tobacco. But is this advice as wise as it may seem?

In part because the answer to the latter question is certainly not entirely positive, in paragraph four we will examine more thoroughly the legalization of cannabis in the two American states, a topic about which we have already provided ample information in Chapter 3. We especially wonder whether in the context of the legalization of this drug the interests associated with it were taken into account in a sufficiently balanced way: the economic interests, the public health interests, the interests of law enforcement. The answer to this question is rather negative. After all, the economic interests have prevailed over the interests of public health.

Finally, in paragraph five we will outline the contours of a proposal for the discussion in the (member states of the) European Union about a well-balanced policy regarding the regulation of cannabis. Of course, not only the forms of regulation developed in North and South America are taken into account. To be sure, the proper developments in the European member states function as a source of inspiration as well. Because of the “coffeeshops”, the situation in the Netherlands differs strongly from that in the other member states, which explains why this peculiar situation will be discussed separately.

6.2 A Preliminary Matter: The Reconsideration of the Drug Treaties

The legalization and regulation of cannabis in some American states and in Uruguay suggest that such a radical revision of the cannabis policy is possible without any consideration for the drug treaties of the United Nations. Indeed, the examples show that this is actually possible. But is it, viewed from an international legal perspective, also appropriate and desirable? Do states, when it suits them, have the right to simply ignore treaties they have ratified? No, they don't. That is not appropriate. And it is definitely not desirable too, because on the one hand it undermines the credibility of the United Nations, and on the other hand it harms the international reliability of the countries involved. Civilized states do not act that way. The fact that, in this context, the United States plays an ambiguous role – the federation does not denounce the concerning treaties, but at the state level it allows practices which are at variance with the treaties – is certainly no reason at all to follow the example of Washington State, Colorado or Uruguay.

But what could be considered as an acceptable approach? Is it possible to revise the drug treaties in a rather short period of time, in such a way that, for all countries or at least a group of countries, they no longer apply to cannabis? Yes, that is possible, as demonstrated by the Single Convention on Narcotic Drugs, adopted in 1961. In 1971 this treaty was changed and made applicable to psychotropic substances. So it could as well be changed to remove cannabis from the accompanying prohibitive regime. Also in the light of the actual development of the cannabis problems in the (Western) world, especially with regard to the production and distribution of cannabis, the subsequent question automatically arises: how can this possibility become a factual reality?

In the past years many supporters of legalization have racked their brains over this question. Which options are available to revise the concerned treaties with respect to the production and distribution of cannabis, particularly for recreational use? In 2008, Room et al. discussed these options in a report for the Beckley Foundation.[1] Recently, M. Jelsma, T. Blickman and P. Bewley-Taylor examined the same problem.[2] Their inventory shows there are different methods to organize the legalization of cannabis by treaty.

The first method implies that states denounce the concerned treaties and subsequently ratify them again, though with a reservation regarding the use of certain drugs without a medical or scientific purpose. However, it remains to be seen whether other countries would accept such a reservation. Moreover, this method would diminish the pressure to proceed towards a complete functional revision of the drug treaties.

The second method therefore consists of a revision of the treaties themselves. However, in practice this method could call forth so many counter-arguments

1 Room, Fischer, Hall, Lenton and Reuter, 2008, p. 151–168. See also Room, 2013, p. 348–349.

2 Jelsma, Blickman and Bewley-Taylor, 2014.

and could result in so many amendments of the initial proposal that, in the end, little or nothing of the intended revision would be left.

The third method implies that a number of parties conclude a treaty which enables them to change certain clauses in the treaties of the United Nations. Such a method looks attractive, but is hard to realize overnight. Just to mention one problem: changes of the treaties which hinder the actual attainment of the aim of the treaties are not permitted.

The fourth method is a rather radical one: a group of countries can decide to simply denounce the treaties. The problem is that the application of this method can have serious political, economic and social consequences for the concerning countries.

The fifth method boils down to this: a group of consentient countries decides to entirely replace one of the treaties by another treaty. Such an approach is imaginable, but not easily realizable because it implies new negotiations about several issues.

Since all the mentioned methods are difficult to apply, some people think that in practice, the only remaining solution may be to actually suspend the treaty by no longer investing in its maintenance. If an influential country such as the United States or a country which is well-known in this context such as the Netherlands, would make use of this method, other countries no doubt would follow that example. It is clear and obvious, however, that at the same time this method would face opposition from other parties associated with the treaties and from institutions, which on behalf of the treaties, are responsible for their maintenance.

Nevertheless, some authors believe we have reached the point where a *de iure* legalization of the cannabis market by means of a reconsideration of the treaties has become inevitable, because in the Americas as well as in Europe it is increasingly considered as politically desirable or necessary.[3] But is this really true? As described earlier, up to now there is not any room for such a development at the level of the (member states of the) European Union. Furthermore, not all American states do accept it to the extent the concerned authors try to make us believe. Furthermore, within the United Nations there is still a lot of opposition against the course followed by countries such as Uruguay and the American states of Colorado, Washington and recently Nebraska.[4] So, maybe these predictors prematurely take their wishes for granted?

In our opinion, too, it is beyond any doubt that the legalization of cannabis requires a revision of the treaties of 1961 and 1988. A recent study by Van

3 Jelsma, Blickman and Bewley-Taylor, 2014, p. 14.

4 Caulkins, Hawken, Kilmer and Kleiman, 2012, p. 146–150.

Kempen and Federova has once again demonstrated this.[5] The best way to adapt the treaties, is by removing cannabis from them by means of a protocol. A crucial question, of course, is whether this protocol will come into operation only after all parties have accepted it, or as soon as a minimal number of parties has done so. In the second case, and given the worldwide spread of cannabis, the international impact of the treaties would be seriously undermined. Inevitably such an arrangement would call forth a lot of protest within the United Nations. For this reason, it is almost certain that only the other option, an unanimous approval of the protocol, stands a chance. And it is also immediately clear that the application of this method will demand a huge collective political effort from a group of countries.

From the point of view of Belgium and the Netherlands this means that if at a given moment they would indeed consider the concerning revision desirable, they could, for instance together with the other countries – Germany, France and Luxembourg – with which they concluded in 1985 the Schengen Agreement, take the initiative to put this matter on the political agenda of the European Union. Of course, by doing so, things would be far from settled. The legalization of cannabis is not at all an issue in the drug policy of the European Union and, as already explained in Chapter 4, up to now important member states such as Germany, France and the United Kingdom have radically rejected it. Nevertheless, for the aforementioned reasons it is more than desirable that the European Union speaks frankly about its cannabis policy and the legalization option. Assuming that the European Union would want to legalize and regulate cannabis, then, with the aid of the United States, Canada and South American states, maybe it would be possible to convince the world community of the desirability to adapt the drug treaties of the United Nations to certain actual developments in the field of cannabis.

Small member states of the European Union such as the Netherlands and Belgium also have other than international political reasons to follow this royal road, instead of imitating some American states by legalizing cannabis on their own.[6]

A first good reason is that the production and distribution of cannabis in the member states of the European Union is to a large extent a cross-border phenomenon. This implies that any member state that would try to legalize cannabis in "splendid isolation" could easily collide with other member states that do not want to take that step. For example because in these member states there is some illicit cannabis production by which the

5 Van Kempen and Federova, 2014.

6 Fijnaut, 2014, p. 215–216.

local legal market in the state concerned is supplied. Or because that legal market, in different ways, supplies cannabis – on a large or a small scale – to the illicit market in the other countries. This means that, when a member state that legalizes cannabis, wants to avoid cross-border market activities and the political conflicts they could evoke, it will have to take drastic measures, even more drastic than in the context of the Schengen Implementation Agreement. Such a member state shall have to establish an integrated production and distribution system, which allows the licensed factories to sell their cannabis only to licensed shops, which, in their turn, are allowed to sell only that particular kind of cannabis, and this only to the inhabitants of the member state and not to non-residents. Which member state is prepared and capable to construct and maintain such a system?

The second reason is an offshoot of the first. A country that has legalized cannabis and as a consequence has regulated the production and distribution of the product in a certain way, will inevitably be confronted with an illicit cannabis market and therefore with criminal organizations which – in terms of production and distribution – want to retain or acquire key positions on that market. This is rather evident for various reasons. The minimum age for cannabis consumers, for instance 18 or 21 years, almost automatically leads to an illicit demand for, and also an illicit supply of, cannabis. And for criminal organizations it is rather easy to sell cannabis below the official price and to win over a lot of customers by doing so. But these criminal organizations will not only set up their production facilities in the member state which has legalized cannabis. Definitely not! To avoid the undermining of their infrastructure by the authorities of the concerned member state, they will also set up production facilities beyond the borders of that state. Within the European Union this implies that, for an effective fight against these criminal organizations, a member state which has legalized cannabis often will need the help of other member states. But will these other states be ready and capable to sufficiently provide that support to a member state which, against their will, has legalized cannabis and so in a way is itself at the root of the problem?

The third reason is linked to the second. Any state which, following the example of Colorado and Washington State, wants to legalize cannabis, has to realize that up to now the federal authorities in the United States are opposed to legalization. As sufficiently demonstrated in Chapter 3, the United States, purely legally speaking, therefore remains party to the drug treaties. This is a very important point, not only in the international legal context but also with regard to domestic politics. It implies that on the whole territory of the United

States, the federal authorities by means of the FBI, the Drugs Enforcement Administration, the Internal Revenue Service and other federal agencies can radically intervene in the production and distribution of cannabis whenever the authorities think there are good reasons to do so – for example the inadequate functioning of the production and distribution system in a state which has legalized cannabis. The past months, the authorities have declared loud and clear – even in Congress – that they will not hesitate to act this way. In comparison with the situation in the European Union, the differences become apparent: the European Union is not a federal state, let alone that the European Commission has federal investigation and prosecution services at its disposal, enabling it to intervene independently in the territory of member states when anywhere in the Union, the cannabis problem runs out of control. This means that in the European Union an adequate control of this particular problem totally depends on good, permanent cooperation between the member states. But such a cooperation is unthinkable when individual member states on their own authority proceed to the legalization of cannabis. In that case every member state above all things will tackle the problems that cause the most trouble to its inhabitants, its authorities and/or its legal economic sectors.

Not only because of international political and international legal reasons a member state of the European Union should never on its own initiative proceed to the legalization of cannabis, but also because of important practical reasons – possibly just out of sheer self-interest. At once, this conclusion also makes it clear that we totally disagree with individuals in Belgium and the Netherlands, who call for the legalization of cannabis in their own country but apparently take no account of the negative consequences a solo action in this area inevitably will have.

Countries who want to legalize cannabis, should at the same time explain how they will organize the production and distribution of the product. Otherwise it is obvious that the real impact of the legalization will not at all be clear. And the opposite is also true. The way cannabis will be regulated, can strongly influence the willingness of people to legalize the drug. If the regulation will occur in a way many people do not agree with, the resistance against legalization, of course, will be bigger than if the opposite is the case. Just shouting out loud that cannabis has to be legalized, without indicating how, it will subsequently be regulated in practice, is a rather pointless and even an easily counterproductive shot in the air. In the discussion about the regulation of cannabis, people frequently refer to the way alcohol and tobacco are regulated. But is that example really as good as is often suggested?

6.3 The Regulation of Alcohol and Tobacco: A Good Example?

The supporters of legalization often and gladly refer to the Prohibition Era in the United States. They consider the associated ban on alcohol as a proof that prohibition can never be effective and creates more problems than it solves. In their view, especially the problem of organized crime is a convincing proof of this thesis.[7] As demonstrated earlier, this representation of the facts is at least one-sided and definitely does not do justice to the positive effects the Prohibition has also generated. However, some outspoken supporters of legalization do acknowledge that the Prohibition has had positive effects on public health and family life. Caulkins etc. refer to the decline in the number of cases of liver cirrhosis as a result of the decreasing number of heavy drinkers, and to the drop in domestic violence, due to the reduction of alcohol misuse in households.[8]

This was not a new finding, on the contrary. The "enforced" prohibition of alcohol in Belgium during the First World War had an impressive positive effect on the physical and mental health of the Belgians. Nevertheless, it is true that, certainly in the days of the "war on drugs" in the United States, the Prohibition has caused a number of negative effects, not least among the users. A simplistic, one-dimensional policy can never be successful because generalizations and stereotypes leave little or no room for the development of appropriate approaches for specific problems. This holds good in the case of the use of illicit drugs, but also with regard to alcohol addiction.

Anyway, many people who support the legalization of cannabis like to refer to the current regulation of the alcohol and tobacco markets as a good model for the regulation of the cannabis market. They argue that it is certainly possible to regulate cannabis according to that model.[9] This is an understandable line of thought. The starting point for the regulation of cannabis in Colorado and Washington State was the way alcohol was regulated in these states. Even so, the question arises whether this example is worth to be followed without any reserve. Maybe the defenders of legalization too easily ignore the treaties and laws which are applicable in this area, as well as the many facts and figures which do not paint such a positive picture of the regulation of alcohol, tobacco and, by extension, psychoactive medication. Are these regulations really as big a success as is often suggested? Or to put it more generally: perhaps the supporters neglect the fact that it is difficult to keep a social phenomenon such as

7 Dupont and Voth, 1995, p. 461.

8 Caulkins, Hawken, Kilmer and Kleiman, 2012, p. 115.

9 Decorte, 2014, p. 35–40.

illicit drugs, – especially a multidimensional and international drug such as cannabis – within manageable proportions once it is legalized.

The past years, in the context of the *Groupe Pompidou* of the Council of Europe, a measurement and evaluation system has been developed which makes it possible, at the national level, to measure and evaluate the coherence between the strategies against various licit and illicit drugs.[10] In the meantime, this model has been tested in quite a number of member states of the Council of Europe. The results reveal that the objectives formulated in the context of the control strategies are very similar for the licit and the illicit drugs. This does not come as a surprise. The distinction between licit and illicit does not affect the objectives in the realm of, for instance, public health:

> There is a growing convergence of perceptions and approaches within the domains of illicit drugs and alcohol policy, though the political will to combine the domains has not been so strong, unless within a wider substance-misuse policy domain. Tobacco control remains a separate and distinct policy domain.[11]

This finding, which dates from a few years ago, is still valid. In recent years the alcohol and the drug policy have converged even further, as demonstrated by the country reports of the *Groupe Pompidou.*[12]

In itself, this convergence of policies is not so strange. It is self-evident that in the concerned strategies the health dimension prevails. This dimension forces the authorities to protect risk groups, such as minors, and to limit the freedom of users, including those of so-called legal drugs. The ban on smoking in enclosed public spaces is an obvious example. Also in relation to the safety policy the drugs and the alcohol policy have strongly converged. Taking action against the users is not a priority for the authorities, unless the act of using leads to dangerous situations such as driving under the influence of such stimulants or trespasses the boundaries of individual freedom and causes public nuisance or endangers minors by using drugs in their presence or pushing them to use such products themselves. This applies as much to the use of alcohol or tobacco as it does to the use of cannabis.

Furthermore it is a fact that the trade of alcohol and tobacco becomes more and more restricted and that, in this area, unlimited economic freedom is a

---

10 Muscat and Pike, 2010, p. 65, and De Ruyver, Vander Laenen and Eelen, 2012, p. 33–42.

11 Pike, 2008, p. 91.

12 Muscat and Pike, 2010, p. 11–15; Eisenbach-Stengl, 2012, p. 21–31; Pike, 2012, p. 43–63; Trigueros, 2012, p. 101–114; and De Ruyver, Vander Laenen and Eelen, 2012, p. 33–42.

thing of the past. So it is no coincidence that the illicit trade of cigarettes has become a worldwide, lucrative and low-risk business, which in many respects easily bears comparison with the international drug traffic. In particular the huge price differences between countries – which are mainly the result of different tax rates – make it very tempting for smugglers to transport large quantities of cigarettes from one country (where cigarettes are relatively cheap) to another (where they are much more expensive). A price comparison between for example Poland and Great Britain gives an idea of the extent of the temptation: in 2013 a pack of cigarettes costed 1.57 pounds in Poland and 6.29 pounds in the United Kingdom.[13]

The way cigarette smuggling is organized has a lot in common with the way illicit drugs are transported across the world: via local gangs which form a well-integrated transport chain, reaching from the places where the cigarettes are deposited or produced to the places where they will finally be distributed.[14] This parallel is not really surprising. In both cases we have to do with the smuggling of valuable goods across borders, which, at least in the Western world, are increasingly well-guarded in every possible way.

In addition, we may not forget that the use of cannabis and the use of alcohol and tobacco very often go together. That is also a reason why in the development of prevention strategies it is better not to make a distinction between licit and illicit drugs. The increasing convergence between the strategies against illicit drugs (especially cannabis) and the strategies focussing on alcohol, tobacco and psychoactive medication is, certainly in the EU, a fact nobody can ignore:

> There has been a shift in national drug strategies – at least in Europe – to erode the substance-specific approach which traditionally segregated activity on licit psychoactive substances from activity on illicit drugs. Politically, it is no longer taboo to compare legal and illegal substancy. The recent advert of smoking bans in Europe represents a golden opportunity to measure the knock-on effects on consumption of other substances.[15]

---

13 See in this connection the short article in *The Guardian*, "New effort to stop fake cigarettes filled with excrement, mould and asbestos", 23 August 2014.

14 Hornsby and Hobbs, 2007; Antonopoulos, 2008; L'Hoiry, 2013; and Fix, Hyland, O'Connor et al., 2014. See also Stijn Cools, "Slimme criminelen smokkelen sigaretten", *De Standaard*, 8–9 March 2014.

15 Sznitman, Olsson and Room, 2008, p. 119.

There are two ways to look at the convergence of the control strategies. To the supporters of the legalization of cannabis it will be obvious to provide cannabis the same legal status as alcohol and tobacco. On the other hand, the opponents of legalization will not hesitate to emphasize that the convergence only demonstrates that the actual policy has nothing at all in common with the picture painted by the supporters of legalization: an inefficient repression which also hurts the users, as is the case in a war on drugs. The truth, as so often, lies in the middle.

An alcohol or a tobacco policy prioritizing health objectives, inevitably involves restrictions on individual liberty and a more rigid regulation of demand and supply. And those who think health arguments are not sufficiently convincing to pursue such a restrictive policy, should also take into account the financial-economic reality of unsustainable health care costs and, by extension, the social costs related to alcohol and tobacco in our society. That is why in a large number of countries, authorities have tightened the rules and set bounds to the freedom of action. Some people are delighted that such interventions in economic life do not occur by means of criminal law but by means of economic, fiscal, social and administrative law.[16] However, that is not always the way it goes. In a lot of countries trespassers of the rules of fiscal, economic and social law end up in the criminal justice system.

Anyhow, the regulation of alcohol and tobacco, as it has evolved over the past decades, pushes these legal luxuries more and more in the direction of a prohibitive regime. The fact that according to the prevailing opinion young people should have no access to the regulated market, has resulted in a regulatory framework for alcohol and tobacco which, at least in this respect, very closely resembles the legal status of cannabis. Since, in this area, all member states of the European Union develop a similar policy, it is more than clear that at the European level a tighter regulation of alcohol and tobacco enjoys broad political and social support.

It is striking that certain countries, in spite of poignant reports about the health risks associated with the use of alcohol and tobacco, find it difficult to reduce the supply of especially alcohol. A telling example is Belgium, where the alcohol lobby last year managed to persuade a political party, belonging to the majority, to block a proposed "alcohol plan" containing several supply-limiting measures. The minister of Public Health, president of the Interministerial Conference on Drugs, subsequently decided to withdraw the alcohol plan.[17] The retraction of the concerning supply-limiting

16 Decorte, 2014, p. 35–36.

17 I. Ghys, "Jongeren drinken minder maar nog te veel", *De Standaard*, 17 December 2013.

measures – more precisely the ban on selling alcohol in filling stations or by means of drink machines – disturbed the equilibrium between supply and demand reduction measures. So there was no longer room for a balanced approach. It illustrates that in countries such as Belgium, where the production and distribution of alcohol are important economic activities, major health concerns do not easily prevail over purely economic interests. When it really matters, economic interests still predominate. That was already the case more than a century ago, at the time of the alcohol temperance movement, and it still remains so.

Restrictive measures against the distribution of tobacco are much better accepted. The Framework Convention on Tobacco Control (FCTC), which was adopted by the General Assembly of the World Health Organization (WHO) on May 21, 2003 and which entered into force in February 2005, is, to put it mildly, a remarkable realization in this context. In a time of harsh criticism of the drug treaties of the United Nations, 178 countries were willing to ratify the framework convention. The objective of this convention is as simple as it is clear: protecting present and future generations from the effects of tobacco use and from exposure to smokers. In other words: a choice has been made for a broad, integral approach of the worldwide tobacco problem, with attention to the entire supply chain and everything connected with it, such as publicity and taxes. The standards contained in the treaty usually are considered to be minimum rules, and the states which are a party to the treaty are encouraged to take additional measures to limit the availability of tobacco.

This inevitably leads to two conclusions. The first conclusion is that the regulation of the production and distribution of tobacco increasingly acquires prohibitive features. This evolution is already going on for a long time. In 2003, the then director of the United Nations Office on Drugs and Crime, A. Costa, summarized it as follows:

> The fight against dependence and abuse is progressing in areas other than illicit drugs. Public health history was made as countries recently completed negotiations at the WHO for the Framework Convention on Tobacco Control, meant to reduce related deaths and illnesses. Occasional calls for the reconsideration (i.e. relaxation) of current drug control legislation are hardly consistent with member countries' stated objective of protecting present and future generations from the devastating consequences of nicotine addiction, itself not an illicit substance.[18]

---

18 Speech A. Costa on the occasion of the *International symposium on cannabis*, organized by the *United Nations Office on Drugs and Crime* in Stockholm on 7 March 2003.

What Costa wanted to bring to our notice, is the need for consistency in the (inter)national policy regarding the use of substances. From a health perspective, this is obvious. Just as it is obvious that the same attitude should be adopted in the prevention, assistance and harm reduction strategies in which the distinction between licit and illicit luxuries almost does not matter anymore.

The second conclusion is related to the first. Nationally and internationally, the use of tobacco and everything associated with it, encounters much more headwind than the use of alcohol. This is quite embarrassing for the supporters of legalization and regulation of cannabis, because the way tobacco and cannabis are used, is in most cases identical. It is not obvious to discourage tobacco smoking in every possible way, while at the same time the smoking of cannabis is legalized and regulated. If that happens, the consistency of the dissuasive policy message will be completely undermined.

Nevertheless, once the decision is taken to legalize and regulate cannabis, the question arises what can be learned from the interventions developed and implemented in order to control alcohol and tobacco? There already have been executed quite many cost-effectiveness studies, which have provided a rather unequivocal picture of which interventions are effective and which are not.[19]

As to alcohol policy, the following measures yield the best results (in descending order): raising taxes, a ban on advertising, compulsory closing times, and breath testing in traffic. Large-scale media campaigns and alcohol education at school score weak on cost-effectiveness. The facts show that also in the context of the tobacco policy the rule applies: the higher the taxes, the more effective the policy. A ban on advertising, the use of counter-advertising and the enforcement of the smoking ban in publicly accessible premises are much less cost-effective.

These experiences seem to indicate that the supporters of cannabis regulation are right when they say that by raising taxes on the purchase of cannabis within a regulated distribution system, under certain conditions a double success can be scored: on the one hand there will be some room for education, on the other hand the taxes will generate revenues for the government. However, whether these two goals will actually be achieved, is another question. To what extent will cannabis users in highly commercialized distribution systems such as the cannabis shops in Colorado or, closer to home, Dutch coffeeshops be receptive to dissiduading messages? And as far as the government revenues are concerned, it has to be taken into account that high taxes will raise the

19 Room, 2008, p. 122–125.

purchase price of cannabis. So one of the main objectives of the regulation of cannabis, namely to oust the illicit production and distribution of cannabis from the market, is jeopardized.

In addition, it needs to be emphasized that, although raising taxes can sometimes be effective, this is certainly not the case when we are dealing with highly developed international markets such as the tobacco market and the alcohol market. In particular, this becomes clear when we look at the illicit trade in cigarettes, which not only encompasses cigarettes that are smuggled from a legal market with rather low tax rates to another legal market with much higher tax rates, but also cigarettes that are illegally produced and distributed in one and the same market. It is obvious that high taxes or tax increases can easily cause an activation and reinforcement of the illicit cigarette trade.

Dependent on the source, the illicit market for cigarettes in Belgium is estimated to account for 1 to 7 per cent of the total turnover.[20] The highest estimate is that of the producers. Probably they want to give a sign to the Belgian authorities that there are limits to the systematic raising of taxes on cigarettes. Internationally, sometimes even higher percentages are mentioned. In a recent working paper of the European Parliament, for example, the trade in illicit cigarettes is estimated to account for 11,1 per cent of the total cigarette market. However, it should be noted that in this and other reports of the European Parliament it is stated, on good grounds, that the large amounts of illicit cigarettes sold in the member states of the European Union, are not only due to smuggling organizations which take advantage of the price differences between legal packs of cigarettes or which, on a large scale, produce counterfeit cigarettes ("illegal whites"), but also to well-known global cigarette manufacturers such as Philip Morris, British American Tobacco and Japan Tobacco International. These and other producers are accused of deliberately encouraging this smuggling:

> Overproduction and oversupply of cigarettes to some countries exceeds the legitimate demand and fuels the black market.

In consequence of the smuggling, not only the European Union itself but also its member states miss a lot of tax revenues. To such an extent that the concerned enterprises have been pushed to conclude a deal with the European Union in which they promise a certain financial compensation for the tax losses. A compensation that, among other things, will be used to finance the struggle against the illicit cigarette trade. Up to 2029 a total amount of 1.7 billion euros has to be paid.[21]

20 *De Standaard*, 8 March 2014.

21 European Parliament, 2013, p. 7 and 9, and European Parliament, 2014, p. x.

Since cannabis is a drug which nowadays can be produced, rather easily, almost everywhere in the world and which is consumed all around the world, the foregoing also applies to a legalized cannabis market – though within certain limits: the production of cannabis will not be dominated by just a few international companies anytime soon. As in the case of tobacco, raising taxes on cannabis could unintentionally enhance the illicit production and the illicit trade. The fact that raising taxes on cannabis products is not a simple thing to do, makes this problem even more complicated than it already is in itself. On what should the taxation be focussed: on the strength of the drug (the amount of THC in it) or on the combination of psychoactive components?[22]

This kind of difficulties automatically raises the question: what, in general, is the best way to regulate cannabis? Caulkins et al. are discerning two main currents in the group of supporters of legalization and regulation:

> Public-health advocates of legalization see great potential for careful regulation to mitigate the harms of marijuana use, while libertarian advocates are suspicious of regulation generally.[23]

In Colorado, the second main current seems to have prevailed over the first one, because its regulated market is offering entrepreneurs pretty much room to set up their company. Not so in Uruguay, where the authorities worked out a much stricter regulation, which, among other things, includes a pricing method that is tailored to the prices at the illicit market.[24] As already described in Chapter 4, different models of regulation are at hand.

It is clear that a state monopoly has the advantage of ensuring a stronger hold on the distribution system. The same is true for the pricing method and the control of the access to the system. The stricter the regulation, the tighter the grip on the functioning of the system and the smaller the risk for abuse and violation of the rules of the game. The disadvantage is easy to guess: the revenues the system generates for the authorities are (much) smaller than in case the market can play its role to the full, for example by issuing an unlimited amount of licences for the production and distribution of cannabis. In the short term, this way of regulating might generate quite a lot of revenues.

The other side of the coin, however, is the danger that such a system completely derails and/or that the illicit market infiltrates in the regulated system. If that happens, supply and demand can evolve in a direction which no longer has anything to do with the original objectives. This is what occurred after

22 Caulkins, Hawken, Kilmer and Kleiman, 2012, p. 153–154.

23 *Ibid.*, p. 154.

24 See also the short article on this subject in *Knack*, 27 November 2013.

the legalization of medical cannabis in a number of American states and in Canada at the beginning of this century. Something similar also occurred in the Netherlands as a result of the policy of tolerance regarding coffeeshops. And at the same time the Canadian as well as the Dutch example demonstrates how difficult it is to get a system that has escalated under control again, especially when the effects of the escalation reach far beyond the country's borders.

The foregoing leads to the conclusion that in the context of the legalization of cannabis we indeed can learn something – as well in the positive as in the negative sense – from the regulation of alcohol and tobacco. It would be strange if we could not. It is in a way an obvious consequence of the convergence of the various control strategies for these substances in the member states of the European Union. Whereas the prohibition policy regarding cannabis, certainly at the level of the user, has been softened significantly, the regulation of alcohol, and especially tobacco, becomes stricter and stricter. The distinction between cannabis on the one hand and alcohol and tobacco on the other hand, is increasingly a legal distinction.

Finally, this brings us to the following question: based on the experiences with alcohol and tobacco, is it desirable or necessary to regulate cannabis? Or, to put it another way and more generally: is a regulation of alcohol and tobacco better for society than the ban on cannabis?

Public expenditures and social costs are important indicators for the impact of the use of substances on a society. Alcohol and tobacco consumption are more widespread than the use of illicit drugs. As already emphasized elsewhere, there is a link with the factor of availability. Regulated luxuries are available at the legal market. Maybe not for everybody in the same way and it is true that the distribution is often subjected to several restrictions, but nevertheless there is a leading principle: everybody who meets the conditions, has access to the available supply. In the case of illicit psychoactive substances the situation is completely different. People who want to use these, have to rely on the illicit market or the "tolerated market". Only a minority is willing to cross that threshold.

In Chapter 6 (see 6.4.) public expenditures research learns what the Belgian authorities, as a whole, spend on the problem of licit and illicit drugs. In this context it is relevant to underline that, as to the use of licit and illicit drugs, Belgium is an average European member state.[25] To answer the question formulated a few lines higher, it is, however, important to examine the ratio between the public expenditures associated with the problem of illicit drugs and the expenditures associated with the use of regulated substances: alcohol, tobacco and psychoactive medication.[26] This yields the following pie chart:

25 European Monitoring Centre on Drugs and Drugs Addiction, 2014, p. 33–52.

26 Vander Laenen et al., 2011.

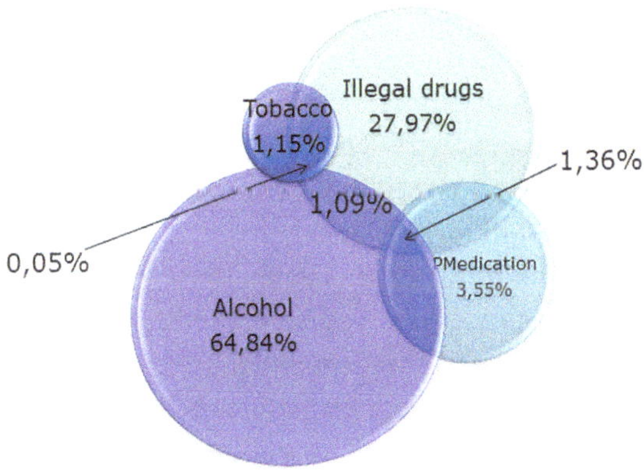

FIGURE 1 *Public Expenditures 2008, by Substance (Vander Laenen, De Ruyver, Christians and Lievens, 2011)*

The chart discloses a remarkable fact: the alcohol-related expenditures account for almost two thirds of all public expenditures, whereas the expenditures related to illicit drugs comprise less than one third.[27] By comparison, the expenditures to restrain the negative effects of tobacco and psychoactive medication are very limited. As to the expenditures related to the tobacco problem, we need to point out that the expenditures for the treatment of the health damage caused by tobacco use are not included in the public expenditures, because they are external expenditures. These expenditures, along with the private expenditures, are contained in the social costs of the use of tobacco.

The high expenditures related to the alcohol problem are due to the costs of hospital treatment of alcohol-dependent people.[28] No less than 57.41% of all expenditures for the policy regarding illicit drugs, alcohol and psychoactive medication goes to the treatment of alcohol dependency. That tells a lot about the extent of the alcohol problem in Belgium. So it is not surprising that at the previous pages we have repeatedly pointed to the increasing cannabis dependency, not only in the European Union but also in the United States. It is for sure that a greater availability of cannabis leads to a greater use, especially when such a use becomes more socially acceptable and no longer carries the stigma of illegality. And a greater use inevitably results in an increasing number of cannabis-dependent people. This, in turn, has repercussions for the amount of public expenditures that have to be used for the treatment of cannabis-related problems.

No recent figures are available about the extent of the social costs associated with the use of licit and illicit drugs in Belgium. At the moment, a scientific study is being carried out by the Belgian Science Policy Office, but the results

27 Vander Laenen, De Ruyver, Christiaens and Lievens, 2011.

28 Vander Laenen, De Ruyver, Christiaens and Lievens, 2011, p. 146.

of that study are not yet known.[29] In an earlier study about the social costs of alcohol use, a study executed by the Higher Institute of Labour Studies, these costs were estimated at almost 6 billion euros for the reference year 1999, which, adjusted for inflation, corresponds with 8.07 billion euros in 2014.[30] After subtraction of the gross revenues of 2.07 billion euros (mainly VAT and excise duties) the net social costs amount to 5.9 billion euros.[31] More recently, in 2013, in the design of a programme to tackle the alcohol problem, it was assumed that the social costs amount to 4.4 billion euros, 2.23 billion euros of which were attributed to more illness-related absences and more absenteeism in general, lower production, more labour accidents and higher unemployment.[32] This calculation is close to the amount of 4.2 billion euros recently mentioned by health economist Annemans.[33]

At the European level, in the year 2003 the total social costs of alcohol use were estimated at 125 billion euros.[34] In 2010 the total social costs of the alcohol consumption in the European region amounted to 155.8 billion euros.[35] According to P. Anderson and B. Baumberg, the social costs of tobacco use are comparable with the social costs of alcohol use.[36] The social costs of the use of illicit drugs, though, are significantly lower. If we rely on the calculation made by Single, who states that public expenditures represent 5% of the social costs, and if we know the proper ratios, we get an idea of the order of magnitude of the social costs of illicit drugs.[37]

Summarized, we can draw several conclusions from these facts and figures. The data about the public expenditures for, and the social costs of, alcohol demonstrate that the regulation of this legal luxury in terms of the cost to society is not at all a model for the regulation of cannabis and definitely not for the possible regulation of other illicit drugs. As some authors point out, from a legal viewpoint the regulation of alcohol, tobacco and psychoactive medication certainly can be a source of inspiration.[38] But the reality is, that we

29 This study is executed under the supervision of professors Vander Laenen, Pauwels, Annemans and Putman and will be completed in 2015.

30 Converted in euros.

31 Degreef, Pacolet and Bouten, 2003, p. 480–481.

32 Ministerie van Sociale Zaken, Algemene Cel Drugs, *Alcoholplan 2013* (internal document).

33 X, "Drankmisbruik kost maatschappij 4.2 miljard euro", *Knack*, 25 April 2013.

34 Anderson and Baumberg, 2006, p. 64.

35 Rehm and Shield, 2012, p. 72.

36 Anderson, 2006, p. 70.

37 Single, 2003, p. 43.

38 Decorte, 2014, p. 35–40.

have to deal with stimulants. The consumption of the concerned substances is rarely based on a rational choice. Which translates itself into prevalence figures that, for many years already, are downright alarming and therefore lead to higher public expenditures than the current public expenditures related to cannabis use.

As a consequence the call to tighten the regulation of these legal drugs is more powerful than ever, and the use of tobacco has even ended up in the sphere of criminalization. Health considerations prevail, but the affordability of health care and the growing accountability of the users also play an important role, as well as the consistency of the health care-related signals the authorities are sending out. It sounds trivial, but it is a real problem: how could we explain in a reasonable way that tobacco smoking is not allowed, whereas the smoking of cannabis is? We have to take into account that the legalization of cannabis will increase its availability and therefore will influence its use. This will also have consequences for the cost of health care and social security. Furthermore, there is only a small chance that after the legalization of cannabis the cost of law enforcement will go down. The result of all this will be that the social costs of cannabis use will increase.

As explained in the introduction of this book, in the paragraph about the concepts, and demonstrated in publications of the *Groupe Pompidou*, certainly in the European Union there is a growing convergence between the policy regarding legal drugs and the policy regarding illicit drugs.[39] This is a completely logical development when the choice is made for an integrated and integral approach and for a well-balanced policy directed at both demand and supply. And, also important in this context, this policy choice is widely supported at the level of the European Union.

6.4 The Legalization of Cannabis in the European Union: The American Way?

In the sketches of the drug policy in the European Union and the United States that we made in the previous chapters, it was made clear, explicitly and implicitly, that in the context of the regulation of cannabis, three different types of interests have to be weighted against each other: the economic interests of the authorities and the individuals, the interests of individual and collective health, and the interests of a fair and effective law enforcement. In view of the regulation of cannabis, the way these interests are weighted against each other

39 Muscat, 2008; Muscat, Van de Mheen, Barendregt et al., 2010; and Muscat and Pike, 2012.

is obviously a crucial question. In line with the outcome of this process, certain interests will prevail in the regulation and others won't.

In the previous paragraph we concluded that the way these interests were weighted against each other in the case of the regulation of alcohol and tobacco is not a good example for the way cannabis should or could be regulated. Inevitably the question arises: what then would or could be the right way to do it? To answer this question, we shall examine whether the way cannabis is at present regulated in two American states, deserves to be imitated by the member states of the European Union.

Of course, in this context we shall implicitly and explicitly make use of the analysis of the developments in both states as presented in Chapter 3. We will not focus on the legalization of cannabis in Uruguay. The reason is that for the moment it is not yet clear how the plans devised by the Uruguayan government will work out in practice.

6.4.1 *The Green Gold Rush*

For those who still have doubts: the legalization of cannabis in Colorado and Washington State is quickly becoming an economic success story. On 18 July, 2014 on the website of *The New York Times* an article was published under the following heading:

> Next gold rush: legal marijuana feeds entrepreneurs' dreams.[40]

The article describes how the young cannabis industry in Colorado, as a kind of magnet, is attracting fortune-hunters from all over the United States. Colorado already counts more than 200 shops selling marijuana for recreational use. In the first six months after the legalization, employment almost doubled, from 6,000 people with a licence to work in the marijuana business to 11,290 people. Besides this, a lot of suppliers are creating jobs in support of the cannabis business. Cannabis plantations are an essential part of the whole trade and so their number is rapidly increasing.[41] By the way, mainly new companies are trying their luck in this booming business. Established companies remain a little hesitant, also because at the federal level cannabis is still an illicit drug and the sector for that reason still bears a stigma. Nevertheless, it seems that in the concerned states the legal cannabis market – in terms of its turnover- and the number of people employed in it- will soon be comparable

40 J. Healy and K. Johnson, "Next gold rush: legal marijuana feeds entrepreneurs' dreams", *The New York Times*, 18 July 2014.

41 K. De Ruyter, "Marihuana wordt big business in vs", *De Standaard*, 5 August 2014.

with the illicit cannabis market. At this moment, the entire legal cannabis sector in the United States is estimated to account for around 2.6 billion dollars. By the year 2018 this amount could rise to 10 billion dollars.[42]

As remarked earlier, the flourishing of the cannabis market is not confined within the borders of the concerned states. Because of the possibilities created for non-residents to buy limited amounts of cannabis in Colorado, the drug tourism, from at least nearby states, flourishes as well. It is not yet clear how much of the cannabis for recreational use, which is sold in Colorado, is destined for neighbouring or other states. But without any doubt large quantities are involved. After the industry was set up in Colorado, The Marijuana Policy Group, on behalf of the Department of Revenue of Colorado (which is responsible for both the regulation of cannabis for recreational use and the regulation of alcohol, tobacco and medical cannabis), has published a report about the situation. In that report, the investigators have estimated the demand from outside the state at about 10 tons.[43] Note that this only refers to the demand for licensed cannabis for recreational or medical use, not to the demand for illicit cannabis. The total turnover in Colorado is estimated at 121.4 tons.

According to other sources the part of the demand from outside the state is higher and comprises about half of all cannabis sold in the state.[44] So, the cannabis business is thriving in Colorado. And it seems that it will also thrive in Washington State, where the sale of cannabis for recreational use has started on July 8, 2014. Up to now, 25 retailers there have been granted a licence. The licence applications of 300 other retailers are pending.[45]

We also have to bear in mind that the legal sale of cannabis in Colorado and Washington State is not limited to rather small amounts of uncut cannabis. At the moment, cannabis is already offered for sale in a wide range of forms. We mentioned earlier that cannabis cannot be used as an ingredient in all sorts of food or drink. But any ambiguity is not far away. On the one hand, to protect the youth, it is not permitted to put cannabis in sweets or lollies. On the other hand cannabis may be added to cookies, brownies and other sorts of pastry.[46] As if children do not feel attracted to cookies and are able to make the right distinction between the mentioned products.

42 E. Zimmerman, "Starts-ups seize marijuana opportunities as big companies hold back", *The New York Times*, 6 August 2014.

43 Light, Orens, Lewandowski and Pickton, 2014, p. 1.

44 K. De Ruyter, "Marihuana wordt big business in VS", *De Standaard*, 5 August 2014.

45 Reuters, "Marijuana cookies to hit Washington shops but cannabis lollies are banned", *The Guardian*, 18 July 2014.

46 *Ibid.*

The large assortment of marijuana products demonstrates that the rules of marketing dominate the cannabis industry. This means that the producers and the sellers of cannabis are doing their utmost to put their products as much as possible in the market. And, in addition, it means that these producers and sellers will not just try to meet the existing demand, but will also make great efforts to increase the demand and, as a consequence, their earnings.

So it is not really surprising that Caulkins, who presented himself in the past as supporter of legalization, a few months ago talked about a "dangerous corporate takeover of the legal marijuana market" in Colorado and Washington State.[47] Instead of cautiously following a third way in the legalization of cannabis, these states have gone from one extreme to the other:

> Colorado and Washington have chosen to swing from close to one end of the spectrum (prohibition except for a quite permissive medical system) to close to the other end (for-profit enterprise subject to standard regulations plus some regulations particular to marijuana). They have skipped over several viable intermediate alternatives.

6.4.2 *The One-sidedness of the Economic Approach*

In this context it is appropriate to remind the reader that in the United States, in particular economists have often defended the legalization of cannabis. Not everyone of them had the same narrow view on the matter, but in general the economic approach of legalization often comes down to the expectation or conviction that savings realized this way in the area of law enforcement can be transferred to prevention and care.[48] However, the economists never succeeded in convincing the general public and each other. M. Thornton puts it as follows:

> The set of policy judgments (of economists) do not present a clear and unified perspective that the general public can understand, trust and willingly accept.[49]

But this did not prevent authoritative economists to get a grip on the legalization debate. Already in the early nineties some in their midst were pleading for

---

47 J. Caulkins, "How to avoid a likely and dangerous corporate takeover of the legal marijuana market", *The Washington Monthly*, March-April-May 2014.

48 Thornton, 2004, p. 82.

49 *Ibid.*, p. 100.

a solution akin to what nowadays is practiced in the states of Colorado and Washington, although it was even more drastic. P. Benjamin and R. Miller, for instance, at that time proposed the following:

> Our proposal – the Constitutional Alternative – is that the power to control the manufacture, distribution and consumption of all psychoactives revert to the states, under provisions identical to those of the Twenty-first Amendment.[50]

Also in Europe leading economists support the idea of ignoring, if needed, the treaties of the United Nations and proceeding to legalization.[51] And also these economists mainly use economic arguments. Of course it is not illogical that they fall back on theories they are acquainted with. In the case of the drugs phenomenon, however, this results in a downright one-sided approach. Mastering a complex and multifaceted problem requires a holistic approach which integrates all, or anyway most, of the dimensions of the drugs phenomenon. Economic interests have to be taken into account, but not at the expense of public health and – not to forget – law enforcement.

The global illicit drugs economy is dominated by criminal organizations which have immense financial resources at their disposal. It is not possible to expel these organizations from a market by simply legalizing it. The global nature of the drugs phenomenon asks for an international approach which is global too. So we have to tackle this phenomenon at a geographic scale that at least spans a continent, and preferably the whole world. And to be successful at that scale, one has to take into account the political opinions and relations which are circulating at that level. When the former British ambassador to Afghanistan, Sir W. Patey, suggests to bring the opium trade under state control,[52] or when a Moroccan political party wants to legalize the cannabis production in the Rif area,[53] such proposals only have a chance if they enjoy enough international support.

It is really not possible to explain the quantitative and qualitative aspects of the cannabis problem exclusively by means of economic analyses and

---

50 Benjamin and Miller, 1991, p. 194.

51 Collins, 2014, p. 84.

52 E. MacAskill, "Former UK ambassador to Afghanistan calls for legalization of drugs", *The Guardian*, 25.6.2014.

53 P. Schemm, "Moroccan party holds hearings for legalising cannabis", *Business Day Live*, 4.12.2013.

models.[54] Or, as M. Cleveland – an opponent of drug prohibition – remarked in 1998:

> Legalization in any of its many possible variations cannot solve family and social problems either, any more than repeal of alcohol prohibition solved the problems leading some individuals to become alcoholics.[55]

This is an important issue because it establishes the link with the fact that today cannabis is the world's most popular illicit drug. The figures speak for themselves. For various reasons, the ban on cannabis has not prevented cannabis consumption to assume such big proportions. Moreover, the supporters of legalization and regulation do not hesitate to stress that prohibition has made cannabis a lucrative business for organized crime.

Yet there is much reason to doubt whether the fervent supporters of legalization and regulation will succeed in realizing what the prohibition movement, and certainly the "war on drugs" strategy, has failed to accomplish: a worldwide reduction of the use of drugs, including the use of cannabis. This for the simple reason at least in the United States, reducing cannabis use is not a priority for the authorities that have legalized this drug.

6.4.3 *The Main Objectives of Legalization*

This is clearly demonstrated by the analysis Caulkins, Kilmer, MacCoun, Pacula and Reuter – all of them for years already defenders of a drastic reversal of the drug policy – have made in 2011. They listed the reasons why authorities in the United States want to create a legal cannabis market.[56] It is appropriate to mention that their inventory of reasons is completely in line with the descriptions in Chapter 3 of the way the legalization has been put into practice some time later in Colorado and Washington State.

In the first place legalization is a means to increase tax revenues. The authors frankly state that this was the main motive behind the failed attempt in 2010 to legalize the cannabis market in the impoverished state of California through *Proposition 19*. The attempt narrowly failed because the growers of medical marijuana turned against the proposal because of fear to lose their privileged market position.[57] In 2012 the same happened in the state of Oregon. The narrow defeat in the vote was the result of the commotion caused by the composition of the Oregon Cannabis Commission, the body that would be responsible for

54 Van Laar, Cruts, Van Ooyen-Houben et al., 2013, p. 73–167.

55 Cleveland, 1998, p. 573.

56 Caulkins, Kilmer, MacCoun, Pacula and Reuter, 2011, p. 866.

57 Crick, Haase and Bewley-Taylor, 2013, p. 5.

the delivery of licences. Growers and sellers would constitute the majority of the board of directors of that commission. This provoked a lot of protest. Furthermore, an important sponsor of the project, a big entrepreneur in medical marijuana running hospitals in several states, has put himself in a difficult position by pleading guilty for tax evasion.[58]

This, by the way, is a constant in the breakthroughs the legalization movement has been able to accomplish the past years. In part the activists had the necessary funds at their disposal thanks to the support of spirited philanthropists such as G. Soros as well as financiers mainly geared to a high return on investment. In this context it is also relevant that the entwinement between the former lobbyists and the new cannabis industry is sometimes very close. Until the successful vote for legalization of cannabis in Colorado in November 2012, the director of communications of the aforementioned Marijuana Policy Group in Colorado was a recruiter of votes. After the vote he has started to capitalize on his lobbying work.[59] These are not just minor facts. They reveal what it is really all about: financial gain for entrepreneurs and additional revenues for the authorities. In this respect there is not much difference between licensed entrepreneurs in the medical and recreational cannabis business in the United States and Dutch coffeeshop owners who have the necessary means to carry on a legal battle against local and national authorities.

The second reason why some authorities decide to legalize the cannabis market is their wish to reduce the number of arrests for the possession of small amounts of cannabis and all the negative consequences related to it. Certainly in the United States, though not so in many member states of the European Union, this is a valid reason.[60] In its plea to legalize cannabis *The New York Times* argues that the social costs of cannabis prohibition are enormous:

> There were 658,000 arrests for marijuana possession in 2012, according to F.B.I. figures, compared with 256,000 for cocaine, heroin and their derivatives. Even worse, the result is racist, falling disproportionately on young black men, ruining their lives and creating new generations of career criminals.[61]

In these circumstances the legalization of cannabis is of course an effective way to reduce the number of arrests for the possession of cannabis and to considerably unburden the criminal justice chain. This frees up space for higher priorities.

---

58 *Ibid.*, p. 5.

59 R. Caroll, "Big cannabis: will legal weed grow to be America's next corporate titan?", *The Guardian*, 3.1.2014.

60 Ballota, Bergeron and Hughes, 2008, p. 99–117.

61 The Editorial Board, 2014, "Repeal Prohibition, again", *The New York Times*, 27.7.2014.

The third reason why authorities in the United States sometimes opt to legalize cannabis is the struggle against the criminal organizations that are controlling the black market. Once again, and certainly in the case of the United States, this is an understandable reason. It is known that "whitening" such a market through legalization is an approved method to withdraw at least a part of that market from the influence of the concerned organizations. This method was not only applied at the federal level at the occasion of the abolition of alcohol Prohibition in 1933, but also in the past decades at the level of states in the context of the establishment of a legal gambling market with casinos and lotteries.

Of course, also in this case the question arises whether in Colorado and Washington State the intended objective will actually be attained. As indicated in the description of the developments in both states, a lucrative black market such as the cannabis market does not disappear like snow before the sun, once it is legalized. This is confirmed by the first reports. No wonder, because for cannabis users who have no access to the legalized distribution system, such as all users under 21 years of age in Colorado and Washington State, the illicit market remains the only place where they can get what they want. It is obvious that criminal organizations are aware of this and will take maximum advantage of it. A small comparison with the Netherlands is appropriate in this context: since many years illicit points of sale are an important distribution channel and have always ensured people under 18 years of age, who cannot buy cannabis in coffeeshops, easy access the drug.

Needless to say, the concerned authorities know this too. It explains why a part of the new revenues is legally reserved to finance the enforcement of the new regulation. Within that regulation, ways and means have been created for a thorough screening of the criminal and financial past of licence applicants. And of course we should not forget that the federal police services are also still there and are entitled to take action against criminal organizations on the territory of states.

Nevertheless, the question remains how all these provisions will work out in practice. It is meaningful that a number of governors – including members of the Democratic Party – prefer to take a wait-and-see attitude towards the actual impact of the legalization in Colorado and Washington State before possibly passing on to legalization in their own states. Even the governor of California has taken this stand: "I think we ought to kind of watch and see how things go in Colorado."[62]

62 A. Nagourney, "Despite support in party, democratic governors resist legalizing marijuana", *The New York Times*, 5.4.2014.

Furthermore there are of course a number of derived secondary objectives such as a better monitoring of the quality of cannabis and cannabis products and an improvement of the possibilities to deny young people access to the cannabis market. Whether all of these secondary objectives are really attainable remains to be seen. In any case, as Caulkins et al. say, some objectives are more attainable than others, depending on the chosen model of regulation.[63] This nuance, although correct in itself, at the same time demonstrates the weakness of the legalization concept. This concept is a flag that covers many cargoes. In order to be able to evaluate the legalization of cannabis, we have to examine on a case by case basis, the way the concept has actually been defined. Otherwise we do not know what we are talking about and soon get caught in a hopeless discussion.

6.4.4 *The Real Consequences of Legalization*

Almost all drug experts who, over the past years, have repeatedly supported a general legalization of cannabis, have warned against high expectations, irrespective of the chosen legalization model:

> The nature of the legalization debate can be summarized in one word: ignorance. Therefore, the most important choice of legalization is the flexibility to adjustment, allowing for learning by doing.[64]

Essential parts of the cannabis policy, from the production up to and including the consumption of the drug, are affected by uncertainty. How, for instance, will (potential) cannabis users react? Will the intensity and the frequency of cannabis use among current users remain the same? And what are the possible health effects related to it?[65] Because of this reason Caulkins et al. in 2011 joined the call for a regular evaluation and, if needed, an adjustment of the legalization model:

> No modern affluent nation has ever legalized commercial production and distribution, so the chance that a proposed regulatory system picks the ideal approach from the outset is very small. There will probably be surprises, large and small, and it would only be through a process of trial and error and incremental adjustment that jurisdictions could determine the best way to regulate this new industry.[66]

63 Caulkins, Kilmer, MacCoun, Pacula and Reuter, 2011, p. 866.
64 Van Ours, 2012, p. 873.
65 Hall and Degenhardt, 2009, p. 1383–1391.
66 Caulkins, Kilmer, MacCoun, Pacula and Reuter, 2011, p. 869.

The uncertainty regarding the ideal legalization model automatically implies that the legalization which is now occurring in the United States (and elsewhere) is based on a number of assumptions.

In the first place it is assumed that thanks to the legalization and regulation the current prices at the different levels of the illicit supply chain will drastically decrease.[67] This obviously has to do with the proceeds and profit margins at the illicit market. Empirical studies demonstrate these are very huge.[68] Though this is not the place to focus on the price setting at the different levels of the illicit supply chain (production, wholesale trade, retail trade), it is demonstrated that the actual cost price, at each level, is much lower than the prices charged on the black market. The calculations have been made.[69] In particular the production costs are much lower, as shown by a number of simulation exercises.[70] Before cannabis was legalized in Colorado and Washington State, supporters of legalization had made estimates of future employment in the legalized cannabis production.[71] It was thought that 16,000 jobs, spread over 8,000 production sites, would suffice to meet the entire demand for cannabis in the United States. However, the distribution would become the main economic engine. Thanks to product diversification and good marketing it was expected to create big economic opportunities. It seems that Colorado is well on its way to fulfil these expectations. A distribution that is a booming business implies a corresponding increase in demand.

Which brings us to the second assumption the supporters of legalization have made: legalization will advance the use of cannabis. Empirical research shows that this, indeed, is true:

> A decriminalization policy leads to greater smoking participation. It indicates that on average, living in a decriminalized state significantly increases the probability of smoking marijuana by 12.6%.[72]

---

67 Caulkins, Hawken, Kilmer and Kleiman, 2012, p. 31–41, and Caulkins, Kilmer, MacCoun, Pacula and Reuter, 2011, p. 867.

68 Vanhove, Van Damme, Surmont, Van Puyenbroeck and De Ruyver, 2012, p. 89–101, and Vanhove, 2014, p. 101–125.

69 Caulkins, Kilmer, MacCoun, Pacula and Reuter, 2011, p. 867, and Kilmer and Burgdorf, 2013, p. 390–391.

70 Bryan, DelBono and Pudney, 2012, p. 54–56, and Caulkins, Hawken, Kilmer and Kleiman, 2012, p. 160–164.

71 Caulkins, Kilmer, MacCoun, Pacula and Reuter, 2011, p. 867.

72 Damrongplasit, Hsiao and Zhao, 2009, p. 355.

Earlier research in Australia led to the same conclusion.[73] Most authors – supporters of legalization as well as more neutral economists and drug experts – foresee an increase in the use of cannabis.[74] This prediction is clearly at odds with the positive effects of legalization the supporters of legalization like to bring to our attention. According to the researchers the expected increase in the use of cannabis will manifest itself among various categories of cannabis users. It is the result of a combination of price-related and not price-related effects.

As to the first-mentioned effects, an increase of new users under 18 years of age and regular users is expected. And since more people will start using cannabis at a young age, the length of time of the use will extend.[75] Bretteville-Jensen discerns a double effect: one on the extent of the drug use and another on the number of drug users. These effects of a fall in prices are easy to understand.

However, other effects such as the impact of publicity for cannabis products, or the decrease in social disapproval and stigmatisation that up to now are linked with the use of cannabis, are not at all price-related. These effects amount to the removal of the threshold that deters potential users from buying cannabis at the illicit market. Other factors could play a part too, such as the fact that after legalization cannabis can be purchased in safe surroundings where the quality of the product is assured.[76] But nobody dares to estimate the impact of the use of cannabis on both the price-related and not price-related effects. In the recent past there have been attempts to estimate the impact, but the concerned authors used broad margins.[77]

In this context it should not be forgotten that in the United States medical cannabis is in many states very easily available. A recommendation, delivered by a doctor on request of the patient, suffices. No medical investigation is needed. This has even given rise to a practice of, so to say, prescriptions on command, comparable with the way in which in the middle of the 1980s every week a few thousand French heroin addicts came to Brussels to get methadone prescriptions from some cooperative doctors; prescriptions that in many cases were afterwards converted into cash at the French drug markets. In 2012,

73 Williams, 2004, p. 123–137.

74 Caulkins, Kilmer, MacCoun, Pacula and Reuter, 2011, p. 867–868; Caulkins, Hawken, Kilmer and Kleiman, 2012, p. 172–175; Van Ours, 2012, p. 872–873; Pacula, 2010, p. 17–19; MacCoun and Reuter, 2001, p. 356–366, and Bretteville-Jensen, 2006, p. 562.

75 Pacula, 2010, p. 17, and Caulkins, Kilmer, MacCoun, Pacula and Reuter, 2011, p. 867–868.

76 Surmont, 2007, p. 73–74.

77 MacCoun, 2010; Pacula, 2010, p. 1–22; Bretteville-Jensen, 2006, p. 562, and Caulkins, Hawken-Kilmer and Kleiman, 2012, p. 172–175.

Caulkins et al. described the following striking practices in states such as Colorado that have a loose regulation:

> The medical-marijuana-recommendation business starts with permission to use marijuana as its goal. The physicians who write most of the recommendations openly advertise, promising not to diagnose and treat illness but simply to provide a recommendation. Some even advertise that the visit is free unless it results in a recommendation. Others have advertisements, or even storefronts, that list a range of conditions for which they will write marijuana recommendations. It's hard to take this seriously as the practice of medicine.[78]

One may wonder whether such a state of affairs can still stand the test of medical ethics. But apart from that, the large-scale use of medical cannabis in the United States has acted as a lubricant for the introduction of recreational cannabis. In this connection M. Kleiman remarks the following:

> The big advantages to consumers of the taxed and regulated market compared with the medical market are testing and labelling, most of the (other) advantages are already there. The other advantage is that you don't have to be a liar. You don't have to go to some doctor and say you're anxious or something.[79]

The quotation applies to the United States. In the European Union the provision of medical cannabis occurs in a completely different, much more stringent way. Anyhow, the past years the legal sale and use of cannabis in the United States have spread so wide that one of the pioneers of the American legalization movement, E. Nadelman, speaks of the "Marlboroization of marijuana".[80]

6.4.5 *The Neglect of Public Health*

For years already, the cannabis policy in the United States is in a spiral of proceeding commercialization. Authorities that love to bite in the carrot the supporters of legalization are dangling in front of them – the prospect of high revenues thanks to the taxes that can be raised on the various parts of the industry – are objective allies of the cannabis industry. It is really no coincidence

78 Caulkins, Hawken, Kilmer and Kleiman, 2012, p. 104.

79 Kleiman, in Crick, Haase and Bewley-Taylor, 2013, p. 9.

80 Nadelman, in Lenton, 2014, p. 354.

that in an impoverished state such as California the supporters of legalization in 2010 almost won the majority of the vote.[81]

But commercial considerations do not only prevail in the legal market for recreational cannabis. They dominate all three of the existing cannabis markets: apart from this legal market the illicit market of course and, as we just have seen, the medical cannabis market as well. Everything is put at the service of a growing turnover. For the legalized markets the consequences are twofold. On the one hand, the situation leads to a considerable tension between a stringent regulation of the market and the commercial space in which the industry wants to operate freely. This conflict is easy to understand when one realizes that Colorado in the short term expects *to collect* 60 million dollars tax money from the legalized market for recreational cannabis, an amount that supposedly will have doubled after 2017.[82] Room, in this connection, makes the following comparison with the alcohol market:

> The Colorado and Washington cannabis control systems are more stringent than the much looser alcohol control systems of today, which often serve private interests more than public health.[83]

On the other hand, if it turns out to be impossible to raise a barrier against the commercialization, soon a second consequence will manifest itself: the use of cannabis, as well as the health risks and health problems related to it, will increase. But, as Reuter remarks, the supporters of legalization do not bother about this:

> Public health is not prominent on the list of factors discussed by the legalization advocates. Oddly enough, the findings linking marijuana and psychosis that emerge around 2005, have not generated much lasting concern.[84]

A number of drug experts, not unwilling to support legalization, were very well aware of the risk the health policy would be subordinated to financial interests. Therefore they recommended, well before the beginning of the legalization process in Colorado, to clearly define the commercial playing field.[85]

81 Crick, Haase and Bewley-Taylor, 2013, p. 4–8.
82 *Ibid.*, p. 9.
83 Room, 2014, p. 347.
84 Reuter, 2014, p. 353.
85 Caulkins, Kilmer, MacCoun, Pacula and Reuter, 2011, p. 868–870.

In the first place they emphasized the huge importance of the tax rates. Generally speaking, these rates have to be high enough in order not to stimulate the use of cannabis too much, but at the same time not too high in order to ensure the regulated market remains competitive against the illicit cannabis market and, in the United States, also against the market for medical cannabis. High tax rates for recreational cannabis undermine this competitiveness.[86] Moreover the levels of tax raising need to be in line with the different profit margins at the various levels of the supply chain.[87] That is why Caulkins et al. propose to attune the tax level to the level of cannabinoids (THC, CBD).[88] This way, financial thresholds are built-in which, in all their relativity, correspond with the health risks. The same should happen with the substances and products that are used in the cultivation of cannabis.

In the second place there are still other possibilities to restrict the commercial playing field. To a certain extent, for example, home growth is an alternative for the profit maximization the commercial market is aiming for. Also restrictions on advertising for recreational cannabis products are an option to try to reach this goal. Hence the restrictive advertising provisions that are in force in Colorado and Washington State. However, these restrictive provisions may not go too far. In similar cases the Supreme Court has often given priority to the freedom of economic activity, including advertising, over the protection of public health.[89]

But even if these and other measures are taken at a certain scale and have a certain impact, it remains to be seen whether the recreational cannabis market can really compete with the two other markets. This, anyhow, is the opinion of Kleiman, who in the state of Washington assists the Liquor Control Board in the implementation of the legislation concerning the production, distribution and consumption of cannabis:

> It's not clear that the commercial market can compete with the medical marijuana market and the illicit market.[90]

Not much imagination is needed to predict what will be considered in case it turns out that the struggle cannot be won by using the existing marketing tools. Entrepreneurs, evidently focussed on profit maximization, will revert to classical strategies such as product diversification and more points of sale in

86 Kleiman, in Crick, Haase and Bewley-Taylor, 2013, p. 9.
87 Caulkins, Hawken, Kilmer and Kleiman, 2012, p. 164–172.
88 Caulkins, Kilmer, MacCoun, Pacula and Reuter, 2011, p. 868.
89 Room, 2014, p. 348.
90 Kleiman, in Crick, Haase and Bewley-Taylor, 2013, p. 9.

order to expand their market share. To keep the selling price low enough, they will push the authorities to decrease the taxes, and for the rest they will hope for a lenient level of law enforcement, like it is the case with regulated alcohol and tobacco.

By the time entrepreneurs resort to these methods, public health will have completely disappeared from the agenda.[91] The policy of the United States will then be diametrically opposed to the policy pursued by the United Nations and the European Union, which is aimed at avoiding the harmful physical and mental effects related to the use of drugs. At that moment, the United States will have gone from one extreme to the other:

> In current US thinking, there seems to be a tendency to a Manichean split between prohibition and the free market in the handling of problematic commodities: either it should be forbidden, or any effort to "grow the market" must be allowed.[92]

The consequences of this reversal, in terms of public spending and social costs, will certainly manifest themselves by then. A. Uchtenhagen gives a clear indication in this context:

> It is surprising how little attention is given to this aspect. The intended taxation does not consider the scope of administration and control resources needed or the increased demand in the education and health sectors.[93]

In Chapter 3 we reported that, with regard to the legalization of cannabis, Uruguay has chosen for an entirely different model than the much discussed model of the American states. The Uruguayan model is plainly not aimed at securing commercial interests, but more than in the United States, aimed at the public health interests. It is in any case important to keep an eye on how this model will be applied in practice, due to the fact that the philosophy behind it, as well as the way the model is worked out, closely resemble the Norwegian model regarding alcohol:

> In the alcohol field, the Norwegian state-owned wine monopoly, with no private commercial interests, no advertising, regulated opening hours and high prices, is an interesting model.[94]

---

91 Room, 2014, p. 346–347.

92 *Ibid.*, p. 348.

93 Uchtenhagen, 2014, p. 357.

94 Pedersen, 2014, p. 352.

There are indeed arguments in favour of this policy. A recent international large-scale study demonstrates that a greater availability of alcohol increases the risk that people start drinking heavily.[95] Therefore some drug experts rightly regret that, in the course of the design of legalization models for cannabis, too little attention has been paid to the rich experience gained from the production and distribution of licit drugs, alcohol and tobacco.[96]

6.4.6 *The Harmfulness of Cannabis Use*

One can ask oneself whether it is really so bad that the way the legalization of cannabis is put in practice in the United States threatens to undermine public health over there. In essence, the answer to that question is rather simple. Such a development neglects the social costs associated with irresponsible drug use and, moreover, stands in glaring contrast to the drug policy of the United Nations and the European Union, which aims to keep social costs as low as possible.

However, it is not surprising that the concerning development takes place in the United States. In this state supporters of legalization usually avoid discussions about the impact of legalization on the health of cannabis users. MacCoun in any case perceives the following constant in the American legalization debate:

> Those who are in favour of legalization tend to ignore the negative health effects of cannabis use. Those who are against legalization, ignore the fact that legal substances such as alcohol and tobacco also have bad health effects.[97]

The latter, by the way, explains why it is better not to use the regulation of legal substances such as alcohol and tobacco as a source of inspiration in the context of the legalization of cannabis. Why would we deliberately lift the social costs related to cannabis use to the level of the social costs of alcohol and tobacco use?

Up to now, scientifically it is not yet possible to accurately determine the extent of the negative consequences of cannabis use for the physical and mental health of the user.[98] Furthermore, it is not easy to find out whether certain physical and/or mental health problems are caused by cannabis use or

---

95 Casswell, 2014, p. 1425–1431.

96 Room, 2014, p. 347; Uchtenhagen, 2014, p. 357, and Reuter, 2014, p. 354.

97 MacCoun, 2012, p. 872.

98 Caulkins, Hawken, Kilmer and Kleiman, 2012, p. 54–81.

"simply" appear – for whatever reason and without any causal relation – in combination with the use of cannabis. However, it is widely or even generally agreed upon that the harmfulness of cannabis – from bronchial damage to addiction and psychoses – particularly manifests itself when this drug is used by very young people and in case of intensive, almost daily use over a longer period of time.[99]

This finding explains why, especially with respect to young people, the greater availability of cannabis due to legalization is such a controversial issue in the debate about this policy topic. The greater the availability – also as a result of efforts to keep the price low enough to hamper the illicit trade –, the greater the risk the mentioned factors will have an effect, primarily among young people.[100] Recently, a journalist of *The New York Times* remarked in an article that fits in the newspaper's campaign in favour of federal legalization of cannabis, that although cannabis in several respects is less dangerous than alcohol and tobacco, it is nevertheless clear:

> that marijuana is now far too easy for minors to obtain, which remains a significant problem. The brain undergoes active development until about age 21, and there is evidence that young people are more vulnerable to the adverse effects of marijuana.[101]

It is not explicated on which studies the allegations of this journalist are based. But without any doubt his opinion is shared by well-known researchers. In 2009, N. Hall and L. Degenhardt, for instance, wrote the following:

> Regular cannabis use in adolescence might also affect mental health in young adults, with the strongest evidence for an increased risk of psychotic symptoms and disorders.[102]

Lately, in a profound literature review, N. Volkow and her colleagues have expressed themselves in a similar way about this problem:

---

99 Van den Brink, 2006, p. 83, and Room, Fischer, Hall, Lenton and Reuter, 2008, p. 56–57.

100 See Volkow, Baler, Compton and Weiss, 2014; Van Ours and Williams, 2007, p. 593–594, and Van Ours, 2012, p. 872.

101 Ph. Boffey, "What science says about marijuana", *The New York Times*, 30.7.2014. In this connection, see also S. Boseley, "Cannabis more damaging to under-18 s, study suggests", *The Guardian*, 27.8.2014.

102 Hall and Degenhardt, 2009, p. 1389.

> Repeated marijuana use during adolescence may result in long-lasting changes in brain function that can jeopardize educational, professional and social achievements.[103]

For reasons like these, it is very important to ponder about the best ways to realize a balanced regulation of cannabis. In particular one should think about the ways – such as targeted education, timely assistance and the struggle against the illicit supply – by which we can avoid that adolescents – who usually have no access to the regulated market till they are 18 or 21 years of age and thus are a very attractive target group for black marketeers – start using cannabis at a very young age. In this context it is appropriate to refer to the figures presented in Chapter 4, about the gravity of the cannabis problem in the European Union. The research data show that relatively large numbers of young people in Europe – in some countries more than in others – starting from age 15 incidentally or regularly use cannabis. Also in view of the extent of the problem, there is plenty of reason to resolutely undertake a struggle against cannabis use by young people.

But apart from this important specific problem it will be clear that if in the process of regulation the emphasis is placed on the realization of commercial objectives, as happened in Colorado, an entirely different situation will arise than in the case a much more directive system such as in Uruguay is installed. In our opinion it is obvious that if one wants to limit, for reasons of public health, the availability of cannabis, it is wise to withdraw this problematic consumption product as much as possible from the free play of market forces. Previously, MacCoun and Reuter had come to a similar conclusion when they were looking for an explanation for the big increase in cannabis use in the Netherlands in the period 1984–1996. In their opinion the increase was mainly the result of the extensive commercialization of the cannabis market through the explosively growing number of coffeeshops in that period. To be honest, we have to add that the named authors softened this explanation by remarking that in the first years of that period the use of cannabis also strongly increased in countries without any coffeeshops, such as Canada and the United Kingdom – but anyhow.[104]

The extent to which cannabis is a problematic substance can in particular be deduced from the help cannabis users are asking for. In the European Union member states, for example Belgium, cannabis users nowadays are prominently present in the drug treatment system. Once the situation was

103 Volkow, Baler, Compton and Weiss, 2014, p. 2225.

104 Van den Brink, 2008, p. 124.

different: until well into the nineties problematic cannabis use and everything associated with it – dependence, mental and physical damage – were rather exceptional. That is why in the Netherlands already very early, in 1976, and later also in Belgium, cannabis was assigned a special status in the drug policy and the drug legislation. But only in the middle of the past decade, the first reports arrived about the increasing number of cannabis-related calls for help in the drug care system. If this development had manifested itself for example five years earlier, maybe the Belgian policy makers would have decided otherwise.

In the case of Belgium and the Netherlands the increase in the number of cannabis users in the drug treatment system is sometimes attributed to the high THC level of "nederwiet" – the Dutch variety of marijuana. According to T. Decorte, the high THC level is the result of the repressive policy in both countries, which by encouraging home cultivation has led to the rising strength of cannabis.[105] However, this explanation is very doubtful. To begin with, W. Van den Brink points out that the rise of the number of cannabis-dependent people is closely connected with the rise of the THC level:

> This increase had been attributed to increasing tetrahydrocannabinol (THC) concentrations in many countries, prohibitionist (USA) and liberal (the Netherlands), but the specific increase in deprived groups seems to point to sociocultural factors as the main cause.[106]

However, this observation does not tell anything about the cause(s) of the increase of the THC level at the end of the 1990's and the beginning of the 2000's. Actually, the increase was the result of the market strategy of the criminal organizations which at that time to a large extent had got hold of the Dutch cannabis sector – from producer to coffeeshop and illicit point of sale. By producing cannabis with a high THC concentration they created a means to bind regular cannabis users in a durable manner to them.[107]

The Trimbos Institute's latest annual measurement (2014) of the THC concentrations in the cannabis varieties offered for sale in coffeeshops indirectly confirms this thesis.[108] A review of the results of the past 15 years shows that up to 2004 the average THC level in "nederwiet" increased (<20%). But since

105 Decorte, 2014, p. 15.

106 Van den Brink, 2008, p. 123.

107 Van de Bunt, 2006, p. 17; Bovenkerk, 2003, p. 143, and Snippe, Bieleman, Naayer and Ogier, 2004, p. 57–65.

108 Rigter and Niesink, 2014, p. 30–33.

then it has gradually decreased, and since 2013 it has fallen below 15%. This was no coincidence: a short time before, the Dutch authorities had announced that coffeeshops no longer were allowed to sell cannabis with a THC level above 15%.

However, the anonymous sampling by the Trimbos Institute reveals big differences. The average THC concentration in the most popular cannabis variety rose from 13.5% in 2013 to 14.6% in 2014. In the most potent variety the concentration remained more or less the same (15.6% in 2013; 15.3% in 2014). Though we have to add that in the context of the study also "nederwiet" with a THC level of 26.1% was detected. In 2014, the average THC level of the so-called "nederhasj" amounted to 20.4%. In imported hashish the average THC level was 14.9%, in imported marijuana approximately 5%. It is also interesting that according to the report the coffeeshops mainly sell "nederwiet" and imported hashish, and that in many coffeeshops no "nederhasj" or imported marijuana is available.[109]

Van den Brink's previously mentioned finding about the link between cannabis addiction and the THC level is supported by data of the European Monitoring Centre on Drugs and Drug Addiction. The reports of 2013 and 2014 contain data with regard to the cannabis users that signed up for treatment in the period 2006–2012. These data demonstrate that the growing presence of problematic cannabis users in the drug care system is a European reality, although the percentages differ strongly (2% in Bulgaria, 66% in Hungary).[110] The figures in relation to Belgium are in line with the European findings. In April 2014 the Vlaamse Vereniging van Behandelingscentra Verslaafdenzorg (Flemish Association of Addiction Treatment Centres) published a review of the registration data for the period 2011–2012.[111] Within the group of people starting therapy, the users of cannabis (or mainly cannabis) had replaced the users of heroin as the largest subgroup. In 2011 the share of both subgroups was 33% cannabis users and 32.2% heroin addicts. In 2012 the difference was a lot more distinct: 34.1% cannabis users versus 29.1% heroin addicts.

These and other figures deserve more attention than they usually receive. They point to a development, field workers have been noticing for about ten years and which reflects an underlying structural problem related to cannabis use. For a long period, cannabis has enjoyed a special status that goes back to the time when it was considered to be a harmless, psychoactive substance and was cherished by alternative social movements. But in the meantime it has

109 Rigter and Niesink, 2014, p. 41.

110 European Monitoring Centre on Drugs and Drug Addiction, 2014, p. 35.

111 Vlaamse Vereniging van Behandelingscentra Verslaafdenzorg, 2014, p. 3.

become clear that an unproblematic use of cannabis is not reserved for everyone. The figures about new enrolments in the drug care system demonstrate this. Precisely because for many years cannabis use was surrounded by an aura of innocence, the threshold to ask for help was high. Today the situation is quite different, which makes the figures even more significant.

6.5 The Regulation of Cannabis in the European Union: A Proposal for Discussion

6.5.1 *The Principles of the Proposal*

In the general introduction we stated that the ambition of this book is to find a way out of the deadlock in which the debate between supporters and opponents of legalization of cannabis, also in Europe, got stuck. A way out, with a proposal for a balanced and therefore realistic cannabis policy. The proposal has been written as if it were a proposal for a discussion that should be embraced by each and every member state of the European Union. The reason for this approach is simple: it is very important that the European Union adopts a cannabis policy that is accepted and supported by all of its member states. By doing so, competition between national systems can be avoided, as well as the transfer of problems – from one country to another –, be it large-scale illicit production of cannabis or serious nuisance caused by excessive distribution and consumption.

It is in the first place useful to recall what was said in the introduction: to be acceptable, the way out has to be embedded in the developments that are taking place in this field in the European Union, the Americas and the United Nations. In the previous chapters this strategic condition has been met to the extent possible: we now have a rather accurate picture of what is happening in the domain of cannabis legalization. And thanks to this knowledge we are also aware of the elements that have to be taken into account in the discussion on legalization and regulation of cannabis in the European Union.

Secondly, it should be noted that the review of the experiments with the legalization of medical and/or recreational cannabis shows that the word "legalization" as such does not mean very much. It only tells us that cannabis is no longer a prohibited drug. The logical consequence of legalization, the regulation of cannabis, is a much more ambiguous matter. As the examples of Colorado, Washington State, Uruguay and Canada clearly demonstrate, cannabis can be regulated in very different ways. The legalization and regulation in these places diverge in a substantial way from each other. And so anybody who, like us, feels concerned about the regulation of cannabis is confronted with the question from which perspective he or she wants to regulate it and how a regulation, within that perspective, can be realized.

In the third place, and in addition to the last point, it seems appropriate to make it abundantly clear that the proposal for discussion, presented below, is in line with the drug policy objectives formulated by the United Nations and the European Union. As described in Chapters 2 and 4, these policy aims are: "a high level of human health protection, social stability and security". That goal has to be reached by decreasing the demand and reducing the supply. This implies that in our proposal we take distance from the American model, which is too much directed at economic objectives, does not primarily serve public health interests, and does not contribute to a reduction of the cannabis supply and demand.

It does not mean – our fourth point – that in the development of a balanced model for the regulation of cannabis American examples cannot – whether in the positive or the negative sense – be an important source of inspiration in certain respects. They never can, however, be the sole examples. It is at least equally important to pay attention to the Canadian example and the Uruguayan example. And last but not least it is obvious that the specific situation in the European Union should be taken into account. In this connection it is significant that up to now, not one single member state, let alone the European Union as such, has called for the legalization of cannabis. On the other hand it is worth noticing that many member states, in line with the possibility offered by the drug treaties of the United Nations, no longer criminally sanction, *de facto* or *de iure*, the possession of cannabis for personal use.

On the basis of these starting points, the following topics will be especially highlighted.

First of all, we shall focus on the possibilities to avoid or reduce cannabis use by young people as much as possible. This topic deserves special attention because cannabis use at an early age can be very harmful to the users themselves. Closely related to this, there is also the burden a society as a whole has to bear, for instance the cost of drug treatment.

In the second place, three forms of growing and using cannabis will be discussed that not only to some extent are compatible with the drug treaties of the United Nations, but are actually practiced in a number of countries of the European Union: small-scale home cultivation of cannabis for personal use, growing and using cannabis in the context of a social club, and providing medical cannabis to seriously ill patients.

In the third place, a highly controversial matter will be considered: the establishment of a closed production and distribution system for cannabis. The polemical character of this issue hardly needs any explanation: such a system is undoubtedly in conflict with the drug treaties of the United

Nations. Nevertheless – taking into account the wide use of cannabis in today's world – the question seems justified whether we might need such a system. And, if that question would be answered affirmatively: what should or could it look like?

In the fourth place, it will be emphasized that although legalization – in whatever form – can make the illicit cannabis market smaller, it cannot conjure away that market. Regulation is not a miracle solution! This means that in the context of the legalization of cannabis attention has to be paid to the importance of solid law enforcement, both at national and international level.

In the fifth place, it will be indicated why we should no longer consider the Dutch coffeeshop model as a good way to give shape to the legalization of cannabis and why, within a reasonable period of time, we should get rid of it.

6.5.2 *The Prevention of Cannabis Use by Young People*

Even if cannabis is legalized, there are two important reasons to take special policy measures regarding young people under 18 or 21 years of age.[112] The first reason is that in all respects – in physical, in mental and in social respect – using cannabis can be very harmful to them. The other reason is that if cannabis is regulated, young people probably more than at present will become the target group of black marketeers, big and small. That is why, from the perspective of public health, it is extremely important not to ignore or abandon precisely this vulnerable group of people.[113]

First of all, it is crucial to give directed and professional information to young people, both at school and in youth associations. In the second place, it is also of great importance to provide young people and their family and social environment with, easily accessible, active aid and assistance. In the third place, we need to work on an effective reduction of the illicit supply around schools, in pubs and restaurants and at festivals.

Moreover, it is obvious that all these measures have to be part of a policy that, in general, aims to dissuade young people from using drugs, be it licit or illicit drugs. As stated several times before, our society not only has to deal with the problem of licit and illicit drugs, but also with the vastly bigger alcohol problem.

---

112 See also T. Parker-Pope, "Legal marijuana for parents, but not for their kids", *The New York Times*, 18.8.2014.

113 Vander Laenen, 2008.

6.5.3 *Three Acceptable Forms of Cultivation and Consumption*

When a cross-section is made of the experiments with legalization in the Americas and the actual developments in the European Union, it is remarkable that three forms of cannabis cultivation and consumption are not only compatible with the room offered by the drug treaties of the United Nations with regard to the personal possession and use of cannabis. Additionally these three forms are also accepted, in several variants, in a number of American and European states or countries: the small-scale domestic growth of cannabis for personal use, the cultivation and consumption of cannabis in a social club, and the provision of medical cannabis to patients. In other words: more and more these three forms of cultivation and consumption can be considered as the common ground for an international cannabis policy, which, above all, should be dominated by public health interests.

Of course, there is more to say about these three forms to give concrete shape to the legalization of cannabis. Once again the question is: how can or should these possibilities be put into practice if only to prevent them from being misused to set up an illicit cannabis market or to provide cannabis to that market. Think of the way home growth of medical cannabis in Canada ran so far out of control the past decade that the federal authorities were obliged to intervene radically and to establish an entirely new system for the production and provision of medical cannabis.

6.5.3.1 The Domestic Growth of Cannabis for Personal Use

As to home growth of cannabis for personal use, it is very important to carefully arrange a number of essential conditions. The following issues certainly deserve special attention.

Above all it is crucial to determine the allowed number and the allowed types of cannabis plants.

Secondly, it has to be stipulated that the produced cannabis is allowed to be used in the grower's small, personal circle, but under no condition is permitted to be sold or traded.

In the third place, it is important to specify which companies are allowed to produce the cannabis seeds and in which ways these seeds can be sold – whether or not directly, in person or through the internet.

In the fourth place, it has to be regulated what will happen with the different types of garbage the domestic growth of cannabis inevitably produces. It may be considered, for instance, to have it delivered to special depots.

And in the fifth place, it is necessary to define the conditions under which officials can pay a visit to a grower's home to verify whether the introduced rules are actually observed. This is an important issue, because experience in

Canada and elsewhere has learned that also the small-scale domestic growth of cannabis can create several types of serious nuisance in the neighbourhood.

6.5.3.2 The Cultivation and Consumption of Cannabis in a Club Context

It is beyond dispute that the cultivation and consumption of cannabis in a club context is almost by definition hard to reconcile with the drug treaties of the United Nations and the legislation in the European Union. Research by Van Kempen and Federova leaves no room for a misunderstanding about this.[114]

On the other hand, if such clubs are not run on a commercial basis, if the cannabis is produced and used – so to speak – in the name of the members, and if the activities of the clubs are stringently controlled by the authorities, a bridge can be built between the letter of especially article 3, paragraph 2, of the Vienna Convention, which deals with the circumstances under which the personal use of cannabis is permitted, and the actual large-scale use of cannabis all over the world. In this connection it is appropriate to refer to the proposal of the Dutch Van de Donk Commission to study the conditions under which social cannabis clubs could be established. With regard to cannabis, that proposal was also a clear effort to bring law and reality closer together.

Anyhow, the possible regulation of cannabis clubs will certainly be more complicated than the regulation of domestic growth. The Spanish example, or more precisely the Catalonian example, or even more precisely the example of Barcelona, shows that at least the following topics could or should be addressed by their regulation.

First, in proportion to the number of inhabitants or the (estimated) number of users in a city or region, the number of clubs that can be granted a licence has to be determined, as well as the allowed size of these clubs in terms of membership. The examples of Uruguay and Spain indicate that opinions differ quite a lot about the preferable size of such clubs.

In the second place, it has to be specified who – in terms of age – can become a member of a cannabis club, how one can become a member, and under which conditions one is allowed to buy within a certain period of time certain amounts of cannabis in the club and to use it on the spot. Special attention should be paid to the question whether only residents can join a club or whether non-residents can also become members.

In the third place, it is necessary to stipulate which amounts of cannabis are allowed to be produced and distributed in the social club context. Equally one has to define the conditions that need to be respected, among others a strict system of registration of the plants that are cultivated and the cannabis that is distributed.

114 Van Kempen and Federova, 2014.

In the fourth place, a scrupulous judicial and financial integrity screening of the management and the people working in the social clubs has to be carried out, in order to preclude criminal groups from getting a grip on their activities. It is also advisable to specify that only residents can participate in the management of the clubs.

In the fifth place, it is important to regulate under which conditions and with which purposes the authorities can supervise and control the activities taking place in the cannabis social clubs. In this context it is rather obvious to determine which sanctions will be imposed on clubs that do not (sufficiently) observe the rules.

6.5.3.3 The Provision of Medical Cannabis to Seriously Ill Patients

The third form of cultivation and consumption of cannabis which is relevant in this connection is the provision of medical cannabis to seriously ill patients. As already amply demonstrated, in medical circles people still have great doubts about the therapeutic value of cannabis. These doubts do not alter the fact, however, that more and more the insight is growing that the targeted use of certain types of cannabis can alleviate the suffering of patients. It explains the increasing goodwill towards this practice, which, on second thoughts, is not automatically in line with the objectives of the drug treaties of the United Nations.

However, in the previous chapters it has been described that such a practice can be regulated in many ways. The way it was regulated in several American states and in Canada the past years, contrasts sharply with the way this matter is dealt with in the Netherlands. To us, the choice between both approaches is not a hard one: from a public health perspective the Dutch approach is definitely the most preferable. Only that way it will be possible to prevent the creation of a market for recreational cannabis disguised as a market for the provision of medical cannabis.

6.5.4 *A Highly Controversial Matter: The Establishment of a Closed Production and Distribution System*

Some countries and states that are regulating recreational and/or medical cannabis – Colorado and Washington State as well as Canada and Uruguay – not only consider the three above-mentioned person-related forms of cultivation and consumption to be acceptable. Regulation there also relates to the establishment of a more or less closed production and distribution system for cannabis. To put it simply: in such a system there are, on the one hand, factories or plantations that are allowed to produce cannabis and, on the other hand, companies that are allowed to distribute the legally grown cannabis.

Without any doubt the establishment of such a system is in conflict with the drug treaties of the United Nations and with European law. Organizing such a production and distribution system for the (member states of the) European Union would be a revolutionary step in the development of its cannabis policy. We do not hesitate to add that such a system is certainly not compatible with our starting point that the legalization and therefore also the regulation of cannabis, should be dominated by public health interests instead of economic and/or fiscal interests. In this context it is worth to refer to the wait-and-see attitude adopted by a large number of governors of American states with regard to the legalization of cannabis in Colorado and Washington State. In our opinion the member states of the European Union should do the same: they should not hastily follow the existing examples of cannabis legalization, but should wait until the impact of legalization in the different policy domains becomes clear. What about the compliance with the rules, the reaction of the black market, the interstate sale of cannabis, the addiction problems, etc.?

But this does not alter the fact that, in case the discussion would be opened at the level of the European Union and maybe also the level of the United Nations, it should also be made clear what an appropriate system could look like. Paradoxical as it may seem, in light of our previous analyses and reservations, it is a good idea to use the models developed and implemented in the Americas over the past years as a source of inspiration. The reason is simple: in a system based on public health interests, to a large extent the same issues have to be addressed as in a system based on economic and fiscal interests. Our mental exercise starts inevitably with the production of recreational cannabis:

- The production is assigned to a limited number of licensed factories who have no economic or financial ties with the distribution companies, in order to avoid the promotion or reinforcement of mutual interests.
- The amount of cannabis the licensed factories are allowed to produce each year, is determined by the authorities on the basis of the estimated needs. The authorities also have to regulate under which circumstances and in which ways the cannabis has to be cultivated and can be processed. Furthermore, the way the factories have to handle garbage should be regulated carefully.
- Very important too is the regulation of the ways in which the factories can deliver their products to their customers. By means of registration and secure packaging the different products should in any case be traceable until delivery to the user.

- To prevent criminal organizations from acquiring direct or indirect control of factories, a thorough screening of the factory owners and their employees is rather obvious. It should be stipulated, by the way, that only residents can play a role in the factories.
- It also has to be determined which authorities are qualified to actually supervise and control the supply in the different stages, which competences they have and which sanctions they can impose in case of irregularities or offences.

As to the regulation of the distribution of cannabis, produced under the conditions mentioned above, it is important to specify what kind of companies are allowed to distribute the legal cannabis. Given the premise that the regulation of cannabis has to be dominated by public health interests, it is certainly not advisable to follow the example of Colorado and Washington State at this point. Neither is it recommendable to follow the example of Uruguay: distribution through pharmacies. In the European Union it is simply not possible to distribute recreational cannabis that way due to specific European rules that need to be respected.

It is worth considering to organize the distribution in a contemporary way: through the internet. In that case purchasers could order – within certain limits – cannabis at a licensed factory, after which the cannabis would be delivered at the customer's home by parcel post. One of the advantages of this approach is that no big monitoring system is needed to watch over the licensed distribution of cannabis. Another advantage is that it is rather easy for the authorities to determine the purchase price of cannabis. Given the importance of price determination as a means to minimize the size of the black market, the value of this advantage can hardly be overestimated.

In case this contemporary distribution method would not be chosen, it will be necessary to establish a network of fixed distribution points. Obviously, in the context of setting up such outlets, a number of matters have to be arranged:

- It has to be determined – in proportion to the number of inhabitants or the number of users – how many shops in a given area are allowed to sell cannabis produced by licensed factories.
- It is important to strictly regulate which shops, under which conditions, can obtain a licence to sell the cannabis and how these shops have to organize the management of their business.
- Also at this stage the judicial past and the financial situation of the owners and their employees need to be screened thoroughly.

- Not less important is to determine the minimum age at which people – i.e. residents – can buy cannabis in licensed shops and the way the buyers have to identify themselves. It should not be permitted to consume the purchased cannabis on the spot.
- It is also necessary to specify which public services will have which competences to control this part of the supply chain. Furthermore the applicable sanctions in case of registered irregularities or offences have to be delineated.

The above-mentioned focal points demonstrate that it is very well possible to establish a closed production and distribution system for cannabis on the basis of a public health perspective. But it remains to be seen whether, at the level of the member states and therefore at the level of the European Union, the political will is present to set up such a system in addition to home grown cannabis and cannabis social clubs and in accordance with the cannabis demand of the population.

6.5.5 *The Needs for (Cross-Border) Law Enforcement*

It almost goes without saying that the legalization of cannabis and the accompanying regulation of the "whitened" cannabis market cannot be realized as planned if the new structure of the market is not protected against people who do not want to comply with it.

In the first place, this means that the authorities should have sufficient personnel at their disposal to supervise and control the compliance with the different rules that constitute the mechanism of regulation. They should be able to powerfully intervene with sanctions whenever and wherever necessary.

In the second place, there should be sufficient law enforcement personnel available to put a brake on the import, production and distribution of illicit cannabis. There is plenty of reason to assume that the criminal organizations, which up to now to a large extent dominate the supply side of the market, will not be willing to give up their illicit but lucrative activities or to cease their criminal practices such as hold-ups on production and distribution facilities. And it is also certain that they will try to infiltrate and to influence the regulated production and distribution system.

In the third place, it should not be forgotten that the legalization of cannabis does not mean that the entire drug business becomes legalized. On the contrary. The other classic drugs – opium, heroin, cocaine – as well as the expanding sector of synthetic drugs will remain illicit and prohibited, like it is the case for synthetic cannabinoids. Therefore, also after the legalization of recreational cannabis, still enough law enforcement capacity has to be available to track down and stop the production and distribution of these and other illicit drugs. Even more so because it is likely that criminal organizations will try to compensate their shrinking share of the cannabis market by increasing their activities in the markets of other, still illicit drugs.

In the fourth place, and for many years to come, a targeted approach to the criminal organizations by the police, the judicial and administrative authorities and the tax services is needed, in order to deprive these organizations, as much as possible, of the criminal income they have gained in the illicit cannabis market. This is mainly necessary to prevent them from investing the money, whether or not by using money laundering constructions, in legal economic sectors such as real estate, catering or transport.

In the fifth place, it is rather obvious that sustained investments in the cross-border fight against the illicit drug traffic are a must. The great importance of intensive cross-border police, judicial and fiscal cooperation to tackle this traffic has previously been demonstrated by our research concerning the joint control of the drug problems in the Euregion Meuse-Rhine.

6.5.6 *The Abolition of the Coffeeshops*

Dutch and foreign supporters of legalization often present the coffeeshops in the Netherlands as the example of a smart cannabis policy. Everyone who has read Chapter 5 of this book, knows better however. He or she knows that the coffeeshops have gradually evolved from small-scale shops for local cannabis users to commercial enterprises causing – partly due to the lax attitude of local and national authorities – serious problems in Dutch society.

The first thing to be mentioned in this context, is the boosting role of the coffeeshops, as a consequence of the so-called backdoor problem, in the flourishing of the large-scale illicit cannabis cultivation and in the development of related social problems, such as organized crime and the deterioration of neighbourhoods.

In the second place, we have to mention the huge public order and safety problems which – especially in the southern part of the country – have manifested themselves at the so-called frontdoor of the coffeeshops and which only recently, thanks to the strict application of the residence criterion, have decreased significantly.

In the third place, it has to be emphasized that coffeeshops do not only create problems at the frontdoor and the backdoor. Everything that occurs in between both doors is problematic as well. It would go too far to say the whole sector is rotten to the core, but undisputably it has a lot of rotten apples.

For the first time and at a large scale, this became clear in Amsterdam, where, in the context of the Emergo project described in Chapter 5, it was discovered that in many cases the coffeeshops downtown are run by people with a serious criminal record. This finding confirmed that the city had indeed good reasons to speak, as it already did for years, of a criminogenic sector and is right to do its utmost to reduce that sector to a "small-scale, transparent and controllable" one of about 150 coffeeshops.[115] It is likely that also at other places the situation is similar to that in Amsterdam. An investigation executed in 2012 by the partners of Regional Information and Expertise Centre Limburg among the coffeeshops and growshops in the province, resulted in an additional tax assessment of four million euros, imposed on 42 coffeeshops because of "hidden revenues".[116]

The best proof of the flawed nature of whole parts of the sector was delivered in the context of the *Project national screening coffeeshops*, carried out in the period 2011–2014 by the National Bureau of the Dutch Ministry of Security and Justice, that is responsible for giving advice to local authorities about the implementation of the special Act, which is aimed at the preservation of the integrity of the public administration. In the context of the project, this bureau screened 71 coffeeshops in 2012 and 39 in 2013. In 54 cases it actually delivered an advice to the related local authorities. In no less than 38 of these 54 cases "a serious risk" of improper use of the granted licences was reported.[117]

In contradiction with many supporters of legalization in the Netherlands, who still believe there is a future for the coffeeshops, we are convinced that this flawed sector has no future at all. The facts mentioned above are a very good reason to proceed as soon as possible to the abolishment of the coffeeshops. Not just the "backdoor" of the coffeeshop is a big problem, as sometimes suggested by supporters of legalization, also other important parts of this tolerated distribution system are problematic and dubious.

The second reason to abolish the coffeeshops is closely related to the first. Nowadays coffeeshops are commercial enterprises and for such enterprises there is simply no place in a cannabis policy dominated by public health interests. Of course, the owners of the coffeeshops and the people who run these

115 See the "Beleidsbrief coffeeshops"/"Policy letter coffeeshops" the mayor of Amsterdam, on behalf of the administration, the judiciary and the police, on December 11, 2012 sent to the Raadscommissie Algemene Zaken/Council's Committee General Affairs (see the website of the city).

116 N. van der Naald and Th. Sniekers, "Wietsector voor 9 miljoen geplukt", *Limburgs Dagblad*, 11.4.2012. See also Regionaal Informatie en Expertise Centrum Limburg, 2014, p. 14–16.

117 See Ministry of Security and Justice, 2011; National Bureau Bibob, 2014. At our request, some data were provided to us by the National Bureau.

shops have a completely different view on cannabis. They are, for obvious reasons, even opposed to the legalization of cannabis, because they are afraid that once the crime-related business risk is taken away, the cost price of cannabis and consequently also the selling price of cannabis in coffeeshops, will drop spectacularly. In April 2014, this fear was publicly expressed by M. Veling, the spokesman of the Association of Cannabis Retailers in Amsterdam.[118]

In sum, in our view it is almost "closing time" for the coffeeshops. There is still another good reason for their abolition: if the legalization of cannabis in the Netherlands would imply that in addition to the existing domestic growth, it will be possible to establish cannabis social clubs and perhaps even a closed production and distribution system for "nederwiet", coffeeshops will no longer be needed to meet the demand for cannabis, on the contrary!

118 X, "Coffeeshophandelaars vrezen voor omzetcijfers bij legalisering wietkweek", *Het Parool*, 7.4.2014.

Bibliography

Addens, T. (1939), *The Distribution of Opium Cultivation and the Trade in Opium*, Haarlem, Joh. Enschedé en Zonen.

Adviescommissie drugsbeleid (2009), *Geen deuren maar daden; nieuwe accenten in het Nederlandse drugsbeleid*, Den Haag, Ministerie van VWS, Justitie en BZK.

Afdeling Onderzoek en Statistiek (2008), *Het coffeeshopbezoek in Nijmegen*, Nijmegen, Gemeente Nijmegen.

Akgul, A. and M. Sever (2014), "Combatting Illegal Cannabis Cultivation in Turkey", *Trends of Organised Crime*, 2014 (published online 11 June 2014).

American College of Physicians (2008), *Supporting Research into the Therapeutic Role of Marijuana*, Philadelphia.

Andersen, P. and B. Baumberg (2006), *Alcohol in Europe: A Public Health Perspective*, London, Institute for Alcohol Studies.

Andreas, P. and E. Nadelmann (2006), *Policing the Globe: Criminalization and Crime Control in International Relations*, Oxford, Oxford University Press.

Antonopoulos, G. (2008), "The Greek Connections): The Social Organization of the Cigarette Smuggling Business in Greece", *European Journal of Criminology*, pp. 263–288.

Asbury, H. (1990), *The gangs of New York: An Informal History of the Underworld*, New York, Paragon House.

Attorney, The, General's Conference on Organized Crime (1950), Washington, Department of Justice.

Ballotta, D., H. Bergeron and B. Hughes (2008), "Cannabis Control in Europe", in: S. Sznitman, B. Olsson and R. Room (eds.), *op. cit.*, vol. 2, pp. 97–117.

Barendrecht, C., G. Meerkerk and D. van de Mheen (2011), *De cannabisclub als experiment; een voorstel tot wetenschappelijk onderzoek*, Rotterdam, IVO.

Becker, H. (1963), *Outsiders: Studies in the Sociology of Deviance*, New York, The Free Press.

Beke, B., E. van der Torre and M. van Duin (2011), *Stads- en regioscan in de grootste Brabantse gemeenten*, Apeldoorn, Politie en Wetenschap.

Benbassa, E. et al. (2014), *Proposition de loi autorisant l'usage contrôlé du cannabis*, Paris, Sénat, Session Ordinaire de 2013–2014, no 317.

Benjamin, D. and R. Miller (1991), *Undoing Drugs: Beyond Legalization*, New York, Basic Books.

Bennett, W. (1992), "Response to Milton Friedman", in: R. Evans and I. Berent (eds.), *op. cit.*, pp. 53–56.

Benschop, A., L. Buijs, L. Engelfriet et al. (2009), *Coffeeshops in het hart van de stad; bewoners en toeristen over postcodegebied 1012 in Amsterdam*, Amsterdam, Universiteit van Amsterdam, Bonger Instituut.

Besteman, K. (1991), "War is Not the Answer", in: J. Inciardi (ed.), *op. cit.*, pp. 130–134.

Bewley-Taylor, D. (2001), *The United States and International Drug Control, 1909–1997*, London, Continuum.

Bewley-Taylor, D. and C. Hallam (2008), *An Overview of Cannabis Policy: Moving Beyond the Stalemate*, Oxford, The Beckley Foundation.

Bieleman, B., P. Goeree and H. Naayer (2005), *Coffeeshops in Nederland 2004: aantallen coffeeshops en gemeentelijk beleid, 1999–2004*, Groningen, Intraval.

Bieleman, B. and H. Naayer (2007), *Onderzoek coffeeshops Terneuzen*, Groningen, Intraval.

Bieleman, B. and R. Nijkamp (2009), *Coffeeshopbezoekers in Venlo 2009: tellingen en enquête coffeeshopbezoekers Venlo*, Groningen, Intraval.

Bieleman, B., R. Nijkamp and A. Buit-Minnema (2010), *Coffeeshopbezoekers Terneuzen najaar 2009*, Groningen, Intraval.

Bieleman, B., R. Nijkamp and K. de Haan (2011), *Lokaal balanceren: onderzoek coffeeshopbeleid Gemeente Groningen*, Groningen, Intraval.

Bieleman, B., E. Spijkers and L. Griesheimer (2001), *Evaluatie coffeeshopbeleid gemeente Heerlen*, Groningen, Intraval.

Bieleman, B., R. Nijkamp, J. Reimer and M. Haaijer (2013), *Coffeeshops in Nederland 2012: aantallen coffeeshops en gemeentelijk beleid, 1999–2012*, Groningen, Intraval.

Blom, T. (2008), *Opiumwetgeving en drugsbeleid*, Deventer, Kluwer.

Bovenkerk, F. and W. Hogewind (2003), *Hennepteelt in Nederland: het probleem van de criminaliteit en haar bestrijding*, Zeist, Uitgeverij Kerckebosch.

Branch, T. (1992a), "Let Koop do it", in: R. Evans and I. Berent (eds.), *op. cit.*, pp. 297–308.

——— (1992b), "The Legalization of Drugs: Why Prolong the Inevitable?", in: R. Evans and I. Berent (eds.), *op. cit.*, pp. 157–180.

Bretteville-Jensen, A. (2006), "To Legalize or Not to Legalize? Economic Approaches to the Decriminalization of Drugs", *Substance Use and Misuse*, pp. 555–565.

Broekhuizen, J., J. Raven and F. Driessen (2006), *Handhaving en naleving van de coffeeshopregels in 2004*, Utrecht, Bureau Driessen.

Brouwer, J. and J. Schilder (2012), "Over de grenzen van gedogen, het failliet van de B en I in het coffeeshopbeleid", *Nederlands Juristenblad*, pp. 3082–3089.

Brown, C. and Ph. Resnick (2014), *The Fiscal Impact of Amendment 64 on State Revenues*, Denver, Colorado State University, Colorado Futures Center.

Brunn, K., L. Par and I. Rexed (1975), *The Gentlemen's Club: International Control of Drugs and Alcohol*, Chicago, Chicago University Press.

Bryan, M., E. DelBono and S. Pudney (2011), *Licensing and Regulation of the Cannabis Market in England and Wales: Towards a Cost-Benefit Analysis*, Essex, University of Essex, Institute for Social and Economic Research.

Bundeszentrale für gesundheitliche Aufklärung (2011), *Der Cannabiskonsum Jugendlicher und junger Erwachsener in Deutschland 2010: Ergebnisse einer aktuellen Repräsentativbefragung und Trends*, Köln.

Bureau voor Medicinale Cannabis (s.d.a), *Medicinale cannabis; informatiebrochure voor artsen en apothekers*, Den Haag, Ministerie van Volksgezondheid, Welzijn en Sport.

Bureau voor Medicinale Cannabis (s.d.b), *Medicinale cannabis; informatiebrochure voor patiënten*, Den Haag, Ministerie van Volksgezondheid, Welzijn en Sport.

Carter III, H. (1992), "We're Losing the Drug War Because Prohibition Never Works", in: R. Evans and I. Berent (eds.), *op. cit.*, pp. 91–94.

Casswell, S., T. Huckle, M. Wall and L. Yeh (2014), "International Alcohol Control Study; Pricing Data and Hours of Purchase Predict Heavier Drinking", *Alcoholism; Clinical and Experimental Research*, pp. 1425–1431.

Caulkins, J. (2014), "How to Avoid a Likely and Dangerous Corporate Takeover of the Legal Marijuana Market", *The Washington Monthly*, <http://www.washington monthly.com/magazine/march_april_may>.

Caulkins, J., A. Hawken, B. Kilmer and M. Kleiman (2012), *Marijuana Legalization; What Everybody Needs to Know*, New York, Oxford University Press.

Caulkins, J., B. Kilmer and M. Graf (2013), "Estimating the Size of the EU Cannabis Market", in: F. Trautmann, B. Kilmer and P. Turnbull (eds.), *op. cit.*, pp. 289–322.

Caulkins, J. et al. (2011), "Design Considerations for Legalizing Cannabis; Lessons Inspired by Analysis of California's Proposition 19", *Addiction*, vol. 107, pp. 865–871.

Centraal Bureau voor de Statistiek, *Nationale rekeningen: revisie 2010*, Den Haag, 2014.

Chatwin, C. (2011), *Drug Policy Harmonization and the European Union*, New York, Palgrave.

——— (2013), "A Critical Evaluation of the European Drug Strategy: Has it Brought Added Value to Drug Policy Making at the National Level", *International Journal of Drug Policy*, vol. 24, pp. 251–256.

Cleveland, M. (1998), "Downsizing the Drug War and Considering 'Legalization'; An Economic Perspective", in: J. Fish (ed.), *op. cit.*, pp. 547–577.

Collins, J. (ed.) (2014), *Ending the Drug Wars; Report of the LSE Expert Group on the Economics of Drug Policy*, London, The London School of Economics and Political Sciences.

Coördinatiepunt Assessment en Monitoring Nieuwe Drugs, *Risicoschatting cannabis 2008*, Bilthoven, Rijksinstituut voor Volksgezondheid en Milieu.

Cornil, P. and Ch. Tisseyre (1972), "Réaction sociale à la déviance; le problème de la drogue en Belgique", in: *Les frontières de la répression, op. cit.*, pp. 223–248.

Costes, J.-M. (ed.) (2007), *Cannabis; données essentielles*, Paris, Observatoire Francais des Drogues et des Toximanies, 2007.

Council of the European Union (2001), *The Schengen Acquis Integrated into the European Union*, Luxembourg, Office for Official Publications of the European Communities.

Crick, E., H. Haase and D. Bewley-Taylor (2013), *Legally Regulated Cannabis Markets in the US; Implications and Possibilities*, Swansea, Swansea University, Global Drug Policy Observatory.

Damrongplasit, K., Ch. Hsiao and X. Zhao (2010), "Decriminalization and Marijuana Smoking Prevalence; Evidence from Australia", *Journal of Business and Economic Statistics*, pp. 344–356.

Dangreau, J., L. Deben and K. de Greve (eds.) (2012), *Drugwetgeving*, Brussel, Larcier.

De Beaufort, L. (1989), "Strafrechtelijke marktbeheersing; over het opsporings- en vervolgingsbeleid inzake drugsdelicten", in: M. Groenhuijsen and A. van Kalmthout (eds.), *op. cit.*, pp. 69–85.

De Bock, G. (1972), "Jeugd en zorg", in: *Les frontières de la répression, op. cit.*, pp. 249–294.

De Bruin, D., M. Dijkstra and J. Breeksema (2008), *Coffeeshops in Nederland 2007: naleving en handhaving van coffeeshopregels*, Utrecht, Stichting CVO.

Decorte, T. and P. Tuteleers (2007), *Cannabisteelt in Vlaanderen: patronen en motieven van 748 telers*, Leuven, Acco.

De Grazia, J. (1991), *DEA; The War on Drugs*, London, BBC Books.

Degreef, T., J. Pacolet and R. Bouten (2003), *Sociale kosten-batenanalyse van alcoholgebruik en -misbruik in België*, Leuven, KULeuven, Hoger Instituut voor de Arbeid.

Deprez, N., J. Antoine and J. Assuete-Lorente (eds.) (2011), *Belgian National Report on Drugs 2011*, Brussel, Wetenschappelijk Instituut Volksgezondheid.

De Ridder, H. and F. Verleyen (1971), "A. Vranckx", in: *10 politieke portretten*, Tielt, Lannoo.

De Ruyver, B. (1982), "De alcoholwet Vandervelde in historisch en ideologisch perspectief", *Tijdschrift voor Sociale Wetenschappen*, pp. 342–369.

——— (1984), "De drugswetgeving in historisch en rechtsvergelijkend perspectief", in: K. Maes, J. Maertens, F. Carlier and B. de Ruyver (eds.), *op. cit.*, pp. 51–90.

——— (1986), *De criminele politiek onder de socialistische ministers van Justitie E. Vandervelde, P. Vermeylen en A. Vranckx*, Gent, Universiteit Gent, Faculteit der Rechtsgeleerdheid.

——— (1988), *De strafrechtelijke politiek gevoerd onder de socialistische ministers van Justitie E. Vandervelde, P. Vermeylen en A. Vranckx*, Antwerpen, Kluwer.

——— (2006), "Drugs in de Lage Landen; de Belgische kant van het verhaal", *Justitiële Verkenningen*, no. 6, pp. 135–145.

De Ruyver, B., J. Casselman, F. Bullens et al. (2000), *Het Belgisch drugbeleid anno 2000: een stand van zaken drie jaar na de aanbevelingen van de Parlementaire Werkgroep Drugs*, Gent, Universiteit Gent, Onderzoeksgroep Drugbeleid, Strafrechtelijk Beleid en Internationale Criminaliteit.

De Ruyver, B. and F. Koekelberg (2003), "De politiehervorming; een tussentijdse evaluatie en aanbevelingen tot bijsturing waar nodig", *Vigiles: Tijdschrift voor Politierecht*, no. 5, pp. 153–159.

De Ruyver, B., J. Pele and D. de Graeve (eds.) (2007), *Drugs in cijfers II*, Gent, Academia Press.

De Ruyver, B. and T. Surmont (eds.) (2007), *Grensoverschrijdend drugstoerisme; nieuwe uitdagingen voor de Euregio's*, Antwerpen, Maklu.

De Ruyver, B., F. Vander Laenen and S. Eelen (2012), "The Long Road to an Integral and Integrated Policy in Belgium", in: R. Muscat and B. Pike (eds.), *op. cit.*, pp. 37–42.

De Ruyver, B., G. Vermeulen, T. vander Beken et al. (2002), *Multidisciplinary Drug Policies and the UN Drug Treaties*, Antwerpen, Maklu.

Deutsche Beobachtungsstelle für Drogen und Drogensucht (2013), *Bericht 2013 des nationalen REITOX-Knotenpunkts an die EBDD: neue Entwicklungen und Trends, Deutschland.*

D'Haenens, J. (1972), "Juridische aspecten", in: *Les frontières de la répression, op. cit.*, pp. 369–386.

Dienst Ipol (2008a), *Nationaal dreigingsbeeld 2008; georganiseerde criminaliteit*, Zoetermeer, Korps Landelijke Politiediensten.

——— (2008b), *Het groene goud; verslag van een onderzoek naar de cannabissector voor het nationaal dreigingsbeeld criminaliteit met een georganiseerd karakter*, Zoetermeer, Korps Landelijke Politiediensten.

Dienst Ipol (2012), *Nationaal dreigingsbeeld 2012: georganiseerde criminaliteit*, Zoetermeer, Korps Landelijke Politiediensten.

Diez-Ripolles, J. (1989), "Huidige trends in de werkzaamheden van het Europese Parlement met betrekking tot verdovende middelen", in: M. Groenhuijsen and A. van Kalmthout (eds.), *op. cit.*, pp. 21–28.

Diplock, J., D. Plecas and L. Garis (2013), *Targeting Marihuana Growing Operations in British Columbia*, Vancouver, University of the Fraser Valley, School of Criminology and Criminal Justice.

Dobbelaar, J., E. van der Torre and A. Besselink (2009a), *Drugsscenes in Breda*, Den Haag, COT.

——— (2009b), *Drugsscenes rondom Breda; Etten-Leur, Rucphen, Zundert, Alphen-Chaam en Baarle-Nassau*, Den Haag, COT.

Dorn, N. (ed.) (1999), *Regulating European Drugs Problems; Administrative Measures and Civil Law in the Control of Drug Trafficking, Nuisance and Use*, The Hague, Kluwer Law International.

Drogenbeauftragte, Die, der Bundesregierung (2012), *Nationale Strategie zur Drogen- und Suchtpolitik*, Berlin.

Drug Enforcement Administration (2013), *National Drug Threat Assessment: Summary*, Washington, US Department of Justice.

——— (2014a), *The Dangers and Consequences of Marijuana Abuse*, Washington, US Department of Justice.

Drug Enforcement Administration (2014b), *Exposing the Myth of Smoked Medical Marijuana*, Washington, US Department of Justice.

Dupont, R. and E. Voth (1995), "Drug Legalization, Harm Reduction and Drug Policy", *Annals of Internal Medecine*, pp. 461–465.

Durney, J. (2000), *The Mob; The History of Irish Gangsters in America*, Naas, Leinster Leader.

Easton, S. (2004), *Marijuana Growth in British Columbia*, Vancouver, The Fraser Institute.

Eisenbach-Stangl, I. (2012), "Integration and Coherence of Policies for Alcohol, Illicit Drugs and Tobacco in Australia: The Past Ten Years", in: R. Muscat and B. Pike (eds.), *op. cit.*, pp. 21–31.

Eldredge, D. (1998), *Ending the War on Drugs; A Solution for America*, Bridgehampton, Bridge Works Publishing Company.

Elsen, Ch. (1995), "Drugs as a Priority in Cooperation in the Fields of Justice and Home Affairs", in: G. Estievenart (ed.), *op. cit.*, pp. 360–368.

Estievenart, G. (ed.) (1995a), *Policies and Strategies to Combat Drugs in Europe; The Treaty on European Union: Framework for a New European Strategy to Combat Drugs?* Dordrecht, Martinus Nijhoff.

——— (1995b), "The European Community and the Global Drug Phenomenon; Current Situation and Outlook", in: G. Estievenart (ed.) 1995a, *op. cit.*, pp. 50–98.

European Monitoring Centre for Drugs and Drug Addiction (2013a), *European Drug Report; Trends and Developments*, Luxembourg, Publications Office of the European Union.

——— (2013b), *Prevalence of Daily Cannabis Use in the European Union and Norway*, Luxembourg, Publications Office of the European Union.

——— (2014), *European Drug Report; Trends and Developments*, Luxembourg, Publications Office of the European Union.

European Monitoring Centre for Drugs and Drug Addiction and Europol (2013), *EU Drug Markets Report; A Strategic Analysis*, Luxembourg, Publications Office of the European Union.

European Parliament (2013), *Working Document on the Agreements with the Tobacco Industry and Fight with the Illicit Tobacco Trade*, Brussels, 2.4.2013 (rapporteur: B. Staes).

——— (2014), *Workshop Cigarette Smuggling; Briefing Papers*, Brussels, 14.1.2014.

Evans, R. and I. Berent (eds.) (1992), *Drug Legalization: For and Against*, La Salle, Open Court Publishing Company.

Expertcommissie Lijstensystematiek Opiumwet (2010), *Drugs in lijsten*, Den Haag, Ministerie van Volksgezondheid, Welzijn en Sport.

Federale beleidsnota drugs; bericht 19 januari 2001 (2012), in: J. Dangreau, L. Deben and K. de Greve (eds.), *op. cit.*, pp. 245–283.

Ferret, J. (2000), *L'autre Europe des drogues; politiques des drogues dans cinq pays d'Europe: Espagne, Portugal, Hongrie, Pologne et Bulgarie*, Paris, La Documentation Française.

Fijnaut, C. (1983), *De zaak-François; beschouwingen naar aanleiding van het vonnis*, Antwerpen, Kluwer Rechtswetenschappen.

——— (2007), *De geschiedenis van de Nederlandse politie; een staatsinstelling in de maalstroom van de geschiedenis*, Amsterdam, Boom.

——— (2009), "Een nuchtere kijk op de Hollandse coffeeshop: het drugsbeleid in revisie", *Socialisme en Democratie*, no. 3, pp. 16–23.

——— (2014), "Legislation of Cannabis in Some American States; A Challenge for the European Union and its Member States?", *European Journal of Crime, Criminal Law and Criminal Justice*, pp. 207–217.

Fijnaut, C. and B. De Ruyver (2008), *Voor een gezamenlijke beheersing van de drugsgerelateerde criminaliteit in de Euregio Maas-Rijn*, Maastricht, Euregio Maas-Rijn.

Fijnaut, C. and J. van Riessen (2008), *Veel te winnen*, Eindhoven, Gemeente Eindhoven.

Fijnaut, C. and I. Zaat (2003), *De sociale (on)veiligheid in Tilburg; een kritische analyse van de problemen en een reeks aanbevelingen voor hun aanpak*, Tilburg, Gemeente Tilburg.

Fish, J. (ed.) (1998), *How to Legalize Drugs*, Northvale, NY, Jason Aronson.

Fix, B., A. Hyland, R. O'Connor et al. (2014), "A Novel Approach to Estimating the Prevalence of Untaxed Cigarettes in the USA; Findings from the 2009 and 2010 International Tobacco Control Surveys", *Tobacco Control*, no. 23, pp. 61–66.

Foot White, W. (1955), *Street Corner Society; The Social Structure of an Italian Slum*, Chicago, The University of Chicago Press.

Fried, A. (1993), *The Rise and Fall of the Jewish Gangster in America*, New York, Columbia University Press.

Friedman, M. (1992a), "An Open Letter to Bill Bennett", in: R. Evans and I. Berent (eds.), *op. cit.*, pp. 49–52.

——— (1992b), "Bennett's 'Public Policy Disaster' is Already Here", in: R. Evans and I. Berent (eds.), *op. cit.*, pp. 57–60.

Friedrichs, J. (2008), *Fighting Terrorism and Drugs; Europe and International Police Cooperation*, Oxon, Routledge.

Frontières, Les, de la répression (1972), Bruxelles, Editions de l'ULB.

Gallup, The, Organization (2011), *Youth Attitudes on Drugs*, Brussels, European Commission.

Gemeenschappelijke verklaring van de Interministeriële Conferentie Drugs; een globaal en geïntegreerd drugsbeleid voor België, Brussel, 25 januari 2010.

Gemeente Heerlen (2001), *Operatie Hartslag; "Naar een veilige en beheersbare binnenstad"*, Heerlen.

Gemeente Heerlen (2002), *Softdrugsbeleid gemeente Heerlen*, Heerlen.

——— (2004), *Softdrugsbeleid gemeente Heerlen; actualisering mei 2004*, Heerlen.

——— (2010a), *Heerlen versnelt; coalitieakkoord Heerlen, 2010–2014*, Heerlen.

——— (2010b), *Meerjarig bestuurlijk programma, 2011–2014; begroting 2011*, Heerlen.

——— (2011), *Kadernota integrale veiligheid 2011–2015, gemeente Heerlen*, Heerlen.

——— (2013), *Handhavingsbeleid drugs en overige (woon)overlast*, Heerlen.

Gemeenteraad Maastricht (2011a), *Expertmeeting drugsoverlast 29 april 2011*, Maastricht.

——— (2011b), *Hoorzitting drugsbeleid 18 mei 2011*, Maastricht.

Ghodse, H. (ed.) (2008), *International Drug Control into the 21st Century*, Aldershot, Ashgate.

Gisle, L. (2010), "Het gebruik van illegale drugs", in: L. Gisle (ed.), *Gezondheidsenquête België, 2008; rapport II – leefstijl en preventie*, Brussel, Wetenschappelijk Instituut Volksgezondheid.

Greenwald, G. (2009), *Drug Decriminalisation in Portugal; Lessons for Creating Fair and Successful Drug Policies*, Washington, Cato Institute.

Groenhuijsen, M. (2013), "Van coffeeshop naar drugscafé? Enkele voetnoten bij de slepende discussie over het huidige Nederlandse drugsbeleid", *Delikt en Delinkwent*, pp. 493–500.

Groenhuijsen, M. and A. van Kalmthout (eds.) (1989), *Nederlands drugsbeleid in Westeuropees perspectief*, Arnhem, Gouda Quint.

Groupe SCR (2011), *Légalisation contrôlée du cannabis*, Paris, Assemblée Nationale.

Grund, J.-P. and J. Breeksema (2013), *Coffeeshops and Compromise; Separated Illicit Drug Markets in the Netherlands*, New York, Open Society Foundations.

Guindon, G., P. Driezen, F. Chaloupka and G. Fong (2013), "Cigarette Avoidance and Evasion: Findings fom the International Tobacco Control Policy Evaluation Project", *Tobacco Control*, pp. 1–10.

Gurule, I. (1998), "The 1998 UN Convention against Illicit Traffic in Narcotic Drugs and Psychotropic Substances – A Ten Year Perspective: Is International Cooperation Merely Illusory?", *Fordham International Law Journal*, pp. 74–121.

Hall, W. and L. Degenhardt (2009), "The Adverse Health Effects of Non-Medical Cannabis Use", *The Lancet*, vol. 374, pp. 1383–1391.

Hibell, B., U. Guttormsson, S. Ahlström et al. (2012), *The 2011 ESPAD Report; Substance Use among Students in 36 European Countries*, Stockholm, The Swedish Council for Information on Alcohol and other Drugs.

Hill, J. (1992), "The Zone of Privacy and the Right to Use Drugs; A Jurisprudential Critique", in: R. Evans and I. Berent (eds.), *op. cit.*, pp. 101–122.

HM Government (2007), *Drugs: Our Community, Your Say; A Consultation Paper*, London, Home Office.

——— (2010), *Drug Strategy 2010; Reducing Demand, Restricting Supply, Building Recovery: Supporting People to Live a Drug Free Life*, London, Home Office.

——— (2013), *Drug Strategy Annual Review: Delivering within a New Landscape*, London, Home Office.

Home Affairs Committee (2012–2013), *Drugs: Breaking the Cycle*, London, House of Commons.

Hornsby, R. and D. Hobbs (2007), "A Zone of Ambiguity; The Political Economy of Cigarette Bootlegging", *British Journal of Criminology*, pp. 551–571.

Hughes, C. and A. Stevens (2012), "A Resounding Success or a Disastrous Failure; Re-Examining the Interpretation of Evidence on the Portuguese Decriminalisation of Illicit Drugs", *Drugs and Alcohol Review*, no. 31, pp. 101–113.

Hulsman, L. and W. Blok van der Velden (eds.) (1971), *Rapport van een werkgroep van de Stichting Algemeen Centraal Bureau voor de Geestelijke Volksgezondheid*, Meppel, Boom.

Inciardi, J. (ed.) (1991), *The Drug Legalization Debate*, Newbury Park, Sage Publications.

Inciardi, J. and D. McBride (1991), "The Case *Against* Legalization", in: J. Inciardi (ed.), *op. cit.*, pp. 45–79.

International Drug Policy Consortium (2013), *IDPC Response to the 2012 Annual Report of the International Narcotics Control Board*, London.

International Narcotics Control Board (2008), *Report 2007*, New York, United Nations.

——— (2013), *Report 2012*, Vienna, United Nations.

——— (2014), *Report 2013*, Vienna, United Nations.

Jelsma, M., T. Blickman and D. Bewley-Taylor (2014), *The Rise and Decline of Cannabis Prohibition*, Amsterdam, Transnational Institute and Global Drug Policy Observatory.

Joffe, A. and W. Yancy (2004), "Legalization of Marijuana; Potential Impact on Youth", *Pediatrics*, vol. 113, pp. 632–638.

Jonas, S. (1991), "The US Drug Problem and the US Drug Culture; A Public Health Solution", in: J. Inciardi (ed.), *op. cit.*, pp. 161–182.

Jong, W. (2014), "Het zou Opstelten sieren als hij zijn standpunt zou bijstellen", *Het Tijdschrift voor de Politie*, no. 3, pp. 10–15.

Junger-Tas, J. (1972), *Schooljeugd en drugs; een onderzoek op enkele Belgische scholen*, Brussel, Studiecentrum voor Jeugdmisdadigheid.

Karel, R. (1991), "A Model Legalization Proposal", in: J. Inciardi (ed.), *op. cit.*, pp. 80–102.

Kazemier, B., A. Bruil, A. van de Steeg and M. Rensman (2012), *The Contribution of Illegal Activities to National Income in the Netherlands*, The Hague/Heerlen, Statistics Netherlands.

Kerr, K. (1985), *Organized for Prohibition; A New History of the Anti-Saloon League*, New Haven, Harvard University Press.

Kilmer, B. and J. Burgdorf (2013), "Insights about Cannabis Production and Distribution Costs in the EU", in: F. Trautmann, B. Kilmer and P. Turnbull, *op. cit.*, pp. 389–404.

Kilmer, B., J. Caulkins, L. Dahlkemper et al. (2013), *Marijuana Consumption in Washington State Twice as Large as Previously Estimated*, Santa Monica, Rand.

Kilmer, B., J. Caulkins, G. Midgette et al. (2013), *Before the Grand Opening; Measuring Washington State's Marijuana Market in the Last Year before Legalized Commercial Sales*, Santa Monica, Rand.

Kilmer, B., K. Kruithof, M. Pardal et al. (2013), *Multinational Overview of Cannabis Production Regimes*, Cambridge, Rand.

Klip, A. (2009), "Op weg naar minder opportuniteit", *Delikt en Delinkwent*, 2009, pp. 185–196.

Knepper, P. (2011), *International Crime in the 20th Century; The League of Nations Era, 1919–1939*, Houndsmills, Palgrave Macmillan.

Korf, D. (1995), *Dutch Treat; Formal Control and Illicit Drug Use in the Netherlands*, Amsterdam, Thesis Publishers.

——— (2008), "An Open Front Door: The Coffeeshop Phenomenon in the Netherlands", in: S. Sznitman, B. Olsson and R. Room (eds.), vol. 1, pp. 137–156.

Korf, D., E. Kleemans, T. Decorte and T. Boekhout van Solinge (2006), "Drugs en drugshandel in Nederland en België", *Tijdschrift voor Criminologie*, pp. 115–130.

Korf, D., G. Müller, M. Freeman and D. Lettink (1993), *Drugstoerisme in de grensstreek*, Amsterdam, Het Amsterdams Bureau voor Onderzoek en Statistiek.

Korf, D., M. van der Woude, A. Benschop and T. Nabben (2001), *Coffeeshops, jeugd en toerisme*, Amsterdam, Rozenberg Publishers.

Landelijk Bureau Bibob (2014), *Jaarverslag 2013*, 's-Gravenhage, Ministerie van Veiligheid en Justitie.

Lenton, S. (2014), "New Regulated Markets for Recreational Cannabis; Public Health or Private Profit?", *Addiction*, vol. 109, pp. 354–355.

Ley, A. (1920), "Alcoholisme et criminalité", *Revue de Droit Pénal et de Criminologie*, pp. 513–526.

L'Hoiry, X. (2013), "'Shifting the Stuff wasn't Any Bother'; Illicit Enterprise, Tobacco Bootlegging and Deconstructing the British Government's Cigarette Smuggling Discourse", *Trends in Organized Crime*, pp. 413–434.

Light, M., A. Orens, B. Lewandowski and T. Pickton (2014), *Market Size and Demand for Marijuana in Colorado*, Colorado, Department of Revenue.

London School of Economics Expert Group on the Economics of Drug Policy (2013), *Ending the Drug Wars*, London, London School of Economics and Political Science.

Maalsté, N., G. van den Brink, G. Brouwer and A. Schilder (2010), *Juridische en praktische haalbaarheid van "Limburg trekt zijn grens"*, Tilburg, Tilburgse School voor Politiek en Bestuur.

MacCoun, R. (2010), *Estimating the Non-Price Effects of Legalization on Cannabis Consumption*, Santa Monica, Rand.

Maes, K., J. Maertens, F. Carlier and B. de Ruyver, (eds.) (1984), *De witte cirkel; het drugsbeleid in Vlaanderen*, Antwerpen, Van Loghum Slaterus.

May, T. and O. Skrine (2013a), "Impact of Decriminalization of Personal Possession Offences in Portugal", in: F. Trautmann, B. Kilmer and P. Turnbull (eds.), *op. cit.*, pp. 407–424.

May, T. and O. Skrine (2013b), "Impact of Changes in the Netherlands Coffee Shop Policies on Local Markets: Politics, Policies, Confusion and Chaos: The Problems Associated with Implementing the Dutch Weed Pass", in: F. Trautmann, B. Kilmer and P. Turnbull (eds.), *op. cit.*, pp. 425–446.

McVay, D. (1991), "Marijuana Legalization: The Time is Now", in: J. Inciardi (ed.), *op. cit.*, pp. 147–160.

Mein, A. and M. van Ooyen-Houben (2013), *Bestuurlijke rapportage coffeeshop Checkpoint*, Utrecht, Verwey-Jonker Instituut.

Melis, S. (2013), *VAD leerlingenbevraging in het kader van een drugsbeleid op school; syntheserapport schooljaar 2011–2012*, Brussel, VAD.

Middelburg, B. (1992), *De dominee; opkomst en ondergang van mafiabaas Klaas Bruinsma*, Amsterdam, L.J. Veen.

Ministerie van Veiligheid en Justitie (2011), *Project landelijke screening coffeeshops, 2011–2014*, 's-Gravenhage, Ministerie van Veiligheid en Justitie.

Mission Interministérielle de Lutte contre la Drogue et la Toxicomanie (2013), *Government Plan for Combating Drugs and Addictive Behaviours, 2013–2017*, Paris.

Moore, M. (1992a), "Actually, Prohibition was a Success", in: R. Evans and I. Berent (eds.), *op. cit.*, pp. 95–98.

Moore, M. (1992b), "Drugs: Getting a Fix on the Problem and the Solution", in: R. Evans and I. Berent (eds.), *op. cit.*, pp. 123–156.

Muscat, R. (ed.) (2008), *From a Policy on Illegal Drugs to a Policy on Psychoactive Substances*, Strasbourg, Council of Europe Publishing.

Muscat, R. and B. Pike (eds.) (2012), *Reflections on the Concept of Coherency for a Policy on Psychoactive Substances and Beyond*, Strasbourg, Council of Europe Publishing.

Muscat, R., S. van de Mheen, C. Barendrecht et al. (2010), *Towards an Integrated Policy on Psychoactive Substances; A Theoretical and Empirical Analysis*, Strasbourg, Council of Europe Publishing.

Nadelmann, E. (1991), "The Case for Legalization", in: J. Inciardi (ed.), *op. cit.*, pp. 17–44.

——— (1992), "The Case for Legalization", in: R. Evans and I. Berent (eds.), *op. cit.*, pp. 19–26.

Nadelmann, E. (1993), *Cops across Borders; The Internationalization of US Criminal Law Enforcement*, Pennsylvania, The Pennsylvania State University Press.

National Conference of State Legislatures (2014), *State Medical Marijuana Laws*, Denver (updated 8 April 2014).

Nelli, H. (1976), *The Business of Crime; Italians and Syndicate Crime in the United States*, New York, Oxford University Press.

Nota integrale veiligheid, 2010–2014, Gemeente Terneuzen.

Office of National Drug Control Policy (2013), *National Drug Control Strategy*, Washington, White House.

——— (2014), *National Drug Control Strategy*, Washington, White House.

Organization of American States (2013), *Scenarios for the Drug Problem in the Americas, 2013–2025*, Washington.

Pacula, R. (2010), *Examining the Impact of Marijuana Legalization on Marijuana Consumption; Insights from the Economic Literature*, Santa Monica, Rand.

Pardoel, K., J. van Haaf, S. Bogaerts and A. van Kalmthout (2004), *Coffeeshops in Nederland anno 2003: aantallen, lokaal beleid, handhaving en naleving*, Tilburg, IVA.

Pedersen, W. (2014), "The Powerful Mix of Capital and Cannabis Culture", *Addiction*, vol. 109, pp. 352–353.

Pike, B. (2008), "Irish Drug Policy and its link with Alcohol and Tobacco Policies", in: R. Muscat (ed.), *op. cit.*, pp. 91–107.

——— (2012), "Coherency of Irish Policies on Illicit Drugs, Alcohol and Tobacco", in: R. Muscat and B. Pike (eds.), *op. cit.*, pp. 43–63.

Plettinckx, E., J. Antoine and P. Blanckaert (eds.) (2012), *Belgian National Report on Drugs 2012*, Brussel, Wetenschappelijk Instituut Volksgezondheid.

Proceedings (1934) *of the Attorney General's Conference on Crime*, Washington, Department of Justice.

Projectgroep Emergo (2011), *Emergo; de gezamenlijke aanpak van de zware (georganiseerde) misdaad in het hart van Amsterdam; achtergronden, ontwikkelingen, perspectieven*, Amsterdam, Boom.

Rangel, C. (1992), "Legalizing Drugs: A Dangerous Idea", in: R. Evans and I. Berent (eds.), *op. cit.*, pp. 13–16.

Regionaal Informatie en Expertise Centrum Limburg (2014), *Jaarverslag 2013*, Maastricht.

Reijnaud-Maurupt, C. (2009), *Les habitués du cannabis; une enquête qualitative auprès des usagers réguliers*, Paris, Observatoire Français des Drogues et des Toxicomanies.

Rekenkamer Maastricht (2010), *Onderzoek spreidingsbeleid coffeeshops*, Maastricht, Rekenkamer.

Reuter, P. (2014), "The Difficulty of Restricting Promotion of Legalized Marijuana in the United States", *Addiction*, vol. 109, pp. 353–354.

Reuter, P. and F. Trautmann (eds.) (2009), *A Report on Global Illicit Drugs Markets 1998–2007*, Brussels, European Commission.

Room, R. (2008), "In Thinking about Cannabis Policy: What Can Be Learned from Alcohol and Tobacco?", in: S. Sznitman, B. Olsson and R. Room (eds.), *op. cit.*, pp. 121–135.

——— (2013), "Legalizing a Market for Cannabis for Pleasure: Colorado, Washington, Uruguay and Beyond", *Addiction*, vol. 109, pp. 345–351.

Room, R., B. Fischer, W. Hall et al. (2008), *Cannabis Policy; Moving beyond Stalemate*, Oxford, The Beckley Foundation.

Rovers, B. and C. Fijnaut (2011), *De drugsoverlast in Maastricht en omliggende gemeenten*, Antwerpen, Intersentia.

Ruggiero, V. and N. South (1995), *Eurodrugs; Drug Use, Markets and Trafficking in Europe*, London, University College London Press.

Serlippens, A. (2012), "Het beleid", in: J. Dangreau, L. Deben and K. de Greve (eds.), *op. cit.*, pp. 1–27.

Siesling, M., B. Smeets and A. Spapens (2011), *Geldbomen op zolder: thuiskwekers van hennep in beeld*, Tilburg, IVA.

Single, E., D. Collins, B. Easton et al. (2003), *International Guidelines for Estimating the Economic Costs of Substances Abuse*, Geneva, World Health Organization.

Single, E., L. Robson, X. Xie and J. Rehm (1988), "The Economic Costs of Alcohol, Tobacco and Illicit Drugs in Canada", *Addiction*, vol. 97, pp. 991–1006.

Smet, V., B. de Ruyver, Ch. Colman et al. (2013), *Het aanbod van illegale drugs in België: wat weten we?; een haalbaarheidsstudie van betrouwbare indicatoren van het drugsaanbod*, Gent, Academia Press.

Snippe, J., B. Bieleman, A. Kruize et al. (2005), *Hektor in Venlo; eindevaluatie: inspanningen, proces en resultaten, 2001–2004*, Groningen, Intraval.

Snippe, J., B. Bieleman, H. Naayer et al. (2004), *Preventieve doorlichting cannabissector c.a.*, Groningen, Intraval.

Snippe, J., A. Kruize and B. Bieleman (2003), *Inspannen tegen XTC: eerste meting*, Groningen, Intraval.

Snippe, J., R. Nijkamp and B. Bieleman (2013), *Onderzoek drugsbeleid Venlo 2012–2013*, Groningen, Intraval.

Société des Nations (1937), *Convention pour limiter la fabrication et réglementer la distribution des stupéfiants du 13 juillet 1931; étude historique et technique par la Section du Trafic de l'Opium du Secrétariat de la Société des Nations*, Genève, Société des Nations.

Spapens, A. (2006), *Interactie tussen criminaliteit en opsporing; de gevolgen van opsporingsactiviteiten voor de organisatie en afscherming van xtc-productie en -handel in Nederland*, Antwerpen, Intersentia.

Spapens, A. and C. Fijnaut (2005), *Criminaliteit en rechtshandhaving in de Euregio Maas-Rijn*, Antwerpen, Intersentia.

Spapens, A., H. van de Bunt and L. Rastovac (2007), *De wereld achter de wietteelt*, 's-Gravenhage, WODC.

Spapens, A., T. Müller and H. van de Bunt (2014), "The Dutch Drug Policy from a Regulatory Perspective", *European Journal on Criminal Policy and Research* (online, august 2014).

State of Colorado (2013), *Task Force Report on the Implementation of Amendment 64; Regulation of Marijuana in Colorado*, Denver.

Stichting Maatschappij en Veiligheid (2014), *Alternatieven voor de aanpak van drugs; achtergrondstudie ten behoeve van een actieplan*, Den Haag.

Surmont, T. (2007), "Het profiel van de coffeeshopbezoeker in Terneuzen", in: B. de Ruyver and T. Surmont (eds.), *op. cit.*, pp. 54–88.

Sutherland, E. (1934), *Principles of Criminology*, Chicago, J.B. Lippencott Company.

Sznitman, S., B. Olsson and R. Room (eds.) (2008), *A Cannabis Reader: Global Issues and Local Experiences; Perspectives on Cannabis Controversies, Treatment and Regulation in Europe*, Lisbon, European Monitoring Centre for Drugs and Drug Addiction, 2 vols.

Thornton, M. (2004), "Drug Policy; Prohibition vs Legalization: Do Economists Reach a Conclusion on Drug Policy?", *Econ Journal Watch*, pp. 82–105.

Tisseyre, Ch. (1977), *La drogue en Belgique*, Bruxelles, J.E.B.

T.M.C. Asser Instituut (2005), *Experimenteren met het gedogen van de teelt van cannabis ten behoeve van de bevoorrading van coffeeshops; internationaalrechtelijke en Europeesrechtelijke aspecten*, 's-Gravenhage.

Tops, P. and W. Gooren (2009), *Een pact van het hart; ontstaan en groei van Operatie Hartslag; aanpak van de drugsproblematiek in Heerlen*, Apeldoorn, Politieacademie.

Transform (s.d.), *How to Regulate Cannabis: A Practical Guide*, Bristol.

Trautmann, F., B. Kilmer and P. Turnbull (eds.) (2013), *Further Insights into Aspects of the EU Illicit Drugs Market*, Brussels, European Commission, 2013.

Trigueros, F. (2012), "A Portuguese Insight into Coherent Policy", in: R. Muscat and B. Pike (eds.), *op. cit.*, pp. 101–114.

Uchtenhagen, A. (2014), "Some Critical Issues in Cannabis Policy Reform", *Addiction*, vol. 109, pp. 356–357.

UK Drug Policy Commission (2012), *A Fresh Approach to Drugs*, London.

United Nations Office on Drugs and Crime (2008), *World Drug Report*, Vienna, United Nations.

Van Amsterdam, J., A. Opperhuizen, M. Koeter et al. (2009), *Ranking van drugs; een vergelijking van de schadelijkheid van drugs*, Bilthoven, Rijksinstituut voor Volksgezondheid en Milieu.

Van Bostraeten, H. (1974), *De jeugdmisdadigheid in België in 1969 en 1970*, Brussel, Studiecentrum voor Jeugdmisdadigheid.

Van Bussel, J. and J. Antoine (2011), "Drugs Use in the General Population and Specific Targeted Groups", in: N. Deprez, J. Antoine and J. Asueta-Lorent (eds.), *op. cit.*, pp. 35–60.

Van Bussel, J. and E. de Donder (2012), "Drugs Use in the General Population and Specific Targeted Groups", in: E. Plettinckx, J. Antoine and P. Blanckaert (eds.), *op. cit.*, pp. 306–384.

Van Cappelle, M. (1989), "Hoofdlijnen van het Nederlandse drugsbeleid", in: M. Groenhuijsen and A. van Kalmthout (eds.), *op. cit.*, pp. 145–152.

Van de Bunt, H. (2006), "Hoe stevig zijn de fundamenten van het cannabisbeleid?", *Justitiële Verkenningen*, no. 1, pp. 10–23.

Van den Brink, W. (2006), "Hoe schadelijk zijn softdrugs?", *Justitiële Verkenningen*, no. 1, pp. 72–88.

Van den Brink, W. (2008), "Decriminalization of Cannabis", *Current Opinion in Psychiatry*, pp. 122–126.

Van der Heijden, A. (2006), *De cannabismarkt in Nederland; raming van aanvoer, productie, consumptie en uitvoer*, Zoetermeer, KLPD.

Vander Laenen, F. (2008), *Drugpreventie voor kwetsbare groepen? Jongeren met een gedrags- en emotionele stoornis aan het woord*, Den Haag, Boom.

Vander Laenen, F. (2012), "Belgische overheidsuitgaven voor drugs; preventie van misbruik en afhankelijkheid van alcohol als kind van de rekening", *Tijdschrift Verslaving*, vol. 8, pp. 13–29.

Vander Laenen, F., B. De Ruyver, J. Christiaens and D. Lievens (2011), *Drugs in cijfers III; onderzoek naar de overheidsuitgaven voor het drugsbeleid in België,* Gent, Academia Press.

Van der Torre, E., B. Beke, E. Bervoets et al. (2013), *Drugsmonitor Midden en West Brabant & Zeeland,* Apeldoorn, Politieacademie.

Van der Torre, E., B. Beke, M. Gieling et al. (2013), *Softdrugsbeleid in Tilburg; een update,* Apeldoorn, Politieacademie.

Van der Torre, E. and S. Gerz (1996), *Drugstoeristen en kooplieden; een onderzoek naar Franse drugstoeristen, Marokkaanse drugsrunners en het beheer van dealpanden in Rotterdam,* Deventer, Kluwer.

Van der Torre, E., R. Holvast, D. Keijzer et al. (2013), *Het nieuwe coffeeshopbeleid; een overzichtelijke tussenbalans in Maastricht,* Apeldoorn, Politieacademie.

Van der Torre, E. and M. Hulshof (2000), *Een drugsscene op Zuid (de Millinxbuurt); een model voor de strategische analyse van drugsscenes*, Samsom, Alphen aan den Rijn.

Van der Torre, E., L. Schaap, B. Beke et al. (2012), *Tilburgse taferelen; de eerste rapportage,* Apeldoorn, Politieacademie.

Van Dijk, J. (1997), "De smalle marges van het Nederlandse drugbeleid", *Tijdschrift voor Criminologie,* no. 1, pp. 2–25.

Van Dijk, P. (2010), *Hennep telen en geweld oogsten?!; een onderzoek naar hennepgerelateerde geweldszaken in de Politieregio Midden en West Brabant,* Rotterdam, Erasmus Universiteit Rotterdam, Faculteit der Rechtsgeleerdheid (thesis).

Van Dijk, W. and L. Hulsman (eds.) (1970), *Drugs in Nederland,* Bussum, Paul Brand.

Van Gemert, F. (1985), *Pushen, versnijden en rippen: dealers in de Amsterdamse binnenstad,* Amsterdam, Universiteit van Amsterdam, Antropologisch-Sociologisch Centrum.

Van Gemert, F. (1988), *Mazen en netwerken; de invloed van het beleid op de drugshandel in twee straten in de Amsterdamse binnenstad,* Amsterdam, Universiteit van Amsterdam, Antropologisch-Sociologisch Centrum.

Van het Loo, M., S. Hoorens, C. van 't Hof and J. Kahan (2003), *Cannabis Policy: Implementation and Outcomes*, Leiden, Rand.

Van het Loo, M., I. van Beusekom and J. Kahan (2002), "Decriminalization of Drug Use in Portugal; The Development of a Policy", *Annals of the American Academy of Political and Social Sciences*, no. 582, pp. 49–63.

Vanhove, W. (2014), *The Agronomy and Economy of Illicit Indoor Cannabis Cultivation,* Gent, Ghent University (PhD thesis).

Vanhove, W., P. van Damme, T. Surmont, L. van Puyenbroeck and B. de Ruyver (2012), *Yican: Yield of Illicit Indoor Cannabis Plantations*, Gent, Academia Press.

Van Kempen, P. and M. Fedorova (2014), *Internationaal recht en cannabis; een beoordeling op basis van VN-drugsverdragen en EU-drugsregelgeving van gemeentelijke en buitenlandse opvattingen pro regulering van cannabisteelt voor recreatief gebruik,* Nijmegen, Radboud Universiteit Nijmegen.

Van Laar, M., A. Cruts, J. Verdurmen et al. (2008), *Nationale drug monitor; jaarbericht 2007*, Utrecht, Trimbos Instituut.

Van Laar, M., A. Cruts, M. van Ooyen-Houben et al. (2013), *Nationale drug monitor; jaarbericht 2012*, Utrecht, Trimbos Instituut.

Van Laar, M., T. Frijns, F. Trautmann and L. Lombi (2013a), "Cannabis Market: User Types, Availability and Consumption Estimates", in: F. Trautmann, B. Kilmer and P. Turnbull (eds.), *op. cit.*, pp. 73–180.

Van Laar, M., T. Frijns, F. Trautmann and L. Lombi (2013b), "Sizing the Cannabis Market: A Demand-Side and User-Specific Approach in Seven European Countries", *Current Drug Abuse Reviews*, no. 3, pp. 1–13.

Van Laar, M. and M. van Ooyen-Houben (eds.) (2009), *Evaluatie van het Nederlandse drugsbeleid*, 's-Gravenhage, Wetenschappelijk Onderzoek- en Documentatiecentrum.

Van Lenteren, P. and J. Büller (2014), "Burgemeester Paul Depla van Heerlen wil een gereguleerde wietteelt", *24/7 Personeelsblad van de Politie*, no. 15, pp. 19–21.

Van Nimwegen, S. (2009), *Tijd om te oogsten...! Onderzoek naar innovatieve interventiestrategieën voor de bestrijding van de georganiseerde hennepteelt volgens de programmatische aanpak*, Tilburg, Politie Midden en West Brabant.

Van Ooyen-Houben, M., B. Bieleman and D. Korf (2013), *Het besloten club- en het ingezetenencriterium voor coffeeshops; evaluatie van de implementatie en de uitkomsten in de periode mei-november 2012*, Den Haag, Wetenschappelijk Onderzoek- en Documentatiecentrum.

Van Ours, J. (2012), "The Long and Winding Road to Cannabis Legalization", *Addiction*, no. 107, pp. 872–877.

Van Ours, J. and J. Williams (2007), "Cannabis Prices and Dynamics of Cannabis Use", *Journal of Health Economics*, pp. 578–596.

——— (2011), "Cannabis Use and Mental Health Problems", *Journal of Applied Economics*, pp. 1137–1156.

Verslag namens de werkgroep belast met het bestuderen van de drugproblematiek (1997), Kamer, *Gedrukte Stukken*, 1996–1997, no. 1062/1.

Vervaeck, L. (1922), "La défense sociale contre le péril toxique", *Revue de Droit Pénal et de Criminologie*, pp. 339–348.

Vervaeck, L. (1926), "Existe-t-il un péril toxique en Belgique?", *Revue de Droit Pénal et de Criminologie*, pp. 312–316.

Vicente, J., D. Olszewski and J. Matias (2008), "Prevalence, Patterns and Trends of Cannabis Use among Adults in Europe", in: S. Sznitman, B. Olsson and R. Room (eds.), *op. cit.*, vol. 2, pp. 6–26.

Volkow, N., R. Baler, W. Compton et al. (2014), "Adverse Health Effects of Marijuana Use", *The New England Journal of Medicine*, no. 370, pp. 2219–2227.

VROM-Inspectie (2009), *Overlast en verloedering; evaluatie wetten Victoria en Victor*, 's-Gravenhage, Ministerie van VROM.

Weijenburg, R. (1996), *Drugs en drugsbestrijding in Nederland*, 's-Gravenhage, VUGA.

Werkgroep drugsoverlast (2007), *Drugsoverlast; samenvattend rapport*, Gent-Terneuzen.

White House (2010), *A Drug Policy for the 21st Century*, Washington.

Wiarda, J. (1989), "Mogelijkheden en beperkingen van de repressie-strategie", in: M. Groenhuijsen and A. van Kalmthout (eds.), *op. cit.*, pp. 49–59.

Wickersham Commission (1931), *Enforcement of the Prohibition Laws of the United States*, Washington, Government Printing Office.

Williams, J. (2004), "The Effects of Price and Policy on Marijuana Use: What Can Be Learned from the Australian Experience?", *Health Economics*, vol. 13, pp. 123–137.

Wisotsky, S. (1989), "Recente ontwikkelingen in de Amerikaanse *war on drugs*", in: M. Groenhuijsen and A. van Kalmthout (eds.), *op. cit.*, pp. 29–48.

Wisotsky, S. (1991), "Beyond the War on Drugs", in: J. Inciardi (ed.), *op. cit.*, pp. 103–129.

Woodiwiss, M. (1988), *Crime Crusades and Corruption: Prohibitions in the United States, 1900–1987*, London, Pinter Publishers.

World Health Organization (2003), *WHO Framework Convention on Tobacco Control*, Geneva, World Health Organization.

Index

Andersen, P. 178
Andreas,P. 11
Anslinger, H. 11, 21

Baumberg, B. 178
Belgium 2–3, 24, 72, 77–79, 88, 100, 112–113, 116, 121–125, 146–147, 161–162, 165, 167–168, 171–172, 174, 176–178, 189, 196, 197
Beckley Foundation 17, 163
Benjamin, D. 183
Berent, I. 26
Bewley-Taylor, D. 17, 163
Blickman, T. 163
Bovenkerk, F. 103, 105, 107
Breeksema, J. 33
Brink, Van den, W. 197
Bunt, Van de, H. 104

Canada 22, 24–25, 51–55, 65, 165, 176, 196, 199–200, 202, 204
  British Columbia 22, 51, 55–57, 60, 64, 176
Caulkins, J. 39, 79, 168, 175, 182, 184, 187, 190, 192
Cleveland, M. 184
Cooney, P. 68, 70
Council of Europe 66, 73, 169
  Groupe Pompidou 66, 169, 179
Crick, E. 4

Decorte, T. 197
Degenhardt, L. 195

European Union 1–3, 24, 65–88, 93, 99, 117, 126, 154, 157, 159, 161–162, 164, 167, 170–171, 174, 176–179, 185, 190, 193–194, 196, 199–200, 202, 205–206
  Barrot, J. 76
  European Commission 76, 88, 167
  European Monitoring Centre for Drugs and Drug Addiction 5, 77–80, 198–199
  European Parliament 67–68, 70, 72, 174
  Europol 77
  Schengen Agreement and Implementation Convention 66, 70–72, 88, 117–118, 124, 166
  Treaty of Amsterdam 72
  Treaty of Lisbon 75, 88
Evans, R. 26

Fedorova, M. 74, 140, 165, 203
France 66, 70, 72, 78–79, 83–84, 88, 105, 112–113, 116, 122, 124, 165, 189
Fijnaut, C. 123, 125–126

Geneva, The, Conventions 1925, 1931 and 1936 9–11
Germany 66, 70, 78, 82–83, 100, 105, 124, 165
Grund, J-P. 33

Hague, The, Convention 1912 9
Hall, N. 195
Hallam, C. 17
Heijden, Van der, A. 103–104
Hogewind, W. 103, 105, 107

Inciardi, J. 26
International Control Committee 12
International Drug Policy Consortium 19
Internationale Kriminalpolizeiliche Kommission 10
Italy 70, 78, 105

Jelsma, M. 163

Kempen, Van, P. 74, 140, 165, 203
Kilmer, B. 77, 79, 184
Kleiman, M. 190, 192
Korf, D. 103

League of Nations 9, 20–21

MacCoun, R. 184, 194, 196
Miller, R. 183

Nadelmann, E. 11, 190

Organisation of American States 30

Pacula, R. 184
Patey, W. 183
Portugal 5, 80–81

Rand 50
Rastovac, L. 104
Reuter, P. 184, 191, 196
Room, R. 44, 163, 191
Rovers, B. 123, 125–126
Ruyver, De, B. 123

Single, the, Convention on Narcotic Drugs 1961 11–12, 20, 102, 163
Soros, G. 185
Spain 66, 78–79, 81, 146–147, 203
Spapens, A. 104

The Netherlands 1–3, 5, 17, 24, 57, 59, 67, 70–72, 77–80, 83, 88–160–165, 167, 176, 186, 197, 204, 208–210
  Amsterdam 97, 106–108, 127–130, 209–210
  Bergen op Zoom 112–113, 126, 138, 145, 157
  Borst, E. 102
  Breda 113, 142
  Depla, P. 146, 149–151
  Donner, P-H. 119–121
  Eindhoven 113–114, 146
  Euregion Meuse-Rhine 108, 123, 125, 208
  Eijsden 122
  Frissen, L. 123
  Heerlen 115, 149
  Helmond 115
  Hirsch Ballin, E. 95–96, 151
  Hulsman, L. 90–93, 107
  Korthals, B. 99
  Leers, G. 117, 120
  Maastricht 97, 100, 115–126, 141–144, 157
  National Police Force 103, 150
  Office for Medicinal Cannabis 102
  Opium Act 90, 94, 106–107, 118, 129, 136, 141, 148, 151
  Opstelten, I. 89, 136–137, 139–140, 143, 148–149, 152–155, 158
  Research and Documentation Centre 139–140
  Roosendaal 112–113, 126, 138, 145, 157
  Rotterdam 97–98
  Stoffelen, P. 96–97
  Task Force B5 112–115
  Terneuzen 108–112, 116, 126, 145, 157
  Tilburg 99, 113, 115, 141–142, 144–145
  Utrecht 103, 105, 138
  Van de Donk Committee 89, 132–135, 146–147, 203
  Van Traa Committee 156
  Veling, M. 210
  Venlo 106–107, 115, 157
  Weijenburg, R. 93
Thornton, M. 182
T.M.C. Asser Institute 100
Trautmann, F. 77
Turnbull, P. 77

Uchtenhagen, A. 193
United Kingdom 66, 70, 77–79, 84–87, 105, 165, 170, 196
United Nations 1–2, 3, 9, 31, 68–69, 71, 74, 100, 126, 154, 159, 161, 164, 172–173, 199–200, 205
  Commission on Narcotic Drugs 18, 87
  International Narcotics Control Board 16, 18–19, 59
  Office on Drugs and Crime 16–17, 172–173
  Yans, R. 18, 59
United States 9, 11, 21–22, 24–25, 27, 31–55, 60–61, 64–65, 73, 147, 149, 160, 162, 165, 177, 179–182, 185–186, 188, 190, 193–194
  American College of Physicians 31
  California 18, 31–32, 37–38, 184, 186, 191
  Colorado 17, 22, 30–31, 36–47, 63, 163–164, 166, 168, 173, 175, 180–186, 188, 191–192, 199, 204–206
  Controlled Substances Act 32
  Department of Justice 32, 35
  Drug Enforcement Administration 35–37, 167

United States (cont.)
- Eighteenth Amendment 23
- Federal Bureau of Investigation 37–38, 167
- Federal Bureau of Narcotics 11
- Harrison Narcotic Act 9
- House of Representatives 36
- Marihuana Tax Act 21
- National Institute on Drug Abuse 38
- National Prohibition Act 23–24
- Obama Administration 32–35, 37
- Open Society Foundations 33
- Oregon 184–185
- Prohibition 22–27, 37, 60–61, 161, 168
- Treasury Department 11
- Washington State 17, 22, 30–31, 36–37, 47–51, 63, 163–164, 166, 168, 180–184, 186, 188, 192, 199, 204–206
- Wickersham Commission 22, 61, 161

Uruguay 17, 22, 30–31, 57–60, 63–64, 147, 149, 160, 162–163, 175, 180, 193, 199–200, 203–204, 206

Vienna, The, Convention against Illicit Traffic etc. 1988 13–15, 26, 68, 73, 141, 148, 203

Volkow, N. 195–196

World Health Organization 172

www.ingramcontent.com/pod-product-compliance
Lightning Source LLC
Chambersburg PA
CBHW071439230926
51846CB00001B/280
* 9 7 8 9 0 0 4 2 9 3 1 8 2 *